A
Zora Neale Hurston
Companion

Photo by Carl Van Vechten, courtesy of the Van Vechten Trust. Used with permission from the Beinecke Rare Book and Manuscript Library, Carl Van Vechten Collection, Yale University.

A
Zora Neale Hurston
Companion

ROBERT W. CROFT

GREENWOOD PRESS
Westport, Connecticut • London

Library of Congress Cataloging-in-Publication Data

Croft, Robert W. (Robert Wayne), 1957–
   A Zora Neale Hurston companion / Robert W. Croft.
     p. cm.
   Includes bibliographical references and index.
   ISBN 0–313–30707–5 (alk. paper)
   1. Hurston, Zora Neale—Handbooks, manuals, etc. 2. Women and literature—United
States—History—20th century—Handbooks, manuals, etc. 3. Authors, American—20th
century—Biography—Handbooks, manuals, etc. 4. African American
authors—Biography—Handbooks, manuals, etc. 5. African Americans in
literature—Handbooks, manuals, etc. 6. Folklore in literatuare—Handbooks, manuals, etc.
I. Title
  PS3515.U789 Z464 2002
  813'.52—dc21
  [B]   2002069610

British Library Cataloguing in Publication Data is available.

Library of Congress Catalog Card Number: 2002069610
ISBN: 0–313–30707–5

First published in 2002

Greenwood Press, 88 Post Road West, Westport, CT 06881
An imprint of Greenwood Publishing Group, Inc.
www.greenwood.com

Printed in the United States of America

The paper used in this book complies with the
Permanent Paper Standard issued by the National
Information Standards Organization (Z39.48–1984).

10 9 8 7 6 5 4 3 2 1

As ever,
for my anchors,
Melody, Christian, and Britanny

and

for Vicki, Virginia, and Dennis,
whose lifelong love and support
I will always cherish.

Contents

Preface

This book grew out of a fascination that I developed with Zora Neale Hurston's writing the first time I read an excerpt from *Their Eyes Were Watching God* while I was attending graduate school. Having grown up in the "old Florida" myself, I was surprised, amazed, delighted, and enthralled to discover a writer of such great power and style, who wrote with the cadences of speech and the colorful idioms that I had heard all my life. So, when I began searching for a topic for a new research project, I naturally thought of Zora.

This book begins with an overview of Hurston's life followed by a companion section (arranged alphabetically) on Hurston's works, characters, themes, and motifs. In this section I include entries for all characters from her fictional works, important people from her life, and recurring themes and motifs. In dealing with the characters' race, I chose to put myself in Hurston's world, which for the most part is a world of color. Therefore, in most cases, unless otherwise noted, the characters are African American (or the characters' race is not specified by Hurston and cannot be inferred one way or the other). The major exception to this pattern is Hurston's "white" novel, *Seraph on the Suwanee*, in which almost all of the characters, except for

Joe Kelsey and his family, are white. Therefore, in that novel I identify the race of only the nonwhite characters (except for the Kelseys).

Another issue in identifying characters involved female characters who later marry. In identifying such characters, I have listed them according to the name most often used in the novel or story. Then I have included cross-references to their other name(s), whether it be their maiden name or their married name(s). In some cases, such as Janie in *Their Eyes Were Watching God*, I have listed the character's first name in the main entry, with cross-references to all other names.

The intertextuality of Hurston's writing sometimes made it hard to differentiate between characters since they show up in several stories or novels, often under different names. What I have done in such cases is to list the character first under the title of the work in which he or she plays the most prominent role; following this initial part of the entry come follow-up subentries detailing that character's role in other works in which he or she appears. Likewise, for the entries on Hurston's themes and motifs, I have divided the details of these entries according to their appearance in Hurston's various works.

The next section of the book includes an appendix listing the contents of collections of Hurston manuscripts, correspondence, and other source materials.

The final section of the book is a bibliography. First comes a primary bibliography listing the publication information about Hurston's novels, plays, short stories, nonfiction articles, book reviews, newspaper articles, and poems, including reprints (quite substantial in some cases). Following this part of the bibliography is a secondary bibliography of books, chapters or sections of books, and articles on both Hurston's life and work. In this secondary bibliography, I have attempted to compile an exhaustive listing of all the Hurston criticism and research to date. Such an exhaustive listing is necessary because in my research I found many inconsistencies in previous bibliographies. So I have checked and rechecked the bibliographic information in cases of possible problems to ensure its accuracy. At the end of the secondary bibliography is a list of book reviews on Hurston's various works from their publication to the present. The bibliography is followed by an index.

Acknowledgments

During the four years that I have been researching and writing this book, I have received a great deal of help from a variety of very generous and able people. First and foremost I want to thank the excellent staff (past and present) of the Gainesville College Library, including Rebecca Homan, Angela Megaw, Julie Marlow, Meg Graham, and especially the tireless efforts of Priscilla Rankin, Becky Webb, and Valerie Wood in procuring hundreds of interlibrary loan materials for me.

I also received help from other librarians, including the following: Beth M. Howse, Special Collections Librarian, Fisk University Library; Patrick T. Lawlor, Rare Book and Manuscript Library, Columbia University; Patricia C. Willis, Curator of the Yale Collection of American Literature, Beinecke Rare Book and Manuscript Library, Yale University; Robin Van Fleet, Senior Manuscript Librarian, Moorland-Spingarn Research Center, Howard University; Diana Lachatanere, Curator in the Manuscripts, Archives and Rare Books Division of the Schomburg Center for Research in Black Culture of the New York Public Library; David Wigdor, Assistant Chief of the Manuscript Division of the Library of Congress; Judith A. Gray, Reference Specialist at the American Folk Center of the Library of Congress; Frank Orser from the Special Collections Library at the University of Florida; and at the Harry Ransom Humanities Research Center, University of Texas at Austin, Cathy Henderson, Associate Librarian, and Tara Wenger, Research Librarian.

For help in obtaining the excellent Carl Van Vechten photograph of Hurston, I am indebted to Bruce Kellner, Successor Trustee of the Estate of Carl Van Vechten, and to Stephen Jones at the Beinecke Rare Book and Manuscript Library, Yale University. For permission to reprint the photo, I gratefully acknowledge the Carl Van Vechten Trust. For assistance in obtaining this permission, I wish to thank the Gainesville College Foundation and Sallie Duhling.

Many thanks to Arlene Belzer and Dave Reynhout of Coastal Editorial Services for their excellent copyediting skills, which helped the shape and format of the book.

And as ever, I am grateful to my editor at Greenwood Press, George Butler, for his excellent suggestions for improving the book, and especially for his patience, encouragement, and diligence.

Abbreviations

BOOKS

Eyes	*Their Eyes Were Watching God*
Horse	*Tell My Horse*
Moses	*Moses, Man of the Mountain*
Mules	*Mules and Men*
Seraph	*Seraph on the Suwanee*
Tracks	*Dust Tracks on a Road*
Vine	*Jonah's Gourd Vine*

SHORT STORIES

"Anthology"	"The Eatonville Anthology"
"Black Death"	"Black Death"
"Book"	"Book of Harlem"
"Cock Robin"	"Cock Robin Beale Street"
"Conscience"	"The Conscience of the Court"
"Contention"	"The Bone of Contention"

"Escape"   "Escape from Pharaoh"
"Fire and Cloud"   "The Fire and the Cloud"
"Gas"   "Now You Cookin' with Gas"
"Gaul"   "The Woman in Gaul"
"Harlem Slang"   "Story in Harlem Slang"
"High John"   "High John De Conquer"
"Hurricane"   "Hurricane"
"John Redding"   "John Redding Goes to Sea"
"Light"   "Drenched in Light"
"Magnolia"   "Magnolia Flower"
"Mother Catherine"   "Mother Catherine"
"Muttsy"   "Muttsy"
"Possum"   " 'Possum or Pig?"
"Six-Bits"   "The Gilded Six-Bits"
"Slanguage"   "Harlem Slanguage"
"Spunk"   "Spunk"
"Sweat"   "Sweat"
"Tablets"   "The Tablets of the Law"
"Uncle Monday"   "Uncle Monday"
"Under the Bridge"   "Bridge"
"Veil"   "The Seventh Veil"

PLAYS

Bone   *Mule Bone*
Color   *Color Struck*
First   *The First One*
Spears   *Spears*

NONFICTION

"Art"   "Art and Such"
"Colored Me"   "How It Feels to Be Colored Me"
"Democracy"   "Crazy for This Democracy"

Abbreviations

"Expression"	"Characteristics of Negro Expression"
"Jim Crow"	"My Most Humiliating Jim Crow Experience"
"Pet Negro"	"The 'Pet Negro' System"
"White Publishers"	"What White Publishers Won't Print"

Chronology of Zora Neale Hurston's Life

1891   Zora Neale Hurston is born on January 7 in Notasulga, Alabama.

1894   Hurston family moves to Eatonville, Florida.

1904   Hurston's mother dies on September 18; in October Zora goes to school in Jacksonville, Florida.

1905   Hurston returns to Eatonville; over the next few years she lives with friends and relatives rather than her father, who has remarried.

1915–16   Hurston works as lady's maid for a singer in a traveling Gilbert and Sullivan troupe.

1917–18   Zora attends Morgan Academy in Baltimore, Maryland; in June 1918 she moves to Washington, D.C.

1919–20   She takes classes at Howard University.

1921   "John Redding Goes to Sea" is published in *Stylus*, Howard's literary magazine.

1924   "Drenched in Light" is published in *Opportunity*.

1925   Hurston moves to New York City and wins second place prizes for "Spunk" and *Color Struck* in the *Opportunity* contest; she meets Carl Van Vechten, Langston Hughes, and Fannie Hurst and accepts a position as Hurst's personal secretary; in the fall she enters Barnard College, where she studies with anthropologist Franz Boas.

1926   "Muttsy" wins second-place in the *Opportunity* contest and is published; Hurston collaborates with Langston Hughes and other African American artists to publish *Fire!!*, which includes "Sweat" and the play *Color Struck*.

1927   Hurston travels throughout the South on a research fellowship collecting folklore; on May 19 she marries medical student Herbert Sheen in St. Augustine, Florida; Hurston meets Langston Hughes in Mobile, Alabama, and drives with him to New York; there she meets Hughes's patron, Charlotte Mason, who becomes Hurston's "Godmother" and sponsors her research, albeit with restrictions on Hurston's ability to publish her work.

1928   In January Hurston breaks off her relationship with Herbert Sheen; then she returns to Florida to collect folklore; in May she receives her B.A. degree from Barnard; she spends the rest of the year investigating hoodoo in Louisiana.

1930   Hurston collaborates with Langston Hughes to write *Mule Bone*.

1931   Hurston and Hughes fight over the production of *Mule Bone*, ultimately dooming it to failure; Hurston's contract with Mrs. Mason expires in March, but her financial support continues for another year; Hurston's divorce from Herbert Sheen is finalized on July 7.

1932   *The Great Day* is presented on Broadway on January 10 to favorable reviews, but the show is not picked up by producers; Hurston returns to Eatonville.

1933   "The Gilded Six-Bits" is published in *Story*; Hurston receives a complimentary letter from Bertram Lippincott and, encouraged by his interest, writes *Jonah's Gourd Vine* and submits it for publication.

1934   Hurston works briefly as a drama teacher at Bethune-Cookman College in Daytona Beach, Florida; *Jonah's Gourd Vine* is published in May; Hurston travels, revises the manuscript of *Mules and Men*, and considers accepting a fellowship to work on a doctorate in anthropology at Columbia.

1935	Hurston travels around the South with Alan Lomax and Mary Elizabeth Barnicle collecting folklore; Lippincott publishes *Mules and Men* in October.
1936	Hurston receives a Guggenheim Fellowship to study West Indian folklore; she travels to Jamaica and Haiti; while in Haiti, she writes *Their Eyes Were Watching God* in seven weeks.
1937	*Their Eyes Were Watching God* is published by Lippincott on September 18 and receives mostly favorable reviews.
1938	Hurston works on the Federal Writers' Project in Jacksonville, Florida; she writes *Tell My Horse*, which is published in October.
1939	After marrying Albert Price III on June 27, Hurston leaves him in Florida to take a job as a drama teacher at the North Carolina College for Negroes in Durham, North Carolina; *Moses, Man of the Mountain* is published in November.
1940–41	Hurston files for divorce (February 1940), travels around the country, moves to Los Angeles, where she works for a few months (October 1941–January 1942) at Paramount Pictures as a story consultant, and starts work on her autobiography.
1942	Hurston moves to St. Augustine, Florida; *Dust Tracks on a Road* is published to generally favorable reviews in November.
1943	*Dust Tracks* wins the Anisfield-Wolf Book Award for the year's best book on race relations; Hurston moves to Daytona Beach, Florida; her divorce from Albert Price becomes final on November 9.
1944–46	Hurston is engaged to but never marries James Howell Pitts; she collaborates on the musical comedy "Polk County" with Dorothy Waring, but fails to find backing for the production; her novel *Mrs. Doctor* is rejected by Lippincott.
1947	Hurston travels to Honduras to do research; she works on *Seraph on the Suwanee*.
1948	Hurston returns to New York, where she is arrested on child molestation charges on September 13 but ultimately cleared in March of the next year; *Seraph on the Suwanee* is published on October 11.
1950	Hurston is working as a maid in Miami, Florida when her story "The Conscience of the Court" is published by the *Saturday*

Evening Post; Negro Digest publishes her article "What White Publishers Won't Print."

1951   Hurston publishes conservative political articles in various magazines and moves to Eau Gallie, Florida.

1952–53   Hurston writes articles defending Ruby McCollum for the *Pittsburgh Courier;* she starts working on a biography of Herod the Great.

1955   For her opposition to the Supreme Court's 1954 *Brown v. Board of Education* decision, which she explains in a letter to the editor of the *Orlando Sentinel* published on October 11, Hurston is criticized by civil rights leaders.

1956–57   Hurston works as a library clerk at Patrick Air Force Base in Cocoa Beach, Florida.

1958–59   For the *Fort Pierce Chronicle*, Hurston writes a column on "Hoodoo and Black Magic" and substitute teaches at Lincoln Park Academy, a Negro public school in Ft. Pierce, Florida; early in 1959 she suffers a stroke and enters the St. Lucie County Welfare Home on October 29.

1960   On January 28, Hurston dies impoverished and is buried in an unmarked grave in the Garden of Heavenly Rest, a segregated cemetery in Fort Pierce, Florida.

Zora Neale Hurston's "Big Association of Living"

In the opening chapter of Zora Neale Hurston's masterpiece *Their Eyes Were Watching God*, her protagonist, Janie, who has just returned to her home after a sojourn away filled with pinnacles of happiness and pits of despair, tells the story of her life to her "bosom friend," Pheoby Watson. Janie tells Pheoby that she has been to "de big association of living" and wouldn't give anything for the experience. Such a term aptly describes Zora Neale Hurston's own life, which started humbly but led her to great heights and then brought her back down to the depths of poverty.

Although she was later to claim to be ten years younger, Zora Neale Hurston was actually born on January 7, 1891, in Notasulga, Alabama, the fifth of eight children of John and Lucy Hurston. John, a preacher and carpenter, had married Lucy Potts when she was only 14, despite the objections of her family, a situation that Hurston was to portray very faithfully in her semiautobiographical novel *Jonah's Gourd Vine*.

In 1894, Hurston's family made a very important move, one of the most significant and influential events in Zora's entire life. John Hurston moved his growing family to Eatonville, Florida, an all-black town near Orlando. At the time the Hurston family moved to Eatonville, the town was still young, having been incorporated only six years earlier in 1886. John Hurston, however, took full advantage of the town's newness and availed himself of the opportunities it offered. Hurston quickly made himself a major figure in the town and was eventually elected mayor three times, beginning in 1897.

Growing up in Eatonville proved to have a profound effect on Zora. There, immersed in African American folk culture and sheltered from the harsher aspects of white racism, Zora flourished, developing the innate self-confidence and self-assurance that were to become her hallmarks as a writer and as an individual. Hurston's fairly idyllic childhood and her parents' influence probably prompted her relatively benign, even conservative views on race, which she expressed years later in her 1928 essay, "How It Feels to Be Colored Me," in which she professed herself not to be "tragically colored." Rather she considered herself simply an individual, the "cosmic Zora."

In Eatonville, this "cosmic" child attended school, developed an avid interest in reading, and hung at the gate watching the world go by. Here Hurston began to dream of launching out into the world so that she could, in her mother's words, "jump at de sun." Her later successes in reaching such heights and living such adventures all stem from her beginnings in Eatonville, for Eatonville was also to provide a source for Hurston's intimate knowledge of folktales and folk language, indispensable to her later writing and her work as an anthropologist.

Unfortunately, reality came crashing down on Zora's awakening dreams on September 18, 1904. The death of her mother at age 38, which Hurston describes in her autobiography, *Dust Tracks on a Road*, profoundly transformed Hurston's safe, secure world. At first she was sent away from Eatonville to attend school in Jacksonville. But when her school fees were not paid, she was sent home to Eatonville only to find that her home had been inalterably changed by her father's remarriage to a stepmother whom she could not get along with. Ultimately, this marriage resulted in the breakup of the Hurston family. At different times during the next several years, Zora was sent off to live with her older brothers or various friends and relatives. Perhaps these years when she learned to "lick the pots in sorrow's kitchen" were necessary to develop her sensitivity as an artist. Or perhaps they helped her to find herself and to determine that she would rise above her situation and realize her dreams.

Another turning point in Hurston's life occurred in 1915, when she took a job as a lady's maid to a singer in a traveling Gilbert and Sullivan repertory company. Traveling around the South with the show, Hurston broadened her horizons and eventually landed in Baltimore, where she started school again in September 1917 at Morgan Academy, from which she graduated in June 1918.

Hurston's next move in 1918 took her to Washington, D.C. Here she worked as a waitress and manicurist before starting classes once again, this time at Howard University, the most prestigious African American college in the United States, from which Hurston earned an Associate's degree by 1920. At Howard, Hurston broadened her horizons further in several ways. From a social standpoint, she met her first husband, Herbert Sheen, a fellow Howard student. From a literary standpoint, Howard provided Hurston contact with influential writers, most notably Alain Locke, a Howard philosophy professor. Eventually, Hurston joined the campus literary club, the *Stylus*, which published her first story, "John Redding Goes to Sea," in May 1921. Other literary successes followed, including the publication of several of her poems and then another short story, "Drenched in Light," which was published in *Opportunity* in 1924.

Albeit limited at this time, Hurston's literary success prompted her to move to New York City, home of the burgeoning Harlem Renaissance. In January 1925, with only $1.50 in her pocket, Hurston relocated to New York. Almost from the first day of her arrival in town, Hurston became part of the center of literary and social activities of the Harlem Renaissance. In May she won two second place prizes in the first literary contest sponsored by *Opportunity* for her story "Spunk" and her play *Color Struck*. Best of all, Hurston began to make contacts with other writers, such as Carl Van Vechten, Langston Hughes, Fannie Hurst (who was to give her a job as secretary and then companion/chauffeur), and Annie Nathan Meyer, who secured her a scholarship to Barnard College, where Hurston started classes in the fall of 1925. Hurston was certainly on the fast track.

At Barnard the direction of the focus of Hurston's life shifted when she met anthropologist Franz Boas. With his encouragement, Hurston began to consider folklore as a valid area of study and an integral aspect of her literary style. Hurston's literary successes continued as she won another second place award in the second *Opportunity* contest in 1926 for her story "Muttsy." Then she and several other notable, up and coming young African American writers and artists collaborated to publish *Fire!!*, a magazine devoted entirely to African

American art and literature without the extra trappings of politics and polemics of other African American publications of the day. The magazine, whose one issue appeared in November 1926, included two works by Hurston: her short story "Sweat" and her play *Color Struck*.

The next year, 1927, really launched Hurston's career as a budding anthropologist. With a fellowship from the Association for the Study of Negro Life and History, obtained with Boas's help, Hurston traveled throughout the South collecting folklore. The first part of her trip turned out to be a learning experience, for it proved less successful than she had hoped, perhaps because she was not completely focused on collecting folklore. In fact, on March 19, 1927, she took a break from collecting and married Herbert Sheen in St. Augustine, Florida. But by August, when Sheen returned to medical school in Chicago, Hurston had resumed her tour. In Mobile, Alabama, Hurston ran into Langston Hughes, and the two of them decided to ride back to New York together in Hurston's car, "Sassy Susie." This trip cemented the two writers' growing friendship.

Back in New York, Alain Locke introduced Hurston to the woman who was to become her patron, Charlotte Mason (Mrs. Rufus Osgood). Mrs. Mason, who was patron to several other African American writers and artists, including Locke and Hughes, contracted with Hurston to provide her with a $200/month stipend to collect folklore. But there was a catch—Mason insisted that Hurston give her ownership of the material that she collected, as well as control over its publication. This relationship with the woman whom Hurston was to come to call "Godmother" later turned out to be both boon and bane for Hurston. While allowing her the finances to travel and research, this deal ultimately held Hurston back by preventing her from publishing her material when and how she wanted.

By January 1928, Hurston's relationship with her husband had disintegrated, due mainly to the demands of her work, his studies, and distance. So Hurston resumed her folklore gathering and over the next few years took several trips to the South, most notably Florida and Louisiana, collecting material that she would ultimately use in *Mules and Men*. Between trips, Hurston managed to graduate from Barnard in May 1928, publish several articles, including one on "Hoodoo in America" in the *Journal of American Folklore* in 1931, and to co-write a play, *Mule Bone*, with Langston Hughes, based on her story "The Bone of Contention." Disagreements over the production of the play, however, resulted in the collapse of her friendship with Hughes.

During this period of Hurston's life, she was also very active in promoting the need for a genuine African American theatre. She wrote and produced a series of shows, besides the unsuccessful *Mule Bone*, that presented Negro folksongs and dance in authentic formats. One of these shows, *The Great Day*, was actually presented on Broadway on January 10, 1932. Although it played only that single performance, Hurston was encouraged to continue working on the show. When she moved back to Florida later that year, she reworked the show as *From Sun to Sun* and put it on first at Rollins College and then, over the next year, in several Florida cities, including Eatonville. In 1934, she helped stage another version of the program, *Singing Steel*, in Chicago.

In August 1933 Hurston's story "The Gilded Six-Bits" was published in *Story* magazine. After publisher J.B. Lippincott read it, he was so impressed that he wrote Hurston to ask if she was working on a novel. Not one to say no to an opportunity, Hurston returned home to Florida, rented a room in Sanford, and in less than four months had produced *Jonah's Gourd Vine*, her first novel. The novel, somewhat autobiographical, nevertheless allowed Hurston to make her first extensive fictional use of her growing knowledge of folklore.

With the momentum established by *Jonah's Gourd Vine*, Lippincott agreed to publish Hurston's folklore book *Mules and Men*. Based on her folklore collecting travels through the South between 1927 and 1929 (with some further work in 1931–32), the book was revised extensively by Hurston before its publication, to good reviews, in October 1935. That same year Hurston renewed her folklore collecting by accompanying legendary folklorists Alan Lomax and Mary Elizabeth Barnicle in a collecting trip through the South for the Music Division of the Library of Congress.

Over the next few years, Hurston's anthropological investigations continued when, after being awarded a Guggenheim Fellowship, she made two trips to Jamaica and Haiti in 1936 and 1937. While on the first trip to Haiti, Hurston, who was recovering emotionally from a failed love affair with a younger West Indian man from New York, wrote her masterpiece, *Their Eyes Were Watching God*, in just seven weeks, finishing the novel on December 19, 1936.

The following year, when the novel was published on September

18, 1937, it was well received by most reviewers, with the notable exception of African American reviewers, most notably Alain Locke, whose caustic review in *Opportunity* bemoaned the book's "oversimplification," and Richard Wright, whose review in *New Masses* condemned Hurston's "minstrel technique" meant to satisfy only her white audience. Although disappointed by such criticism from her fellow African American writers, Hurston was not affected permanently.

Back in the United States, Hurston continued to write. Her next book, *Tell My Horse*, the account of her research in Jamaica and Haiti, however, was a disappointment critically and commercially. When it was published in October 1938, the reviews were disappointing. Eventually Hurston became involved with the Federal Writers' Project in Florida, which was working on a project called "The Florida Negro." Meanwhile, Hurston had also started on her next novel, *Moses, Man of the Mountain*. The idea for this book, which had been in the back of Hurston's mind for quite some time, started with the publication of her short story "The Fire and the Cloud" in 1934. Working intermittently over the next five years, Hurston expanded the story until she had produced a folklore filled, allegorical satire of the fate of African Americans in mid–twentieth-century America in which she transforms the figure of Moses from a Hebrew to an Egyptian of African heritage. Despite her achievement, however, the novel received only mixed reviews when it was published in November 1939.

Hurston's personal and professional life continued to be troubled. After marrying a much younger Works Projects Administration (WPA) playground worker, Albert Price III, on January 27, 1939, Hurston left him to take a job as drama teacher at the North Carolina College for Negroes in Durham. Within a year the marriage was over, and Hurston filed for divorce in February 1940. That same year Bertram Lippincott suggested that Hurston write an autobiography. Hurston considered it, and the following year, while she was in California working in the movie industry as a screenwriter and consultant, Hurston began writing *Dust Tracks on a Road*.

Following the Japanese attack on Pearl Harbor in December 1941, political sentiments shifted irrevocably, forcing Hurston to work further on *Dust Tracks* and edit out some of the anticolonial sentiments critical of the United States. While she revised the book during the early part of 1942, now living back in St. Augustine, Florida, Hurston expunged this material, as well as some of the more controversial racial material. By the time the final version of the book was finished, over 10 percent of the original manuscript had been excised. Perhaps due to her watering down the more controversial material, the book was well received by a mostly white audience and sold well when it was published in November 1942. In fact, it won the *Saturday Review*'s Anisfield-Wolf Book Award of $1,000 for its contribution to the field of race relations.

Ironically, in the next few years after the publication of *Dust Tracks*, her most successful book, Hurston was unable to convince her publisher to publish her next novel, *Mrs. Doctor*, a novel about affluent African Americans. After Lippincott's rejection of Hurston's plans for still another project, she decided to switch publishers. On April 15, 1947, she signed a contract with Scribner's, thanks in part to the influence of successful white author Marjorie Kinnan Rawlings, with whom Hurston had become friends. Thus, Hurston's next novel, *Seraph on the Suwanee*, marked a major departure for her, but not just because of the change of publishers. With *Seraph*, Hurston moved for the first time out of black folklife into mainstream white culture. This move was a conscious decision to try to widen her reading audience and to make an artistic statement that a writer, black or white, had no boundaries constraining a choice of subject matter.

In May 1947, Hurston, who had been planning an expedition to look for a fabled "lost city," left for Honduras. Between May and November Hurston wrote the early versions of *Seraph*, but when she submitted the manuscript for publication, Scribner's asked her to make further revisions, which she completed during the first months of 1948 with the help of editor Burroughs Mitchell. In October 1948, the novel was published and dedicated to Marjorie Kinnan Rawlings and Mrs. Spessard L. Holland (the wife of the governor of Florida).

Unfortunately, the last decade or so of Hurston's life was not as fulfilling, or as successful, as her first sixty years. Perhaps the catalyst of this final downward spiral occurred on September 13, 1948 (just a month before *Seraph on the Suwanee* was to be published), when she was arrested in New York on charges of child molestation. A former landlady accused Hurston of molesting her mentally disturbed 10-year-old son. Hurston's subsequent indictment for the alleged crime, along with the sensationalized (and inaccurate) press coverage that the case received, devastated Hurston. A report in one black newspaper in particular, the *Baltimore Afro-American*, took a tip from a court official and twisted the story completely. Despite the initially promising sales for *Seraph*, Hurston was demoralized. The dismissal of the case in March 1949 did little to turn Hurston's career around or lift her spirits.

Returning to Florida, Hurston attempted to continue writing but met with little success. Her novels "The Lives of Barney Turk" and "The Golden Bench of God" were both rejected by Scribner's. When her short story "The Conscience of the Court" was published in the *Saturday Evening Post*, Hurston was actually working as a maid in Miami to make ends meet. Discouraged, Hurston moved back to Eau Gallie, Florida, and rented the same one-room cabin that she had lived in while finishing *Mules and Men* years before. Here she lived for the next five years.

Increasingly conservative in her political and social views, Hurston, however, did manage to publish a few articles in various periodicals during this period. Articles such as "I Saw Negro Votes Peddled" and "Mourner's Bench, Communist Line: Why the Negro Won't Buy Communism" reflected her libertarian ideals. These articles and most particularly her letter to the editor of the *Orlando Sentinel* (published Oct. 11, 1955) opposing the 1954 Supreme Court decision in the case of *Brown v. Board of Education* express sentiments that seem ultra-conservative, even reactionary, for the times. Yet, as always, Hurston was merely asserting her views on individual freedom and responsibility, choosing not to be bound to any predetermined view because of her race or gender. Unfortunately, such viewpoints, seemingly reactionary yet actually visionary, found few supporters in the 1950s and Hurston was roundly criticized by Civil Rights leaders.

One bright spot during this dark period was Hurston's coverage of an infamous Florida murder trial in late 1952. Ruby McCollum, the black mistress of a prominent white doctor and state senator from Live Oak, Florida, had shot and killed the doctor, who was the father of her youngest child, for attempting to force her to have sex with him in his office. Hurston reported on the trial in several articles for the *Pittsburgh Courier*, a major northern African American newspaper. Following McCollum's conviction, Hurston published an account of the woman's life serially in the newspaper from February 28 to May 2, 1953.

Hurston's last big project, which she had planned but not started working on until 1953, returned her to a biblical theme. She began researching and writing an epic biography of Herod the Great, even going so far as to write Winston Churchill to ask him to pen an introduction for the book. The longer Hurston worked on the project, the larger it grew, ultimately encompassing over a thousand pages. Scribner's, however, rejected the book in 1955. Even so, Hurston continued working on the book.

In the spring of 1956 Hurston was forced to move out of her small house in Eau Gallie, so she took a job as a library clerk at Patrick Air Force Base in nearby Cocoa Beach. Hurston hated the job and must not have been too sorry when she was fired the next year. In December she moved to Ft. Pierce, Florida, where the publisher of the local black newspaper, the *Fort Pierce Chronicle*, asked her to write articles on various subjects for the paper, as well as a column on "Hoodoo and Black Magic."

Over the next two years Hurston wrote for the *Chronicle* while also working as a substitute teacher in the segregated black school, Lincoln Park Academy. Then in 1959 Hurston's advancing age finally caught up with her. She suffered a stroke, debilitating her and forcing her into insolvency and, ultimately, driving her into the St. Lucie County Welfare Home, where she moved on October 29.

On January 28, 1960, less than three months after moving into the home, Hurston was dead of heart disease. With no money to her name, she was buried with funds collected locally from friends and acquaintances. Her resting place was an unmarked grave in the Garden of Heavenly Rest, a grave that remained unknown until Alice Walker located it in August 1973 and erected a headstone with the fitting epitaph: "Zora Neale Hurston: 'A Genius of the South,' 1901–1960, Novelist, Folklorist, Anthropologist."

Such an epitaph can hardly sum up a life that was so full and productive in so many different avenues of life. Although she died in relative obscurity, within twenty years of her death, her literary reputation had been resurrected and raised to a height that she probably would not have dared to dream. Today Hurston stands as a major American writer, whose place in the canon of American literature is unquestioned and whose influence on later writers has been profound. Through taking part in the "big association of living," Hurston managed to achieve more than she ever thought possible and to leave behind a legacy of both great writing and invaluable folklore.

⫸⫷ A ⫸⫷

Aaron.

Moses. Moses' (alleged) Hebrew older brother; he becomes Moses' spokesman and accompanies him on his visits to Pharaoh; later he becomes jealous of Moses' power and does not support his leadership, despite being made high priest; he gives in to the people's demands and builds the golden calf; Moses kills him on Mount Hor and makes Aaron's son, Eleazar, high priest.

Abbie.

Mules. White daughter of planter who goes insane and attempts to murder her father after Dave puts a hoodoo curse on the man.

Abihu.

Moses. One of Moses' oldest sons, who is killed for leading the revolt that led to the building of the golden calf.

A.D.

Mules. Man from Pierce, Florida, who tells the tales of "How the Squinch Owl Came to Be," "The Talking Mule," and "High Walker and Bloody Bones."

Ada.

Color. Dinky's girlfriend, who asks Effie Jones whom she's going to dance with since she has broken up with her old boyfriend Sam.

"Muttsy." One of Muttsy Owens's old girlfriends, who is jealous of his attentions to Pinkie Jones.

Age.

Eyes. Joe Starks begins to mention Janie's advancing age as he gets older. Yet, despite the twelve-year difference in Janie and Tea Cake's ages, age doesn't seem to matter to the younger Tea Cake; he assures her that he doesn't care about the age difference.

Agrippa.

"Gaul." He is made King of Judea by Caligula after he betrays Antipas.

"Veil." Herodias's irresponsible but charming brother, who tells her that Antipas is meeting with John the Baptist.

Alexander.

Mules. Great hoodoo doctor who first senses Marie Leveau's power and convinces her to study hoodoo with him.

Alexander.

"Veil." Herod's son who, along with his brother Miriamne, had plotted to kill their father and was executed.

Hubert Alexander.

Mules. Young boy in the middle of the ring as the children play "Going 'Round de Mountain" in the street on Zora's last day in Eatonville.

Mrs. Bertha Allen.

Mules. Woman who ran the boarding house where Hurston stayed in Loughman, Florida. Her daughter is Babe Hill and her grandson is Cliffert Ulmer.

Jim Allen.

Mules. Old man from Polk County (and Cliff Ulmer's grandfather) who tells the tales of "Why the Sister in Black Works Hardest," "How the Snake Got Poison," "The Hawk and the Buzzard," and "The

Son Who Went to College"; a member of the swamp-gang, he accompanies Hurston on their fishing trip and tells the others how to eat fish.

Tookie Allen.
Mules. Good looking woman who walks past the sawmill in Loughman, Florida in a tight dress, attracting the attention of all the men.

Alligators.
Mules. Folktales related to alligators include such stories as "How the 'Gator Got His Mouth," "How Brer 'Gator Got His Tongue Worn Out," and "How the 'Gator Got Black."

"Uncle Monday." Uncle Monday uses alligators to convince his rival hoodoo doctor, Ant Judy Bickerstaff, that he is superior to her. Hurston was also fond of the phrase, "Go gator and muddy the water," which she used in her dedication to Bob Wunsch in *Jonah's Gourd Vine*, and which the men in the crowd urged Jim Meserve on with in his courtship of Arvay Henson in *Seraph on the Suwanee*.

Amram.
Moses. Moses' (alleged) Hebrew father, who is willing to kill the baby Moses himself rather than have Pharaoh's soldiers do it.

Anderson.
Vine. Member of Zion Hope Baptist Church who sends up a chant following John Pearson's rousing final sermon.

Becky Anderson.
Eyes. According to one of the tales told about Matt Bonner's yellow mule, she is joined under her umbrella by the mule on her way to Maitland.

Dilcie Anderson.
Bone. Woman who wants to testify at Jim Weston's trial, even though she had left ten minutes before the fight started. She is also called Becky Anderson in Act II.

Old Man Anderson.
"Anthology." Man who lives out in the country and has never seen a train; when he finally does, he runs from it.

"Sweat." Man who suggests taking Sykes Jones and his mistress Bertha out and whipping them to teach them a lesson.

Wize Anderson.
"Contention." Methodist court observer who sides with Jim Weston.

Animals.
Of course, animals are ubiquitous in the natural, open settings of Hurston's stories. She uses them as more than scenery, however, as she relates their behavior, tells stories about their relationships to people, uses their characteristics metaphorically to describe her characters, and incorporates them into her folktales.

"Cock Robin." In fable form, Hurston relates the story of the death of the famous bird, but metaphorically satirizes the nature of her people.

Eyes. The behavior of the animals during a hurricane indicates the seriousness of the coming storm.

"Spunk." Joe Kanty gets his revenge on the man who stole his wife; Kanty killed him by returning as a bob cat. (See also entries on Alligators, Bees, Birds, Cows, Dogs, Mules, and Snakes)

Antigonus.
"Gaul." Last of the Asamonean claimants to the throne of Judea.

Antipas.
"Gaul." Antipas plots to assassinate Pontius Pilate and is exiled; he is grieved by John the Baptist's death.

"Veil." Herod the Great's son, prince of Judea and Tetrarch of Galilee, who marries Herodias after his divorce from the daughter of the King of Arabia; he is exiled to Gaul for plotting to overthrow Roman power in Palestine.

Archelaus.
"Veil." Antipas's older brother, whom King Herod the Great named as his successor.

Aretus.
"Veil," and "Gaul." King of Arabia, whose daughter is married to Antipas and who then divorces her so that he can marry Herodias, an action that prompts Aretus to lead an army against Antipas.

Aristobulus.
"Veil." Miriamne's second son; Herodias's father.

Ida Armstrong.
"Six-Bits." Fat woman whom Otis D. Slemmons comments upon when she comes into his ice cream parlor.

"Art and Such."
Hurston's essay on art and literature written for "The Florida Negro" while she was working on the Federal Writers' Project in 1938. In the essay Hurston first discusses impediments to the development of African American art and literature since the Civil War and then asserts the black artist's right to extend the subject matter of his or her art beyond race and repression, subjects then relegated to most black artists and writers. At the end of the essay she mentions a few prominent black Floridian artists and writers, but spends the most time on herself. She credits herself with two innovations: her objective point of view and her use of the Negro idiom in her writing.

⤐ B ⤐

Senator Bailey.
Bone. Young boy and Daisy Taylor's brother who comes to the store to find Daisy.

Joe Banks.
"Six-Bits." Missie May's devoted husband, who works at G & G Fertilizer plant; he returns to her after her affair with Otis D. Slemmons once he sees that the child Missie May bears is really his and not Slemmons's.

Missie May Banks.
"Six-Bits." Joe Banks's young wife, who is happy until Otis D. Slemmons seduces her; she is reunited with Joe after he sees that he is the father of her baby.

Spunk Banks.
"Spunk." Sawmill worker who cuckholds Joe Kanty and later shoots him. Although he is cleared in the subsequent trial by virtue of self-defense, Spunk pays for his crime when Joe returns as a bob-

cat to haunt him and pushes him onto the circle saw, killing Spunk and revenging his loss.

Lonnie Barnes.
Mules. Polk County man and a member of the swamp-gang, who goes on the fishing trip and tells the tales of "The Turtle-Watch" and "How the Woodpecker Nearly Drowned the Whole World."

Johnnie Barton.
Mules. Man from Altamonte who plays guitar for Georgia Burke and George Thomas to sing at the toe-party in Wood Bridge.

Clarence Beale.
Mules. Man who requests more scary stories from A.D. so that Lessie Lee Hudson will want to snuggle up to him.

Clement Beasley.
"Conscience." White loan shark who is attacked by Laura Lee Kimble when he tries to repossess her employer's furniture prematurely.

Emmaline "Emma" Beasely (also spelled Beazeby and Beazeley in the play).
Color. John Turner's dark-skinned girlfriend, who is jealous of his "supposed" attentions to lighter-skinned girls; she breaks off with him at the dance and loses him; twenty years later he returns with the intention of finally marrying her, but she loses him again because of her color prejudice.

James Beasley.
Mules. Man accused of assault and attempted murder and imprisoned, who pays Dr. Duke $185 to keep himself from being convicted.

Rush Beasley.
Vine. Unscrupulous white farmer who cheats Ned Crittenden out of the cotton he raised.

General Beaufort.
"Conscience." Celestine Beaufort Clairborne's father, who gives Laura Lee and Tom Kimble a house on his place so that they can look out for his daughter.

Miz' Beaufort.

"Conscience." Celestine Beaufort Clairborne's mother, who had put Laura Lee Kimble in charge of Celestine's care when Celestine was born.

Beds.

Vine. The walnut bed given to John and Lucy Pearson as a wedding present from Alf Pearson is later taken from Lucy by her brother Bud for a $3 debt. Later she sews for a white woman and gets another bed, which she leaves to her daughter Isis.

Bees.

Eyes. Bees are a symbol of the male aspect of sexuality in both Janie's dream under the pear tree and in her description of Tea Cake as a "bee to her blossom."

Bentley.

"Magnolia." Runaway slave who becomes prosperous down in Florida on the banks of the St. John's River; he marries a Cherokee woman, Swift Deer, but his heart eventually hardens to everyone except his daughter Magnolia Flower; he dies of a heart attack when Magnolia Flower runs off with a mixed-race man named John.

Andrew Berry.

Vine. Member of Zion Hope Baptist Church who warns Rev. Pearson about the plot to replace him with Rev. Felton Cozy. He speaks up in support of Pearson later at the church meeting following Pearson's divorce from Hattie Tyson.

Sister Berry.

Vine. Zion Hope Baptist churchmember who supports Rev. Pearson at the first meeting called to oppose him. Later Pearson's opposition plans to use her involvement with Pearson against him.

Bertha.

"Muttsy." One of the loose young women at Ma Turner's place, who makes fun of Pinkie Jones's appearance.

Bertha.
"Sweat." Sykes Jones's present mistress, a fat, bold woman from Apopka, to whom Sykes promises his wife Delia's house.

Beulah.
"Light." Dog whose chin Joel Watts puts shaving cream on.

Bickerstaffs.
Vine. Poor white tenant farmers who rescue John Pearson from the Alabama River after the bridge collapses.

Ant Judy Bickerstaff.
"Uncle Monday." Rival of Uncle Monday's whose power is tested and broken after she is brought to the lake and overpowered by Uncle Monday and alligators, who force her to acknowledge his superior power.

Ned Bickerstaff.
"Bridge." Conjure man Luke Mimms gets help from to keep his wife faithful.
"Uncle Monday." Ant Judy's son, who sees a huge alligator swim away just as he arrives to rescue his mother from the lake.

Big John de Conqueror.
Eyes, Mules, "High John." Mythic African American folk hero whose amazing feats of daring and strength provide the material for countless stories and folktales.

Big 'Oman.
Eyes. Pretty young girl whom the boys all want to buy treats for.
Vine. Young girl who is interested in John Buddy and with whom John Pearson has an affair after he marries Lucy Potts. John is riding home from Big 'Oman's house when the bridge collapses, plunging him into the Alabama River.

Big Sweet.
Dust, Mules. Rough Polk County woman who helped Hurston collect folk material and who defended her against Lucy in a knife fight. She tells the tales of "Why the Mocking Bird Is Away on Friday" and

"How the 'Gator Got Black." She shacks up with Joe Williard and goes on the fishing trip with the others.

Birds.
Eyes. The buzzards' funeral over the body of Matt Bonner's dead mule mirrors the human funeral that precedes it. Janie describes rumor as a "wingless bird."

Mules. Folktales include stories about the woodpecker and the mockingbird.

Vine. During John Pearson's marriage proposal to Lucy Potts, he asks her if she'd rather be a "lark uh flyin' [or a] dove uh settin'."

Birth.
Although not a mother herself, Hurston includes some accounts of births in her work.

Dust. Hurston recounts the humorous story of her birth, during which her mother was aided by a passing white man.

Moses. The novel opens with a gripping account of Jochebed's harrowing physical and emotional travail in bringing her son into the world while trying to keep quiet and not alert Pharoah's secret police.

Vine. The birth of several of Lucy Pearson's children occurs during the novel.

Black Baby.
Mules. Polk County man and member of the swamp-gang who goes on the fishing trip and tells the tale of "The First Colored Man in Massa's House."

"Black Death."
Hoodoo tale (set in Eatonville) which won Hurston an honorable mention in the first *Opportunity* contest in 1925. The story of Old Man Morgan, a powerful conjure doctor, appeared in essentially the same form in Hurston's 1931 article in the *Journal of American Folklore*, "Hoodoo in America."

Sister Blackbird.
"Cock Robin." Bird who criticizes Brother Owl for not telling the others about the need for money for Cock Robin's funeral.

Blue.
Mules. Fellow card player in game at Loughman with Big Sweet and Hardy.

Blue.
Vine. Fellow worker of John Pearson's in railroad camp who praises John's ability to imitate preachers.

Blue Baby.
Mules. Polk County man and member of the swamp-gang who spars verbally about ugly men with Officer Richardson.

Bluefront.
"Muttsy." Boatman who brings Pinkie Jones to Harlem; he later makes advances towards her at Ma Turner's place but is quickly rebuffed; it is he who starts Muttsy Owens gambling again after Muttsy's marriage to Pinkie.

Daisy Blunt.
Eyes. The prettiest of the town girls, who dresses in white to contrast her rich dark skin; all the boys in town go crazy over her; Charlie Jones and Jim Weston argue over who would do the most for her.

Mrs. Blunt.
Bone. Daisy Taylor's mother, who refuses to allow her name to be mentioned during Jim Weston's trial. Note: Daisy is later given the last names Bailey and Blunt.

Franz Boas.
Professor of anthropology at Barnard College with whom Hurston studied, who influenced her collection of folklore and her ethnographic methodology. In his preface to *Mules and Men*, he praised the book as "an unusual contribution to our knowledge of the true inner life of the Negro."

Docia Boger.
"Black Death." Chambermaid at the Park House Hotel in Maitland who is seduced by Beau Diddely; she moves to Jacksonville after Beau's death and marries.
Color. Contestant from Ocala whose dance partner is Oscar Clarke.

Lum Boger.
"Anthology." Single man engaged to the assistant school teacher.
Bone. Young man who acts as marshall of the court and has trouble maintaining order during the trial; his full name is Columbus; he is Walter Thomas's card partner.
"Contention." Marshall of the court who conducts Joe Clarke into the trial as judge.

Mrs. Boger.
"Black Death." Widow who consults Old Man Morgan after her daughter Docia is seduced and left pregnant by Beau Diddely; Mrs. Boger shoots Beau's image in a mirror and he dies.

Sister Boger.
Vine. Member of Zion Hope Baptist Church who is unimpressed by Rev. Felton Cozy's trial sermon. Without a biblical text, the sermon seems more like a lecture to her.

Mrs. Bogle.
Eyes. Woman who starts singing "We'll Walk in the Light" in her alto voice when the street lamp is lit; the townspeople join in. Her first husband was a coachman who later became a preacher; her second husband was a worker in Fohnes's orange grove who became only a class leader.

"The Bone of Contention."
Story written by Hurston while still a student at Howard University that became the basis for *Mule Bone*, her dramatic collaboration with Langston Hughes.

Bombay.
Spears. Monanga's old councilor, who urges him to accede to the Wahehes' terms, even to the point of selling them some of the tribe's young women.

Matt Bonner
Eyes. Owner of ornery old yellow mule, the source of many jokes; Matt thinks he outwits Joe Starks in trading the mule to him for $5 only to find that Joe has bought the mule to give it a rest from Matt.

"Book of Harlem."
Parody of the biblical story of the prodigal son, which was first published in *Zora Neale Hurston: The Complete Stories* (1995).

Bootsie.
Eyes. Pretty young girl whom the boys all want to buy treats for.
Vine. Young girl who is an acquaintance of John Buddy's. She plays hide and seek with John, Mehaley, Big 'Oman, and the other children.

Bootyny.
Eyes. Migrant worker who plays cards with Ed Dockery and Sop-de-Bottom. He helps run off Mrs. Turner's brother.

Dad Boykin.
Mules. Eighty-one-year-old Polk County man who goes on the fishing trip and tells the tale of "How the Lion Met the King of the World"; he tells the others how to get warm.

Box-Car Daddy.
Mules. Member of the chain gang who leaves the jook when the Quarters Boss comes by but returns and sings.

Dinkie Bradley.
"Uncle Monday." Pregnant young girl whom John Wesley Hogan refuses to marry despite her mother's entreaties.

Janie Bradley.
Color. Contestant from Daytona whose dance partner is Enoch Nixon.

Mrs. Bradley.
"Uncle Monday." Dinkie Bradley's mother, who goes to John Wesley Hogan to ask him to marry her pregnant daughter but is rebuffed, prompting her to seek help from Uncle Monday. She shoots a gun at John Wesley's image in a mirror at Uncle Monday's house and John Wesley falls dead in the road miles away.

Brawley.
Seraph. Oldest son of Minnie Brawley, who is driving the family wagon to church when they pass Arvay Henson and Jim Meserve and offer them a ride, which Jim refuses.

Minnie Brawley.
Seraph. Old busybody riding to church with her family who cranes to see Arvay Henson and Jim Meserve walking together on their first date.

Brazzle.
"Anthology." Biggest liar in the world according to his wife; Brazzle claims to have seen a doctor in Orlando cut open a woman, take out her organs, and then replace them completely.

"Contention." Baptist owner of his Yaller Highness, a mean old mule.

Gene Brazzle.
Mules. Eatonville man who is playing cards on the porch when Zora arrives to collect folktales. He attends the toe-party in Wood Bridge.

Matt Brazzle.
Bone. Old man who was the owner of the yellow mule from which the mule bone weapon was taken.

Caddie Brewton.
"Uncle Monday." Man whom Mary Ella Shaw sees and falls in love with the day before her wedding to Joe Nathan Moss.

Bridges.
"Bridge." Luke Mimms dies just as he goes under the bridge after realizing that his son and wife are in love.

Eyes. Janie and Tea Cake seek safety at the Six Mile Bridge, only to find it already full of refugees.

"John Redding." The washed out bridge over the St. John [*sic*] River carries John Redding's body away.

Vine. the bridge over the Alabama River collapses as John Pearson is riding over it, prompting his "baptism" and subsequent career change to preacher.

Brook.
"Magnolia." Babbling brook that listens to the river tell the story and welcomes the two lovers back to its shores after forty-seven years.

Babe Brown.
Mules. Man who plays the guitar at the toe-party in Wood Bridge.

Donnie Brown.
Mules. Two-year-old boy who is the hindmost chick in the "Chirck, mah Chick, mah Craney crow" game the children are playing in the street on Zora's last day in Eatonville.

Horace Brown.
"Black Death." Man cursed with a traveling curse after Old Man Morgan put a black snake's shed skin in his shoes.

Joe Brown.
"Gas" and "Harlem Slang." Policeman who had beaten Sweet Back and Jelly the previous night; he hates pimps.

Sheriff Joe Brown.
Mules. Sheriff who arrested Sack Daddy for murder barely two weeks after Sack Daddy's luck changed after he killed a cat.

Kitty Brown.
Mules. Catholic New Orleans hoodoo doctor with whom Hurston studied who grows her own herbs.

Jeff Bruce.
Eyes. One of the Eatonville townsfolk who criticize Joe Starks behind his back.

Bull Sparrow.
"Cock Robin." Cock Robin's killer, who later leads his funeral parade.

Bully.
Vine. Man who calls the figures at dances and informs the people at the cotton harvest celebration that the food is ready. He tells John

that Mehaley is the one who erased Lucy's name from Aunt Pheemy's chimney.

Gertie Burden.
Vine. Twenty-two-year-old woman with whom John Pearson carries on an affair. She finally ends the affair when she gets an offer to marry a man who owns an orange grove.

Georgia Burke.
Mules. Woman from Altamonte who sings with George Thomas in her fine alto at the toe-party in Wood Bridge.

Sister Buzzard.
"Cock Robin." Owner of the Shimmy Shack, a high class hotel on Beale Street in Memphis; she is angered that Cock Robin's body is left in front of her hotel.

Henry "Nigger" Byrd.
Mules. Eatonville man who tells the tale of "A Fast Horse."

✴ C ✴

Caleb.
Moses. Hebrew co-worker of Amram; he becomes head military trainer of the young men and is one of the spies who believes that the Israelites can capture the land of Canaan.

Caligula.
"Gaul." Successor to Tiberius.
"Veil." Roman emperor who set Antipas free but later exiled him to Lyons.

Callimander.
"Gaul." A Greek from Corinth, Callimander is Herodias's trusted house steward, whom she sends on a secret mission to locate John the Baptist.

Candles.
Mules. Extensive use of candles is made in the hoodoo ceremonies that Hurston describes. Always the anthropologist, she also alludes to the candles on the altars of churches as vestiges of ancient fire worship.

Candy.
"Six-Bits." Joe Banks throws candy kisses on Missie May's doorstep as a sign of his love; he returns to the practice at the end of the story when he and Missie May are reconciled.

Sister Carey.
Vine. Member of Zion Hope Baptist Church who brings ginger-bread and melon-rind preserves to John Pearson after he quits the pulpit of the church. She and Sister White encourage him to return to the pulpit, but he declines.

Cars.
Eyes. Tea Cake hires a car to take Janie to the picnic and later teaches her how to drive, a sign of her empowerment.

"Light." Isis rides in a car with passing white people, a means of escape for the young child.

Vine. Sally Lovelace buys John Pearson a Cadillac for a first anniversary present, but it turns out to be a coffin for John, who collides with a train.

Dan Carter.
"Bridge." Young man Luke Mimms suggests that his son Artie take hunting, but Artie takes his stepmother Vangie instead.

Dave Carter.
Bone. Jim Weston's Baptist friend and partner in song and dance act who is his rival for Daisy Taylor's atttentions; at the end of the play he and Jim abandon Daisy and renew their partnership.

"Contention." Hunter who is hit on the head with a mule bone by Jim Weston and swears out a warrant for Jim's arrest; he is a Baptist.

"Sweat." One of the men on Joe Clarke's porch; he disparages Bertha after she walks off with Sykes Jones.

Sister Laura Carter.
Bone. Would-be witness at Jim Weston's trial.

Bradford Cary III.
Seraph. Wealthiest man in Sawley, Florida, a banker and later governor of Florida, he helps Maria Henson in order to curry favor with the electorate. His son plays in the same band as Kenny Meserve.

Evelyn Cary.
Seraph. Bradford Cary's wife, who calls the hotel in Sawley to give instructions for Arvay Meserve's care and attention.

"Characteristics of Negro Expression."
One of several essays written by Hurston included in Nancy Cunard's 1934 anthology *Negro*. In this essay, one of Hurston's earliest attempts to incorporate her anthropological fieldwork into her writing, Hurston praises the creativity and unique aesthetics of black language, as well as its impact on the overall American culture.

Charlie.
Seraph. Best turpentine chipper in the camp, whose work Jim Meserve criticizes when he is upset over Arvay Henson.

Charlie.
Seraph. Third man on the *Angeline*, the boat Jim Meserve captains.

Charlie.
Vine. Young man on Pearson plantation who plays hide and seek with the other children and befriends John Buddy.

Checkers.
Bone, "Anthology." The men on the store porch play checkers as they talk.
Eyes. Tea Cake teaches Janie to play checkers, even though her former husband, Joe Starks, had said that she could never learn how.

Uncle Chester.
Seraph. Maria Henson's mentally unbalanced brother, whom Arvay realizes her son Earl favors.

Elder Childers.
Bone. Baptist minister who acts as prosecuting attorney in Dave Carter's case against Jim Weston; he proves that the mule bone is a weapon.

Chimney.
Vine. John Buddy writes Lucy's name on Aunt Pheemy's chimney, but Mehaley erases it.

Celestine Beaufort Clairborne.
"Conscience." Laura Lee Kimble's white employer; she is the widow of J. Stuart Clairborne.

J. Stuart Clairborne.
"Conscience." Young white lawyer without money who had married Celestine Beaufort, but after a few years of relative prosperity he had died, leaving Celestine in financial straits.

Ike Clarke.
"Spunk." Storeowner who lights the town lamp when it gets dark.

Joe Clarke.
"Anthology." Storeowner, mayor, and postmaster of Eatonville, who tries to catch Coon Taylor stealing his watermelons.
Bone. Judge at Jim Weston's trial; Clarke feels threatened by Rev. Simms' encroachment of his authority.
Color. Grand Master of Ceremonies at the cake walk dance contest.
"Contention." Methodist storeowner and mayor who started the town.
Dust. Eatonville storeowner, whose store's porch served as a gathering place for the community and a platform for storytelling.
"Sweat." Storeowner whose porch serves as the town's meeting place; he comments on the negative effects of wifebeating, comparing it to chewing the sweetness out of sugar cane.
"Uncle Monday." First one in town to learn Uncle Monday's name.
Vine. Mayor of Eatonville from whom John Pearson first rents and then buys his first house in town. Clarke owns the town's store, whose porch serves as a meeting place for the townspeople.

Mathilda Clarke.
Color. Winner of the pas-me-la contest.

Mattie Clarke.
Bone. Mayor Joe Clarke's wife, who knuckles under to his bullying.
Vine. Eatonville woman who questions Lucy Pearson about the state of her soul on her deathbed.

Mrs. Clarke.
"Anthology." Joe Clarke's wife who helps him in his store; she is beaten by him when she is younger; she calls him Jody (the same nickname that Janie gives Joe Starks in *Their Eyes Were Watching God*).

Oscar Clarke.
Color. Contestant from Ocala whose dance partner is Docia Boger.

Willie Mae Clarke.
Mules. Woman at the toe-party who likes George Brown.

Clary.
Vine. Young school girl who joins the others in taunting John Pearson the first time he passes the school.

Cock Robin.
"Cock Robin." Philandering bird shot by Bull Sparrow whose funeral turns into a spectacle; although Cock Robin was a member of every fraternal and benevolent order in town, no one wants to bury him.

"Cock Robin Beale Street."
Fable recounting all the other animals' responses to the funeral of Cock Robin. The story was originally one of nine skits in Hurston's dramatic revue "Cold Keener."

Will Cody.
Bone. Man who hangs out at Joe Clarke's store; he is teased because he hasn't brought his "wife" to town.

Lee Coker.
Eyes. One of the first two men to welcome Joe and Janie Starks to Eatonville.

Ned Coles.
Color. Contestant from St. Augustine whose dance partner is Miss Lucy Taylor.

Color Struck.
Hurston's first play; a short work consisting of only four scenes, it depicts the devastating effects of intraracial color prejudice on the lives of a group of African Americans. The play won second place in the first *Opportunity* contest in 1925 and was published in *Fire!!* (1926).

For Further Reading:

Classon, H. Lin. "Re-Evaluating *Color Struck*: Zora Neale Hurston and the Issue of Colorism." *Theatre Studies* 42 (1997): 5–18.

Conjuring.
Eyes. The townspeople think that Janie "fixed" Joe Starks and made him ill. Joe calls a root doctor to help him and ignores the real doctor's advice until it is too late.
"John Redding." Matty Redding fears that her son John has had a spell put on him. (See also Hoodoo)

"The Conscience of the Court."
Hurston's story of the trial of a loyal black family servant on trial for assaulting a white loan shark who attempted to take her mistress's furniture illegally in repayment for a debt. Ironically, at the time of the story's publication in the *Saturday Evening Post* on March 18, 1950, Hurston was herself working as a maid in Miami. When the situation became known, Hurston was interviewed, and the story, by journalist James Lyons, "Famous Negro Author Working as Maid Here Just 'to Live a Little,'" appeared in the *Miami Herald* on March 27, 1950.

Levi Conway.

Mules. Rich ferryman and property owner whose appearance, conduct, and fortune dissipate over a ten-year period and who eventually dies due to Pere Voltaire's curse.

Coodemay.

Eyes. Man who serves as the catalyst for the fight that breaks up Mrs. Turner's restaurant when in his inebriated state he tries to force Sop-de-Bottom out of his seat; after the fight he admits his fault and offers to buy everyone a drink; he comes back on Monday to pay Mrs. Turner $5 for the damages.

Miss Nancy Coon.

"Anthology." Raccoon loved by both Mr. Dog and Mr. Rabbit; she asks them for a week's time to decide whose proposal to accept.

Alfredo Corregio.

Seraph. Portuguese fisherman who moves into Jim Meserve's house in the grove after Joe Kelsey's family moves to town; Jim later puts up the money for a boat, the *Arvay Henson*, for Alfredo to fish with; still later Jim fishes with him in a second boat, the *Angeline*.

Felicia Corregio.

Seraph. The Corregios' younger daughter, who plays with Kenny and Angie Meserve; when she is 15 she accompanies Kenny to a University of Florida football game.

Lucy Ann Corregio.

Seraph. The Corregios' older daughter; she is attacked by Earl Meserve.

Mrs. Corregio.

Seraph. Savannah-born woman who marries Alfredo Corregio; Arvay doesn't like her because she cooks seafood and invites Jim to eat with them.

"Court Orders Races Can't Mix."

Hurston's letter to the editor of the *Orlando Sentinel* published on August 11, 1955, expressing Hurston's conservative (and, according to some, reactionary) response to the Supreme Court's 1954 decision on school desegregation. Hurston based her response on the assertion that African Americans should not be fooled into following the white lead in all areas of life, but instead should concentrate on seeing that "the compulsory education provisions for Negroes in the South [are enforced] as is done for white children." As a person proud of her race, she points out the contradiction of "scream[ing] race pride and equality while at the same time spurning Negro teachers and self-association." Her growing political conservatism is further evident when she predicts that this intrusion of federal control over the states is but the first of many future inroads against the Constitution. Her letter was widely reprinted in Southern newspapers and severely criticized by civil rights leaders.

Courtship.

Hurston's stories portray a full range of courtship rituals, displaying a whole continuum of successful and failed romances.

"Contention," *Bone*. Dave Carter and Jim Weston's rivalry leads them to exaggerate their intentions toward Daisy Taylor during their courtship, although in *Mule Bone* Daisy's charms do not prove as powerful a draw as the two men's friendship.

Eyes. The contrasts between Logan Killicks's noncourtship of Janie through an arranged marriage, Joe Starks's courtship in tempting Janie to run away with him, and Tea Cake Woods's romantic courtship of Janie illustrate the many differences in courtship styles and outcomes. In addition, after Joe's death, Janie is beset by more suitors than Penelope, until Tea Cake comes along and wins her heart. The boys in the town show similar interest in the attractive Daisy Blunt.

Seraph. Jim Meserve's courtship of Arvay Henson is similar to the *Taming of the Shrew*. Hatton Howland's courtship of Angie Meserve ends in an elopement.

Vine. John Pearson's courtship of Lucy Potts is hindered by interference from Lucy's mother.

Cows.

Eyes. Janie holds onto a cow's tail to pull her to higher ground during the flood.

Vine. Lucy Pearson wants her children to grow up to be "bell cows" (leaders, not followers).

Jimmy Cox.
Bone. Bootsie Pitts's new beau from Altamont.

Rev. Felton Cozy.
Vine. Stuffy minister who replaces John Pearson as pastor of Zion Hope Baptist Church. In his trial sermon Rev. Cozy claims to be a "race man."

Janie Mae Crawford.
Eyes. Janie's maiden name; (See also Janie).

Tripp Crawford.
Eyes. Store customer whom Hezekiah castigates in the manner of Joe Starks when Tripp asks for more credit before having paid his previous bill.

"Crazy for this Democracy."
Article published in December 1945 *Negro Digest* in which Hurston included some of the anti-American ideas which her publishers had persuaded her to edit out of her 1942 autobiography *Dust Tracks on a Road.* In this essay she parodies Franklin Delano Roosevelt's phrase "the arsenal of democracy" as "the arse-and-all of democracy" because the country that has fought a war for freedom still tolerates injustice around the world and at home, especially in its Jim Crow laws, which Hurston advocates should be repealed not eventually, but immediately.

Crazy Joe.
"Magnolia." Simple-minded man Bentley plans to force his daughter Magnolia Flower to marry to prevent her from marrying John.

Creation Story.
Eyes. Janie tells the story of how man's spark was eventually covered by mud and that the lonely sparks are in search of each other now.
Mules. Hurston includes folktales about creation in this anthropological work.

Crip.
Mules. New skitter man who throws a razor at Big Sweet's head during her fight with Lucy.

Amy Crittenden.

Vine. John Pearson's mother, who was born on the Pearson plantation in 1853 and bore John sometime after the end of the Civil War. When John was four, she married Ned Crittenden.

Ned Crittenden.

Vine. John Pearson's abusive step-father. Ned beats his wife Amy and disparages John for his light skin color, ultimately prompting John to break away from the family for good.

Ezekial "Zeke" Crittenden.

Vine. Oldest of John Pearson's younger half-brothers; he cries when John first leaves the family to go to Notasulga. John tells Zeke to look out for his girlfriend Lucy when he goes off to the tie camp on the Alabama River. Zeke brings a letter from Lucy to John at the tie camp. Years later Zeke moves to Eatonville a year or two before Lucy dies and is a source of comfort to John in the ensuing years.

Zachariah "Zack" Crittenden.

Vine. One of John Pearson's younger half-brothers, nicknamed Zack.

Albert Crooms.

"Anthology." Fruit picker who has a long affair with Daisy Taylor.

Laura Crooms.

"Anthology." Albert's longsuffering wife, who finally has had enough and beats up her rival Daisy Taylor with an ax handle.

Brother Crow.

"Cock Robin." Crow who claims to have spotted a few of Cock Robin's blue eggs around his nest; he remembers Sister Speckled-Hen's fish fry and barbecue when talk of raising money for Cock Robin's funeral arises.

"Cudjo's Own Story of the Last African Slaver."

Hurston's account of her 1927 interview in Mobile, Alabama, with Cudjo Lewis, the only living survivor of the *Clotilde*, the last slave ship to land on American soil in 1859. Much of the article, published in the October 1927 issue of the *Journal of Negro History*, she plagiarized from Emma Langdon Roche's book *Historic Sketches of the Old South* (1914), but her theft was not detected until 1972 by linguist William Stewart.

Cup-Cake.
Seraph. Third man and cook on the *Arvay Henson* when Jim Meserve takes Arvay out for the first time.

❋ D ❋

Dancing.
Dancing is an integral part of the musical reviews that Hurston produced, *The Great Day*, *From Sun to Sun*, and *Singing Steel*. Dance expresses the African character better than almost any other medium.

Color. A cake walk dance parade is the occasion for the jealousy that leads to Emma Beasely's breakup with John Turner. The third scene of the play consists mostly of the dance contest.

Eyes. John and Lucy Pearson's "grand march" is not considered dancing because they don't cross their feet.

Mules, Horse. Many of the hoodoo ceremonies Hurston describes incorporate dances into their rituals, especially as a means of empowering the participants.

"Veil." Salome's dance of the seven veils results in the death of John the Baptist.

Calvin Daniels.
Mules. Eatonville man who invites Zora to a toe-party in Wood Bridge; tells the story of "John and the Frog."

Dave.
Eyes.   Young man who joins Jim Weston and Charlie Jones in pay-
ing court to Daisy Blunt.
Mules. Servant of white Middle Georgia planter who uses hoodoo
to exact revenge for the man's murder of his daughter.

Brother Davis.
Eyes. Man who leads the town in prayer at the lighting of the street
lamp.

Edna Davis.
"John Redding." Witch Judy Davis's daughter, who had wanted
to marry Alfred Redding, thus prompting her mother's curse on
Matty Redding.

Old Lady Davis.
Eyes. Woman Joe Starks hires to cook for him after he gets sick and
ostracizes Janie.

Witch Judy Davis.
"John Redding." Woman who had sworn to put travel dust on
Matty Redding's son John because Matty stole Alfred Redding from
her daughter Edna.

"De Turkey and de Law."
Hurston's rewrite of *Mule Bone*, emphasizing the hunting prowess
of Jim Weston and Dave Carter as the play's central conflict rather
than their rivalry over the favors of a young woman (which Langton
Hughes had shifted the emphasis to).

Death.
Old "slew-footed" Death sticks his ugly head in at the most in-
opportune moments in Hurston's fiction, although in some cases, the
deaths are inevitable.
Dust. Hurston recounts her own mother's death from the perspective of a young daughter.

Eyes. Nanny's death at the beginning of the book is expected. Joe
Starks's death comes as a result of his way of life. Tea Cake is con-
scripted to help bury the dead following the hurricane. Then his

death comes as a result of the bite from a rabid dog. Death is described as a square-toed monster who lives in a house without a roof.

"John Redding." John Redding's death by drowning in the river sets him free.

Moses. The death of Moses at the end of the novel is preceded by many deaths, starting in Egypt with the plague on the firstborn and culminating in Moses' killing of Aaron.

Seraph. Earl Meserve's violent death is the culmination of years of pent-up violence; Arvay Henson's deathbed visit with her mother brings her life into better focus.

"Spunk." Joe Kanty is shot to death by Spunk Banks but gets his revenge on Spunk by pushing him onto the circle saw.

"Sweat." Sykes Jones's death from a rattlesnake bite is just retribution for his abuse of his wife Delia.

Vine. Lucy Pearson's death causes the breakup of the Pearson family; John Pearson's death is the final punishment for his fatal flaw, infidelity, when he is hit by train.

Della.
Vine. Woman who helps Aunt Pheemy deliver Lucy Pearson's first daughter.

Delphine.
Vine. Woman from Opelika who draws John Pearson's attention away from Lucy at the time of the birth of their first daughter.

Delphine.
"Anthology." Bold woman nicknamed "Miss Pheeny" with whom Mitchell Potts has an open affair.

Aunt Dangie Dewoe.
Vine. Hoodoo doctor whom Hattie Tyson consults to win John Pearson's affections.

Beau Diddely.
"Black Death." Waiter at the Park House Hotel in Maitland who seduces Docia Boger and then refuses to marry her; he dies of heart

failure when Mrs. Boger shoots his image in Old Man Morgan's mirror.

Dink.
Vine. Lucy Potts's older married sister, who attempts to help Lucy and John by distracting her mother's attention.

Dinky.
Color. Ada's boyfriend, who flirts with Effie Jones on the train until Ada shows up.

Disease.
Eyes. Joe Starks dies of a kidney ailment; Tea Cake dies of rabies.

Moses. The land of Egypt is hit by a series of plagues; later Miriam is cursed with leprosy by Moses.

Mules, Horse. Many hoodoo spells bring about or cure various maladies.

Vine. Isie Pearson's bout with typhoid drives her father to the arms of another woman for comfort.

Aunt Diskie.
"High John." Slave whom High John de Conquer takes with him on his journey through heaven and hell in search of a song.

Divorce.
Hurston herself was divorced twice (from Herbert Sheen in 1931 and Albert Price III in 1943).

"Gaul" and "Veil." Antipas divorces his first wife so that he can marry Herodias.

Vine. Hattie Tyson divorces John Pearson, leading to his downfall from the pulpit of Zion Hope Baptist Church.

Ed Dockery.
Eyes. Migrant worker who plays cards with Sop-de-Bottom and Bootyny and beats them; with his winnings he plans to buy some fine clothes from Sears and Roebuck. He fights Dick Sterrett during the fight at Mrs. Turner's.

Do-dirty.
Vine. Supposed Don Juan who works at the tie camp with John Pearson; he takes John to town with him on Saturday nights.

John Doe.
Mules. Rachael Roe's lover who betrays her by marrying another but returns to her thanks to Kitty Brown's Death Dance.

Dogs.
"Anthology." Mr. Dog is a major character in one of the vignettes, a folktale. Tippy, Sykes Jones's thin, thieving, egg-sucking dog, withstands all attempts to kill him in another vignette.
Eyes. A rabid dog bites Tea Cake and gives him rabies, resulting in his death.

Mr. Dog.
"Anthology." Dog who seems to have the inside track in gaining Miss Nancy Coon's heart until he is outsmarted by Mr. Rabbit, who cuts Mr. Dog's tongue.

Dolls.
Vine. John Pearson gives Lucy Potts a large china doll for Christmas and puts it on the tree at Macedonia Baptist Church. This gift is the first sign that he likes her.

Domestic violence.
Wife-beating seems to be ubiquitous in the setting of Hurston's work. Yet, despite its prevalence and seeming social acceptance, Hurston manages to present a strong case against it by showing the consequences of such violence.
"Anthology," "Contention," *Bone.* Hurston includes discussions among the men of the town on the subject of wife-beating in these works. Surprisingly, for the time, however, not all the men are in favor of the practice.
Eyes. After Joe Starks hits his wife Janie, their relationship never recovers, moving out of the bedroom into the living room. To prove his control over her, even Tea Cake beats Janie when Mrs. Turner's brother comes to town and provokes Tea Cake's jealousy and insecurity.

"Sweat." Delia Jones takes revenge on her abusive husband Sykes by killing him with a rattlesnake.

Vine. Ned Crittenden beats his wife Amy. Duke hits Exie after Mehaley tells him that she saw her with John outside at the barbecue. The book's most damaging attack, however, occurs when John strikes Lucy. John never forgets the look in Lucy's eyes. Later John beats Hattie Tyson several times for various reasons. The last time he beats her for putting a hoodoo spell on him.

A'nt Dooby.
"Cock Robin." Uncle July's wife, who listens to him tell the story of Cock Robin.

Double Ugly
Eyes. Sore loser who cuts Tea Cake in the back after Tea Cake beats him at dice; he claims that Tea Cake has switched the dice. Tea Cake gets the better of him in the ensuing fight.

Sister Dove.
"Cock Robin." Widow who is the chief mourner at Cock Robin's funeral.

Dramsleg.
"Muttsy." Cohort of Muttsy Owens's who accompanies him to Ma Turner's place; Dramsleg expresses an interest in Pinkie Jones, but Muttsy soon supplants him.

Dreams.
Eyes. After her marriage to Logan Killicks and Nanny's death, "Janie's first dream was dead, so she became a woman." This statement emphasizes Janie's passage from the unrealistic and overly romantic dreams of her girlhood into the reality of adulthood. Then, after Joe hits Janie the first time after she burns dinner, her dream (image) of him is shattered and she realizes even more clearly that her dreams do not mirror her reality.

Seraph. Arvay's dreams illustrate her emotional concerns. She dreams of slitting Lorraine's throat. She dreams of the danger of Earl drowning in the Suwanee River while he is staying with her mother.

Vine. A dream of killing a snake and then losing Lucy on a road prompts John Pearson to leave Sanford.

"Drenched in Light."

One of Hurston's earliest stories (published in *Opportunity* in December 1924), "Drenched in Light" is the story of a young girl much like Hurston, Isis Watts, who hangs out at the gate of her home waiting for the world to pass by and wishing to go along for the ride. Hurston recounted a similar event from her childhood in *Dust Tracks on a Road*. Both that account and this story reveal Hurston's intense desire to travel and see the world at an early age.

Pop Drummond.

Mules. Man from Fernandina, Florida who is an expert on ghosts.

Drums.

Mules. Drums are played during some hoodoo ceremonies.

Spears. The tribesmen dance to the sound of drums to prepare for battle.

Vine. In a connection to their African heritage, the people dance to the drums of their own clapping rather than fiddles at the celebration following the cotton harvest. John's final sermon mentions the "hammers of creation." Then at the end of the book the drums play at John Pearson's funeral.

Duke.

Vine. Man who complains to Alf Pearson about John Pearson's attentons to his wife Exie.

Dr. Duke.

Mules. A root and conjure hoodoo doctor, known as a "swamper," who gathers his own roots and herbs.

Dust Tracks on a Road.

In 1940 Bertram Lippincott suggested that Hurston write an autobiography, so the following year, while she was in California trying to break into the movie industry, Hurston began writing what became one of the most intriguing autobiographical accounts ever written. The book is intriguing both for what she includes and what she does not, for what she left in and for what was edited out.

Originally the book contained many anticolonial sentiments critical of the United States, but after the Japanese attack on Pearl Harbor on December 7, 1941, the editor suggested that Hurston "eliminate

[such] international opinions as irrelevant to autobiography." So, while she revised the book during the early part of 1942, now living back in St. Augustine, Florida, Hurston expunged this material, as well as some of the more controversial racial material. By the time the final version of the book was finished, over 10 percent of the original manuscript had been edited out. Even so, Hurston was able to salvage some of this edited material and published it later in "The 'Pet Negro' System" (published in the *American Mercury* in March 1943) and "Crazy for this Democracy" (published in *Negro Digest* in December 1945). Note: This edited material has been restored to the appendix of the Library of America edition of *Zora Neale Hurston: Folklore, Memoirs, and Other Writings* (1995).

Perhaps due to her watering down her more controversial material, the book was well received by a mostly white audience and sold well when it was published in November 1942. In fact, it won the *Saturday Review*'s Anisfield-Wolf Award of $1,000 for its contribution to the field of race relations. Most reviews of the book were favorable, although it was criticized for its lack of detail, its tendency to ambiguity, and some occasional abstruseness.

Much of the book, however, is not truly autobiographical. Although some accounts are accurate, Hurston, nonetheless, reveals once again her tendency to appropriate and translate scenes from her own life into her fiction. Here the process seems to be working in reverse, for Hurston's depiction of her mother's death resembles very closely the death scene of Lucy Pearson in *Jonah's Gourd Vine*, which she had published eight years earlier.

One of the most cutting criticism of the book, however, was its inclusion of few, if any, scenes of conflict between blacks and whites, with few indications of prejudice, discrimination, or injustice. In fact, the one scene that comes closest to protest literature (the black men of the town, including Hurston's father, band together to resist a lynch mob) turns out to be a false alarm when the men learn that the man being punished is a white man and return to their homes in festive spirits.

But such criticism was not and is not new to Hurston's writing, so the book must ultimately be viewed for what it is: a glimpse into the mind of a writer who consistently revealed most when she tried not to reveal anything and revealed least when she was ostensibly being the most open.

For Further Reading:

Boi, Paola. "Zora Neale Hurston's *Autobiographie Fictive*: Dark Tracks on the Canon of a Female Writer." In *The Black Columbiad: Defining Moments in African American Literature and Culture.* Ed. Werner Sollors and Maria Diedrich. Cambridge, MA: Harvard UP, 1994. 191–200.

Domina, Lynn. " 'Protection in My Mouf': Self, Voice, and Community in Zora Neale Hurston's *Dust Tracks on a Road* and *Mules and Men.*" *African American Review* 31.2 (1997): 197–209.

Fox-Genovese, Elizabeth. "To Write My Self: The Autobiographies of Afro-American Women." In *Feminist Issues in Literary Scholarship.* Ed. Shari Benstock. Bloomington: Indiana UP, 1987. 161–80.

Hassall, Kathleen. "Text and Personality in Disguise and in the Open: Zora Neale Hurston's *Dust Tracks on a Road.*" In *Zora in Florida.* Ed. Steve Glassman and Kathryn Lee Seidel. Orlando: U of Central Florida P, 1991. 159–73.

Hillman, Michael Craig. "*Dust Tracks on a Road* as Literary Biography." *Zora Neale Hurston Forum* 10 (1996): 7–20.

McKay, Nellie. "Race, Gender, and Cultural Context in Zora Neale Hurston's *Dust Tracks on a Road.*" In *Life/Lines: Theorizing Women's Autobiography.* Ed. Bella Brodzki and Celeste Schenck. Ithaca: Cornell UP, 1988. 175–88.

Robey, Judith. "Generic Strategies in Zora Neale Hurston's *Dust Tracks on a Road.*" *Black American Literature Forum* 24.4 (1990): 667–82.

Snyder, Phillip A. "Zora Neale Hurston's *Dust Tracks*: Autobiography and Artist Novel." In *Critical Essays on Zora Neale Hurston.* Ed. Gloria L. Cronin. New York: G.K. Hall, 1998. 173–89.

Wainwright, Mary Katherine. " 'The Map of Dixie on my Tongue' and Other Challenges to Autobiographical Conventions in Hurston's *Dust Tracks on a Road.*" In *All About Zora.* Ed. Alice Morgan Grant. Winter Park, FL: Four-G, 1991. 117–26.

E

East Coast Mary.
Mules. Woman at the dance at the Pine Mill in Polk County.

Cap'n Eaton.
Eyes. White man for whom Eatonville is named; he donated the fifty acres for the settlement of Eatonville. Joe Starks buys an additional two hundred acres from him. Cap'n Eaton lives in Maitland, the nearby town.

Eatonville.
The setting for many of Hurston's stories and novels, Eatonville, just north of Orlando, Florida, was the first incorporated African American town in the United States (1886). Hurston moved there with her family in 1894; her father was elected mayor three times (first in 1897). Although Hurston left Eatonville after her mother's death in 1904, she returned to the town many times in her life, most notably on her trips to collect folklore. In her introduction to *Mules and Men*, she describes the town as a "city of five lakes, three croquet courts, three hundred brown skins, three hundred good swimmers, plenty guavas, two schools, and no jail-house."

For Further Reading:

Lillios, Anna. "Excursions into Zora Neale Hurston's Eatonville." In *Zora in Florida*. Eds. Steve Glassman and Kathryn Lee Seidel. Orlando: U of Central Florida P, 1991. 13–27.
Nathiri, N.Y., ed. *Zora! Zora Neale Hurston: A Woman and Her Community*. Orlando: Sentinel Communications, 1991.

"The Eatonville Anthology."

Fourteen vignettes about town life in Eatonville published serially in the *Messenger* in September, October, and November 1926. Some of the vignettes are character sketches, some folktales, and some anecdotes from Hurston's own experience. Thus, the anthology is a blend of folklore and autobiography rendered in a series of sketches. Although the story's final section was inadvertently cut short in the November issue of the *Messenger*, Hurston was able to use it later in her autobiography, *Dust Tracks on a Road* (1942), as she did with several other vignettes, which appeared in works as varied as *Mule Bone, Mules and Men, Their Eyes Were Watching God*, and *Seraph on the Suwanee*.

Old Edy.

Vine. Woman who helps Aunt Pheemy deliver Lucy's first daughter.

Eleanor.

Eyes. White granddaughter of the Washburns.

Eleazar.

Moses. One of Aaron's sons, a Levite, who supports Moses in punishing the leaders who built the golden calf; Moses makes him high priest after Aaron's death.

Slim Ellis.

Mules. Guitar player at the dance at Pine Hill in Polk County.

Elopement.

Seraph. Arvay Henson elopes with Jim Meserve before their wedding; later their daughter Angie elopes with Hatton Howland.

Emasculation.
Eyes. Janie's disparaging remarks on Joe's waning manly power shame him before the men of the town, prompting him to strike her and drive her out of the store.

Escape.
A common motif in African American writing, escape figures less prominently but still significantly in Hurston's fiction. For Hurston's characters, escape usually comes not from physical enslavement but in terms of individual choice.
Eyes. Janie dreams of escaping from Joe Starks's control and abuse.
"John Redding." John Redding dreams of escaping from home as a child and as a young man, but achieves his escape only in death by floating up the St. John [sic] River.
Moses. Moses leads the Hebrews out of bondage in Egypt. Here the enslavement is physical as well as cultural, and it does parallel African American history in both those respects.

"Escape from Pharaoh."
Excerpt from *Moses, Man of the Mountain* recounting the Hebrews' flight out of Egypt culminating with Pharaoh's forces drowning in the Red Sea; it was included in *The Complete Stories* in 1995.

Eulalia.
Mules. First hoodoo doctor with whom Hurston studies; Eulalia specializes in cases involving relationships between men and women.

Eve.
First. See Mrs. Ham.

Exie.
Vine. Duke's wife, who chases after John Pearson.

Eyes.
Eyes provide insight into Hurston's characters' souls, their motivations, their concerns, and their characters.

Eyes. Janie's, Tea Cake's and Motorboat's eyes are all watching the storm and God; Janie remembers the look of the rabid dog's eyes.

Seraph. Arvay's eyes turn from blue to green when she is sexually aroused; Jim sees through the mask of her face by looking at her eyes.

"Sweat." Delia Jones runs away from her dying husband's eyes.

of the book, after listening to Janie's story, Pheoby Watson says that she is going to insist that her husband Sam take her fishing with him now. Janie's freedom has inspired her to exert her own independence.

Seraph. Jim Meserve and Alfred Corregio get fishing boats; there is a long description of shrimping; Jim takes Arvay out for her first look at the ocean, allowing Arvay her first glimpse of the freedom represented by the sea.

Vine. John Pearson and Sally Lovelace go fishing after they get married. Here the fishing is a continuation of their courtship but also a measure of freedom for Sally, whose previous husband had not allowed her to go fishing.

Brother Fly.
"Cock Robin." Fly who misunderstands Brother Bull's comment about Cock Robin laying eggs.

Food.
Food, an essential element in African American custom (as well as Southern hospitality in general), in Hurston's work is often equated with love and concern. The lack of food, or the refusal of food, indicates the exact opposite.

Eyes. Pheoby brings Janie a plate of mullato rice to welcome her friend back home to Eatonville. Later in the novel, however, when Joe Starks is sick, he refuses Janie's offer of food. Their relationship has ended at this point.

Mules. Following Hurston's fasting during her hoodoo initiation ceremony, a great feast is then consumed by all the celebrants.

Seraph. Arvay Henson is jealous of Mrs. Corregio's cooking because of her husband Jim's obvious enjoyment of it.

Vine. John Pearson experiences real hunger for the first time after his self-imposed exile from Eatonville, wandering around hungry until he meets Sally Lovelace.

Mack C. Ford.
Mules. Expert storyteller from Pierce, Florida (in Polk County), who recounts the tales of "Why the Porpoise Has His Tail on Crossways," "Why the Dog Hates the Cat," "How Jack O'Lanterns Came to Be," "Why the East Coast has Mosquitoes and Storms," and "How a Loving Couple Was Parted."

Minnie Foster.
Mules. Kitty Brown's best customer who asks for many love charms on her boyfriend Gabriel Staggers.

Frazier.
Mules. Man from Pierce, Florida, who comments on the meaning of squinch (screech) owls.

Freedom.
A key motif in almost all African American literature, freedom plays a similarly important role in Hurston's writing.
Eyes. Janie enjoys her freedom after Joe Starks's death; Nanny had met the challenges of freedom following emancipation differently; she had been concerned only with security.
Moses. The children of Israel are led from bondage in Egypt to the freedom of the promised land, an analogy for the emancipation of African Americans.
Seraph. Arvay Henson's ultimate freedom, ironically, comes from realizing her reliance on her husband Jim.

John French.
Mules. Eatonville man who tells the tale of "How Jack Beat the Devil."

Friendship.
Hurston presents several friendships of lasting significance in her fiction. These relationships provide support to both of the people involved.
"Contention," *Bone.* Dave Carter and Jim Weston's friendship survives despite their interest in the same woman.
Eyes. Janie and Pheoby's "bosom" friendship allows Janie to tell Pheoby her story in its entirety without leaving anything out.
Vine. John Pearson's long friendship with Hambo is close enough to allow for both support and criticism.

From Sun to Sun.
This production of *The Great Day* was staged by Hurston around Florida in 1933 and 1934. Presented first at Rollins College, the program was eventually performed in several other Florida cities, including Eatonville.

Funerals.

Funerals constitute major cultural events in Hurston's stories. A funeral, thus, becomes a communal ritual requiring the participation of an entire community. Afterward the event is often memorialized in myth.

"Cock Robin." The animals seem to be more interested in a fish fry than in Cock Robin's burial.

Eyes. Joe Starks's big funeral emphasizes his social status in the community; Matt Bonner's yellow mule's "funeral" becomes the stuff of legend; Tea Cake's royal funeral indicates the depth of Janie's love for him.

Seraph. Maria Henson's fine funeral (paid for by Bradford Cary) fulfils her dying wish to her daughter Arvay.

Vine. Lucy's funeral marks the turning point of John's life; John's funeral at the end of the novel marks the tragic downfall of this epic character.

✳ G ✳

Gabe.
Eyes. Man standing behind Ed Dockery's chair during the card game.

Gallentins.
"Veil." Roman commanding officer at Lyons.

Carl Galloway.
Seraph. Son of the owner of the general store in Citrabelle; he counts Kenny Meserve and Belinda Kelsey's money after Belinda stands on her head without her panties on for the passengers of the train.

Gambling.
Eyes. Tea Cake is a gambler, who plays cards and dice.
"Muttsy." Muttsy is a successful gambler who promises to give up the lifestyle when he marries Pinkie Jones, but he soon returns to his dice games.

Gates.

Gates serve as doorways to the outside world in Hurston's fiction.

Dust. Hurston recounts her experience of watching the world from her gate as a child.

Eyes. Janie waits at the gate, wondering what will happen in her life. Pheoby Watson goes in the side gate to visit her friend Janie.

"Light." Isis Watts hangs at the gate, watching the world go by.

Gershom.

Moses. Moses and Zipporah's oldest son, who stays with Moses after Zipporah returns to Midian.

George Gibson.

Vine. Man who borrows John Pearson's tools and refuses to return them following John's fall from grace.

"The Gilded Six-Bits."

One of Hurston's most anthologized stories, "The Gilded Six-Bits" recounts the tale of the idyllic marriage of Joe and Missie May Banks, which is tested by Missie May's infidelity with Otis D. Slemmons, a travelling conman who tempts the naive and backwards Missie with his "gilded" jewelry. All's well that ends well, however, in this sentimental, yet entertaining account of what have sometimes been criticized as overly "primitive" characters, for Joe returns to Missie May once the baby she is carrying turns out to look like him, rather than the odious Otis D. Slemmons, whom Joe has earlier run out of town after catching him and Missie May *in flagrante dilecto*. Published in the August 1933 issue of *Story* magazine, the story caught the eye of Bertram Lippincott, who wrote inquiring if Hurston was working on a novel. This inquiry prompted Hurston to start writing *Jonah's Gourd Vine*.

For Further Reading:

Chinn, Nancy, and Elizabeth E. Dunn. " 'The Ring of Singing Metal on Wood': Zora Neale Hurston's Artistry in 'The Gilded Six-Bits.' " *Mississippi Quarterly* 49.4 (1996): 775–90.

Jones, Evora W. "The Pastoral and the Picaresque in Zora Neale Hurston's 'The Gilded Six-Bits.' " *CLA Journal* 35.3 (1992): 316–24.

"Godmother."

Hurston's nickname for her patron, Charlotte Mason, whom she was said to have a psychic bond with. (See also Charlotte Mason)

Gold.

Mules. Eatonville woman who plays the dozens with Gene Brazzle; she tells the tale of "Why Negroes Are Black."

"The Golden Bench of God."

Hurston's unfinished novel based on the life of Madame C.J. Walker, whose invention and marketing of hair-straightening products made her the first African American woman millionaire. Hurston planned, as she wrote in a letter to her literary agent, Jean Parker Waterbury, to make the novel a "truly indigenous Negro novel" in which she would "write truthfully from the inside" as if "no white audience is present to hear what is said." But Scribner's rejected the novel in 1951.

Good Black.

Mules. Polk County man and member of the swamp-gang who goes on the fishing trip and tells the story of rain in slavery days.

Good Bread.

Mules. Large woman who wears men's overalls; she is offended by Mack Ford's joke that the purpose of big women is to show slim ones how far they can stretch without bursting.

Jim Gooden.

"Uncle Monday." Hunter who claims to see Uncle Monday turn from an alligator into a man.

Gossip.

Eyes. The women talk about Janie as she walks back into town, just as they had talked about Janie and Tea Cake during their courtship.

Vine. John Pearson's extramarital affairs provide fodder for the town gossips.

Granny.
"John Redding." Old woman who claims to have seen Witch Judy Davis creeping out of the Reddings' yard the night after John Redding is born.

Mehaley Grant.
Vine. Young girl (nicknamed "Haley"), who becomes interested in John Buddy and becomes his first sexual experience. Her interest in him continues and they continue to sleep together even after John marries Lucy Potts. Finally, however, after John makes it clear that he will never leave Lucy for her, Mehaley marries Pomp Lamar.

Mr. Grant.
Mules. Mrs. Grant's husband who spits tobacco juice on his wife's enemy just as she is throwing war powder on their door.

Mrs. Grant.
Mules. New Orleans woman who lives below Canal St. She takes steps to counteract her enemy's curse and then seeks additional help from Dr. Strong.

Mrs. Grant.
Vine. Woody Grant's wife, who wants a real preacher to perform her daughter Mehaley's marriage ceremony.

Woody Grant.
Vine. Mehaley's illiterate father who insists on performing his daughter's marriage ceremony.

Ike Green.
Eyes. Would-be suitor of Janie's (after Joe Starks's death) who warns her of the danger of other strange suitors (i.e., Tea Cake).

Old Lady Grooms.
"Black Death." Rival hoodoo doctor sent to her death in the lake by Old Man Morgan.

Guitar.
Eyes. Tea Cake pawns his guitar to hire a car to take Janie out, but he pretends to be playing a guitar when he arrives at store one day;

later he buys another guitar with part of Janie's $200. He plays often when they go down on the muck.

Guns.

Eyes. Tea Cake teaches Janie to shoot a pistol, rifle, and shotgun; Janie becomes a better shot than he is. Tea Cake hides a pistol under his pillow when he is delirious from the rabies.

Seraph. Arvay is not used to handling guns. Her son Earl Meserve, however, is fascinated with them. He steals his father's rifle and shoots at him, resulting in his own death from gunfire when the posse shoots him.

"Spunk." Joe Kanty is shot by Spunk Banks.

"Uncle Monday." On the advice of a hoodoo doctor, Mrs. Bradley shoots a gun at a mirror image of John Wesley Hogan and kills him for abandoning her pregnant daughter.

✳ H ✳

Hair.

Eyes. Joe insists that Janie keep her hair up in a headrag while she is in the store. After Joe's death Janie lets down her hair and sees her "glory." By contrast, Tea Cake combs Janie's hair and likes her wearing it down.

Emma Hales.

Vine. Discontented member of Zion Baptist Church who testifies against John Pearson at his divorce trial. Emma acts out of retribution for John's never having paid her any romantic attention.

John Hall.

Vine. Trustee of Zion Hope Baptist Church who pleads with John Pearson to return to the pulpit when he returns to Sanford in style driving his new Cadillac. He also pays John the $4 he owes him for work John had done before leaving town.

Sister Hall.

Vine. Member of Zion Hope Baptist Church who is impressed by Rev. John Pearson's sermon on the day that Rev. Felton Cozy comes to preach his trial sermon in an attempt to displace John.

Eddie Halliard.
Seraph. Man who fishes with Jim Meserve and Alfredo Corregio.

Ham.
First. Noah's youngest and most favored son, who laughs and sings rather than bringing a sacrifice; Noah, in his drunkenness, curses Ham for laughing at his nakedness; Ham's curse, blackness, causes him to be sent away from the rest of his family.

Ham.
"Magnolia." One of Bentley's workers; he helps tie John up and guards him with a loaded gun, but later he frees Magnolia Flower so that she can steal the key to set John free.

Mrs. Ham.
First. Ham's wife, Eve, who remains loyal to him, even after he is cursed with blackness and exiled.

Hambo.
Bone. Bald Baptist deacon who attends the trial; he beats Joe Clarke at checkers.
"Contention." Baptist member of the trial audience who upholds Rev. Long's view that the mule bone is a weapon.
Eyes. Along with Pearson, he is in charge of barbecuing the three hogs for the celebration of lighting the streetlamp; Hambo is the one who puts on the barbecue sauce.
Vine. John Pearson's best friend and chief supporter at Zion Hope Baptist Church, albeit the one person who will tell John when he's doing something wrong. Hambo calls John on the carpet for his hasty marriage to Hattie Tyson, but then he supports John against Deacon Harris's attempts to remove him from the pulpit and offers to testify against Hattie at John's divorce trial.

Sister Hambo.
Bone. Baptist woman who argues with Walter Thomas at the trial.

"Seaboard" Hamilton.
Mules. Eatonville man who is playing cards on the porch when Zora arrives in town to collect folktales; he later attends the big storytelling session.

Hardy.
Mules. Fellow card player with Big Sweet in the game at Loughman.

"Harlem Slanguage."
Hurston's unedited version (complete with sexually explicit defi-
nitions) of the "Glossary of Harlem Slang" printed at the end of
"Story in Harlem Slang," which was published in the July 1942
American Mercury. Note: The unexpurgated version was printed in
The Complete Stories (1995).

Deacon Aleck Harris.
Vine. Chief opponent of John Pearson's. Harris plots time and
again to oust Pearson, finally urging Hattie Tyson to consult hoodoo
men and to divorce Pearson.

Harry.
"Light." Helen's companion (possibly husband?) who remains
rather aloof.

Helen.
"Light." White woman who saves Isis from a whipping and takes
her to her hotel to dance for her because the young girl is "drenched
in light"; the depressed woman badly needs the child's liveliness.

Dr. Henderson.
Eyes. Doctor who attends Joe Starks's funeral in his Lincoln automobile.

Mrs. Laura Henderson.
Mules. Eatonville woman whose testimony Zora can hear from the
church next door.

Julius Henry.
Mules. Young Eatonville boy who, despite his age, tells some of
the longer tales: "Ah'll Beatcher Makin' Money" and "The Workinest
Pill You Ever Seen."

Pa Henry.
Mules. Eatonville man whose prayer, "Pa Henry's Prayer," is heard from the St. Lawrence church next door.

Arvay Henson.
Seraph. Protagonist of the novel, Arvay changes from a lovestruck young girl to a mature woman during the course of the novel; tamed by Jim Meserve, she endures the ups and downs of marriage to a man she loves. She is the mother of three children: Earl, Kenny, and Angie.

Brock Henson.
Seraph. Arvay Henson's father, who works in the turpentine business; he approves of Arvay's marriage to Jim Meserve.

Lorraine Henson.
Seraph. Arvay's older sister, who steals Rev. Carl Middleton from her and exacerbates the sibling rivalry between the two sisters. Years later the tables are turned when Lorraine grows jealous of Arvay's prosperous life with Jim Meserve, while her marriage to Carl has descended to abject poverty.

Maria Henson.
Seraph. Arvay Henson's mother, whom she favors; Arvay's son Earl Meserve goes to live with the widowed Maria for about six months.

Herod.
"Veil." Miramne's son and Antipas's much older half-brother to whom Herodias is married but then divorces so that she can marry Antipas.

Herod the Great.
Hurston's final, unpublished novel, *Herod* is a biography of the ruler of Galilee from 47 to 4 B.C., the father of the king who sent Jesus Christ to Pontius Pilate. The manuscript of the book was partially burned by a janitor in the St. Lucie County Welfare Home, where Hurston died. Luckily, however, a deputy sheriff who had heard that Hurston was a writer put out the fire, thinking that the proceeds from the sale of the manuscript might be used to pay off her debts. The charred manuscript now resides in the Zora Neale Hurston Collection at the University of Florida Library. Unlike her

other novels, *Herod* uses no dialect. Instead, it is written in standard English as an historical text.

Herod the Great.

"Gaul." King of Judea, who marries Antipas to the daughter of the King of Arabia and Herodias to Herod.

Herodias.

"Gaul." Antipas's wife, who decides to follow him into exile in Gaul rather than stay in Rome.

"Veil." Granddaughter of Herod the Great and daughter of Aristobulus; she marries Antipas after her divorce from his half-brother Herod.

Miss Hessie.

Seraph. Maria Henson's neighbor, who tells Arvay about Lorraine and Carl Middleton cleaning out Maria's place after her death.

Hezekiah.

Eyes. Seventeen-year-old store clerk who helps Janie after Joe Starks's death; he imitates Joe's mannerisms and collects rents for Janie; he begins to look on Janie as a little sister.

Guv'nor Amos Hicks.

Eyes. One of the first two Eatonville residents to welcome Joe Starks and Janie to the town; Hicks, a native of Buford, South Carolina, imagines himself to be quite the ladies' man and attempts to smooth talk Janie but is roundly rebuffed.

"High John de Conquer."

Story about the exploits of the legendary slave hero who outwitted his harsh masters. The story was first published in the October 1943 *American Mercury.*

High John de Conquer.

"High John." Mythic African American folk hero who helped lift the slaves' spirits during slavery times; he could outsmart his white masters and could endure all hardships, triumphing in the end by wit and laughter; he came from Africa and eventually returned there, but he left his power in America in the form of a root.

Babe Hill.

Mules. Polk County woman who befriends Hurston; she is Mrs. Bertha Allen's daughter and Cliffert Ulmer's mother; Hurston later finds out that she had shot and killed her husband.

Ezeriah Hill.

Vine. Oldest man at the tie camp who shows John Pearson around and helps him learn the ropes. Nicknamed "Uncle Dump," he warns John that he doesn't know his own strength after John severely injures Coon Tyler in a fight.

Mr. Hill.

"John Redding." White man who asks for John Redding's help in securing a bridge over the St. John (sic) River, just before a flood. The bridge collapses and John is killed.

Deacon Hoffman.

Vine. One of the leaders of Zion Hope Baptist Church opposed to John Pearson. He and several others question John about his marriage to Hattie Tyson. He acts as chairman of the church meeting that attempts, unsuccessfully, to dislodge Pearson as pastor following his divorce from Hattie Tyson. But then he is one of the men who run after Pearson when he walks out of the church following his final sermon and implores him to stay on.

John Wesley Hogan.

"Uncle Monday." Womanizing young man who refuses to marry Dinkie Bradley even after he impregnates her. John Wesley falls down dead after Dinkie's mother seeks Uncle Monday's help in getting revenge.

Hoodoo.

Hurston's folk upbringing and her adult anthropological work brought her intimate knowledge of conjuring and voodoo practices. She included accounts of these powerful elements in her writing.

"Bridge." Artie Mimms turns to a conjure man to keep his wife faithful.

Eyes. Joe Starks consults a root doctor when he is dying.

Horse. Hurston researched extensively on the voodoo practices, rituals, and personages in Haiti.

Moses. Moses learns magic from Jethro, who describes him as "the finest hoodoo man in the world"; he becomes even more powerful after defeating the deathless snake and reading the book of Thoth.

"Mother Catherine," "Black Death." Hoodoo doctors and priestesses exert great power over their followers in both of these works.

Mules. Hurston visited many hoodoo doctors in Louisiana.

"Uncle Monday." The account of a hoodoo doctor extraordinaire.

Vine. Hattie Tyson consults Aunt Dangie Dewoe in her attempt to catch and keep John Pearson's romantic attentions.

For Further Reading:

Dutton, Wendy. "The Problem of Invisibility: Voodoo and Zora Neale Hurston." *Frontiers* 13.2 (1993): 131–52.

Lamothe, Daphne. "Vodou Imagery, African-American Tradition and Cultural Transformation in Zora Neale Hurston's *Their Eyes Were Watching God.*" *Callaloo* 22.1 (1999) 157–75.

Lindroth, James R. "Generating the Vocabulary of Hoodoo: Zora Neale Hurston and Ishmael Reed." *Zora Neale Hurston Forum* 2.1 (1987): 27–34.

Orlow-Klein, Ingrid M. " 'Witnessing the Ceremony': The Writing of Folklore and Hoodoo in Zora Neale Hurston's *Mules and Men.*" *Bulletin of Faculty of Commerce* 38.2 (1994): 33–51.

Southerland, Ellease. "The Influence of Voodoo on the Fiction of Zora Neale Hurston." In *Sturdy Black Bridges: Visions of Black Women in Literature.* Ed. Roseann P. Bell, Bettye J. Parker, and Beverly Guy-Sheftall. Garden City, NY: Anchor Press, 1979. 172–83.

Speisman, Barbara. "Voodoo as Symbol in *Jonah's Gourd Vine.*" In *Zora in Florida.* Ed. Steve Glassman and Kathryn Lee Seidel. Orlando: U of Central Florida P, 1991. 86–93.

Stein, Rachel. "Rerooting the Sacred Tree: Nature, Black Women, and Voodoo in Zora Neale Hurston's *Tell My Horse* and *Their Eyes Were Watching God.*" In *Shifting the Ground: American Women Writers' Revisions of Nature, Gender, and Race.* Charlottesville: UP of Virginia, 1997. 53–83.

Arthur Hopkins.

Mules. Young Polk County man who goes on the fishing trip and tells the tale of "The Goat That Flagged a Train"; Jim Allen pretends to get mad at him for calling him by his first name.

Sam Hopkins.

Mules. Young Polk County man who goes on the fishing trip.

Horizons.

Eyes. The opening to *Their Eyes Were Watching God* discusses the horizon; Janie later realizes that Nanny had shrunk her horizon and put it around her neck to choke off her possibilities. After her return Janie says, "Ah done been tuh de horizon and back." The book closes with the image of her taking up the horizon and putting it around her shoulders like a shawl.

Seraph. At the end of the novel, Arvay Henson watches the sunrise on the eastern horizon, symbolizing the beginning and promise of her new life with her husband Jim Meserve.

Will House.

Mules. Polk County man who goes on the fishing trip; he discusses the heat and relates the story of a hungry black gnat.

Houses.

For many of the characters in the world that Hurston depicts in her fiction, houses are symbols of wealth and accomplishment, as well as places of shelter and comfort.

Eyes. Joe Starks builds a large house and paints it white to show his status in the town.

Seraph. Arvay burns down her mother's dilapidated old house as a symbol of burning the past and gives the land for a park.

"Sweat." Delia Jones had paid for her home with her sweat and now it is all that's left her. So she defends it and kills her husband rather than relinquish it to him and his mistress.

Vine. Sally Lovelace owns several houses and asks John Pearson to help her maintain them. Her property is one of the inducements that she uses to get John to marry her.

"How It Feels to be Colored Me."

This essay, published in *The World Tomorrow* in May 1928, reveals Hurston's nonconfrontational attitudes about race. Confident of her individual identity, she purports not to feel "tragically colored" and refuses to consider herself a victim of racial prejudice. Rather she insists on remaining herself, feeling her racial difference mainly only when she is thrown against a white background. Sometimes, however, she just feels like "the cosmic Zora," a person of no particular race, simply "the eternal feminine with its string of beads."

Hatton Howland.
Seraph. Yankee whom Angie Meserve elopes with; at his father-in-law Jim Meserve's urging, the enterprising young man buys the Big Swamp and prospers in the Florida real estate business, becoming a Babbitt in his own right when he and Angie join the country club.

Mrs. Howland.
Seraph. Hatton Howland's mother of whom Arvay Meserve becomes jealous after her daughter Angie marries Hatton and the couple move in with Mrs. Howland.

Lessie Lee Hudson.
Mules. Woman from Pierce, Florida who likes Horace Sharp's story.

Langston Hughes.
Preeminent poet of the Harlem Renaissance and one-time friend and collaborator of Hurston's, who also enjoyed the patronage of Charlotte Mason. Hughes and Hurston drove back from Alabama to New York together in 1927. Later they collaborated on the play *Mule Bone*, disagreements over which resulted in their permanent estrangement after 1931.

Hunting.
"Contention," *Bone.* Jim Weston and Dave Carter's conflict starts over a hunting dispute.

Eyes. Janie and Tea Cake go hunting around Lake Okeechobee.

Horse. Hurston recounts the hunt for a wild boar during her visit to Jamaica.

Hur.
Moses. Hebrew worker who asks Pharaoh to give the Hebrews another chance and is refused; he becomes head military trainer of the older men. He upholds Moses's left hand to ensure the Israelites' victory over the Amalekites.

"Hurricane."
Excerpt from *Their Eyes Were Watching God* recounting Janie and Tea Cake's flight in the face of the hurricane and Tea Cake's encounter with the rabid dog; it was included in *The Complete Stories* in 1995.

Fannie Hurst.

One of the short story judges at the first *Opportunity* contest in May 1925; she was a popular white novelist, whose most famous novel is *Imitation of Life*; she hired Hurston as her live-in secretary, even though Zora did not type well. Later Hurst fired her as secretary but kept her on as a chauffeur and companion for over a year. Hurston paid tribute to Hurst by including her, along with Ethel Waters, as one of two inspirational women in her chapter entitled "Two Women in Particular" in *Dust Tracks on a Road*. Later Hurston also wrote an article about Hurst in the October 9, 1937 *Saturday Review*. Following Hurston's death in 1960, Hurst wrote a "Personality Sketch" about Hurston in the *Yale University Library Gazette*.

Benjamin Franklin Hurston.

Hurston's fifth brother, born December 7, 1895, in Eatonville. He later became a pharmacist in Memphis, Tennessee.

Clifford Joel Hurston.

Hurston's fourth brother, born March 4, 1893. He later became a principal of the Negro high school in Decatur, Alabama.

Edward Everett Hurston.

Hurston's sixth brother, born October 26, 1898, in Eatonville. He later worked as a postal worker in Brooklyn, New York.

Hezekiah Robert (Bob) Hurston.

Hurston's oldest brother, born November 1882. Bob became a physician, and Hurston lived with him and his family in Memphis, Tennessee, during 1914–15.

John Hurston.

Hurston's father, born January 1861, he was a Baptist preacher, farmer, and carpenter, and mayor of Eatonville for three terms (starting in 1897). He owned five acres of land and an eight-room house in Eatonville, pastored the Zion Hope and Macedonia Baptist Churches, and served as moderator for the South Florida Baptist Association. He is the model for John Pearson in *Jonah's Gourd Vine*. Like John Pearson, he died in an automobile accident.

John Cornelius Hurston.

Hurston's second brother, born January 1885. He later owned a grocery store in Jacksonville, Florida.

Lucy Hurston.

Hurston's mother (maiden name Lucy Ann Potts), born December 1865 and died September 18, 1904. She was a country school teacher. She served as the model (and namesake) for Lucy Potts in *Jonah's Gourd Vine*. Hurston included a touching account of her mother's death in *Dust Tracks on a Road* (1942).

Richard William Hurston.

Hurston's third brother, born January 1887; during 1912 Hurston lived with him and his wife in Sanford, Florida. He became a chef.

Sarah Emmeline Hurston.

Hurston's older sister, born December 1889, whose married name was Mack. Hurston lived with her in Baltimore while she was attending Morgan Academy.

✳ **I** ✳

Identity.

The search for identity is a key theme in Hurston's work. This search leads many of her characters to go on journeys, seeking themselves. This journey to self becomes the inspiriting element in many of her characters' lives. Unfortunately, the road to self-awareness is often obscured or hindered by other people in the characters' lives, particularly for the female characters. Yet, somehow, many of Hurston's characters manage to succeed despite the obstacles placed in their paths and ultimately come away with a better understanding of who they are.

Eyes. Janie's search for identity begins when she sees the photograph taken by a traveling photographer, which reveals to her, for the first time, that she is black; even her nickname, "Alphabet," becomes a metaphor for her lack of identity; she has so many names (and identities) that they cover the alphabet. Janie's search for identity leads her to three very different marriages. In her first marriage to Logan Killicks, she is still too young to realize her self. In her second marriage to Joe Starks, she attempts to assert her identity only to be pushed down by Joe's domineering personality and fear of her power. Therefore, she begins to see herself as split into two parts—public and private—and develops a shadow self. Not until her marriage to Tea Cake Woods does Janie finally discover her true identity. So, by the time she returns to Eatonville following Tea Cake's death, she finally fully understands who she is. With that newfound knowledge she can pass along her insights to her friend Pheoby Watson.

Seraph. A similar search for identity, although with a very different end result, occurs in Arvay Henson's journey to self-awareness. For most of the novel she pits her individual will against her husband Jim Meserve, only to meet with ultimate failure. At the end of the novel, ironically, she finds her self in Jim and in her relationship to him.

Preacher Ike.
"Magnolia." Minister who eats breakfast with Bentley on the morning Bentley plans to hang John and force Magnolia Flower to marry Crazy Joe.

Infidelity.
"Anthology." Cheating husbands fare harshly in several vignettes.

"Bridge." Luke Mimms realizes that his young wife Vangie is actually in love with his son Artie.

"Six-Bits." Missie May Banks's infidelity with Otis D. Slemmons is forgiven very easily by her husband Joe Banks once he sees that her child is really his.

"Spunk." Here the unfaithful partner is the wife, for Lena Kanty's open infidelity leads to the deaths of both her husband Joe Kanty and her lover Spunk Banks.

"Sweat." Delia Jones's cheating husband Sykes receives his just punishment at the fangs of a rattlesnake, hidden in the house by Delia.

Vine. John Pearson cheats on his wife Lucy repeatedly, finally with Hattie Tyson. Then he cheats on Hattie with Gertie Burden and others. His death results from his guilt over cheating on his third wife, Sally Lovelace, with Ora Patton.

Iris.
"Veil." Herodias's maid.

Israel.
"Magnolia." One of Bentley's workers who helps tie John up to prevent him from marrying Magnolia Flower.

Muttsy Ivins.

Mules. Frightened man (afraid for his life because he is sleeping with another man's wife) who pays Anatol Pierre $250 to arrange the other man's death.

✳ J ✳

W.B. Jackson.
Eyes. Owner of a big white house, the color of which Joe Starks's house resembles.

Jacob.
Moses. Hebrew man who is killed by Pharaoh's soldiers when he tries to save his baby son; his wife is also killed.

Jake.
"Light." Puppy Isis Watts lets "swim" over the dishwater.

Janie.
Eyes. Hurston's prototypical African American feminist heroine of *Their Eyes Were Watching God.* Janie's journey "to the horizon and back" chronicles her search for her own identity. Moving from the overprotective maternal control of her grandmother (Nanny) through three very different marriages (the first to Logan Killicks, the second to Joe Starks, and the last to Tea Cake Woods), Janie, having finally found herself, ultimately returns home to Eatonville to relate the story of her journey to her close friend Pheoby Watson.

For Further Reading:

Howard, Lillie P. "Nanny and Janie: Will the Twain Ever Meet?" *Journal of Black Studies* 12.4 (1982): 403–14.

Inman, James A. "Love and Awareness in Hurston's Janie: An Archetypal Connection." *Zora Neale Hurston Forum* 10 (1996): 1–6.

Kayano, Yoshiko. "Burden, Escape, and Nature's Role: A Study of Janie's Development in *Their Eyes Were Watching God.*" *Publications of the Mississippi Philological Association* (1998): 36–44.

Sheppard, David M. "Living by Comparison: Janie and Her Discontents." *English Language Notes* 30.2 (1992): 63–75.

Washington, Mary Helen. " 'I Love the Way Janie Crawford Left Her Husbands': Zora Neale Hurston's Emergent Female Hero." In *Invented Lives: Narratives of Black Women 1860–1960.* Ed. Mary Helen Washington. New York: Doubleday, 1987. 237–54. Reprinted in *Zora Neale Hurston: Critical Perspectives Past and Present.* Ed. Henry Louis Gates Jr. and K.A. Appiah. New York: Amistad Press, 1993. 98–109; and *Zora Neale Hurston: "Sweat."* Ed. Cheryl A. Wall. New Brunswick, NJ: Rutgers UP, 1997. 193–209.

Japheth.

First. Noah's second son, who along with his brother Shem is jealous of Noah's favoritism toward their younger brother Ham; Japheth and Shem cover their drunken father after Ham laughs at his nakedness, hoping that Noah will now favor them. But after Noah curses Ham, they implore him to revoke his curse.

Mrs. Japheth.

First. Japheth's wife, who, jealous of Ham's favor in Noah's eyes, encourages her husband to help his brother Shem in covering their father Noah after Ham laughs at his nakedness, so as to share in the credit and gain favor with their father.

Jealousy.

Jealousy is a potent emotional factor in many of Hurston's stories. Often the cause for jealousy is unfounded, yet the damage done by the emotion still wreaks havoc.

"Bridge." The father/son/stepmother love triangle results in the father's death.

Color. Emmaline Beasely's jealousy over color causes her to lose John Turner twice.

Eyes. Janie's jealousy over Tea Cake and Nunkie causes Janie to doubt Tea Cake; Tea Cake's jealousy of Janie and Mrs. Turner's brother stems from his own insecurities. His jealousy grows even worse when he becomes crazed from rabies.

Moses. Ta-Phar is jealous of Moses; Aaron and Miriam are jealous of Moses' power; Miriam is also jealous of Zipporah, Moses' beautiful wife.

"Veil." Herodias's jealousy of John the Baptist's influence over her husband Antipas ultimately leads to John's death.

Brother Jeff.
Vine. Member of Zion Hope Baptist Church who believes that Rev. Felton Cozy will not be able to surpass John Pearson's preaching performance.

Jelly.
"Gas," "Harlem Slang." Harlem pimp whose real name is Marvel; he lives off women but is now broke; he brags about his sexual prowess with women.

Christopher Jenkins.
Mules. Man who attempts to calm Good Bread down and avoid a fight after she takes umbrage to Mack Ford's joke about her size. He sings in a deep baritone voice.

Pat Jenkins.
Bone. Would-be witness at Jim Weston's trial.

Dr. Samuel Jenkins.
Mules. Hoodoo man from Marrero, Louisiana, whose specialty is reading cards.

Jesus Christ.
"Gaul." Man brought to Antipas during Passover, whom Antipas assumed to be John the Baptist until Jesus refused to speak.

Jethro.
Moses. Chief of the Kenites who becomes Moses' father-in-law and mentor; he urges Moses to follow his mission to deliver the Israelites from Egypt.

Mules. Hurston describes him as "a great hoodoo man" in her work on folklore.

Jim.
"Magnolia." One of Bentley's workers who helps tie John up to prevent him from marrying Magnolia Flower.

Jochebed.
Moses. Moses' (alleged) Hebrew mother, who insists on sparing his life.

Jody.
Eyes. Janie's nickname for Joe Starks, which she uses when she feels close to him. (See also Joe Starks)

John.
"Magnolia." Light-skinned school teacher who falls in love with Magnolia Flower and vows to marry her despite her father's objections; he and Magnolia Flower flee northward by boat and return forty-seven years later.

John.
"Possum." Trusted house slave who steals a young pig and gets caught when his master comes to his cabin; through his wit he escapes punishment, however.

John Buddy.
Vine. John Pearson's nickname as a boy. (See also John Pearson)

"John Redding Goes to Sea."
Hurston's first published story, first printed in the Howard University literary magazine the *Stylus* in May 1921 and then reprinted in *Opportunity* in January 1926. The story incorporates folklore beliefs and familiar Hurston themes of dreams, escape, rivers, and bridges in telling the tale of a young man who yearns to travel and explore the world only to be held back by family ties. In the end he escapes only in death.

John the Baptist.
"Veil." Young Essene religious prophet for whom Antipas and Herodias are waiting in Gaul; he had denounced Antipas's marriage to Herodias and incurred her wrath.

Albert Johnson.
Bone. Teets Miller's new beau, who works as head bellman at the hotel in Apopka.

Charles S. Johnson.
Organizer of the *Opportunity* literary contest, in which Hurston won prizes in 1925 and 1926; he also acted as editor of the National Urban League's magazine *Opportunity: A Journal of Negro Life*, which published five of Hurston's early works, "Drenched in Light," "Spunk," "John Redding Goes to Sea," "Muttsy," and *Color Struck.* He also included Hurston's play *The First One* in his 1927 anthology, *Ebony and Topaz.* He appears in *Mules and Men*, where he is told by hoodoo doctor Samuel Jenkins that he will go on a long trip and the next day he receives notice of a trip to West Africa.

Oral Johnson.
Vine. Member of the church choir that John Buddy joins to be close to Lucy Potts.

Jonah's Gourd Vine.
After reading Hurston's story "The Gilded Six-Bits" in the August 1933 issue of *Story* magazine, J.B. Lippincott wrote her to ask if she was working on a novel. Never one to pass up an opportunity, Hurston immediately headed home to Florida, rented a room in Sanford, and in less than four months had produced *Jonah's Gourd Vine*, her first novel. It was accepted for publication on October 16, 1933, and published in May of the following year.

The novel begins in Macon County, Alabama, where Hurston was born. There, after fighting with his abusive stepfather, Ned Crittenden, 16-year-old John Buddy journeys away from home for the first time, crossing the Big Creek and leaving behind his mother, Amy Crittenden, his stepbrothers and stepsisters. On his mother's advice he seeks employment from her former slaveowner (and possibly John Buddy's biological father), Master Alf Pearson, whose surname John Buddy eventually takes as his own.

With Pearson's help John Buddy attends school, where he meets the girl he is to marry, the much younger Lucy Potts. Before and after the two marry, however, John displays a weakness for infidelity that continues to plague him even after he and Lucy have a growing family. His indiscretions eventually result in his getting into a fight that causes him to have to leave the county in the dead of night.

As chance would have it, John winds up heading for Florida, where he hears about the all-black town of Eatonville, near Orlando. After saving enough money for their train fare, John moves Lucy and the children to Eatonville, where he prospers first as a carpenter and then as a preacher, eventually rising to the position of State Moderator. But John's weakness for women continues to hound him. So when a woman named Hattie Tyson uses hoodoo charms to gain his attention, he succumbs to temptation. The town begins to talk and John's star, which had risen so fast and so far, begins to fall. The change in John is most apparent when, after Lucy chastises him about his affair with Hattie and its consequences, he strikes her on her deathbed.

Following Lucy's death, John's fortunes plummet. His family falls apart and Hattie Tyson turns out to be a shrewish wife. After he begins beating her, she turns once again to hoodoo for protection. In the midst of all this personal turmoil, certain factions in John's church begin to plot to replace him, and although with the help of some of his loyal friends and supporters he manages to hold his opponents off, even after Hattie divorces him, John finally preaches his last sermon and leaves town in disgrace.

Wandering around jobless and hungry, John winds up in Plant City, where he meets a wealthy and lonely widow named Sally Lovelace. With Sally's help John regains his position and even begins pastoring a church again. After a year he returns to Eatonville in triumph driving the new Cadillac that Sally had purchased for him.

Back home old friends who had deserted him in his time of need are suddenly going out of their way to be nice to the newly prosperous John, even going so far as to offer him the position of pastor at his old church. Although John refuses this offer, he stays in town too long and falls prey to the attentions of the vampish Ora Patton. After his tryst with Ora, John is so distraught over his betrayal of Sally that he does not notice the train that strikes his car, killing him, as he hurries home to Sally the following morning.

In death John Pearson is mourned and memorialized as a great man in services all over the state. At the Eatonville service, attended by both Sally Lovelace and Hattie Tyson, the preacher's sermon praises John's accomplishments and ends in a rhythmic, drumlike beat.

Hurston explained the title of the novel (which had originally been titled *Big Nigger*) in a letter to Carl Van Vechten written February 28, 1934, thusly: As Jonah sat under a gourd vine (that had grown up overnight to protect him from the heat), a worm came along and cut it down. After this "great and sudden growth" (i.e., John Pearson's rise to fame and prosperity), "one act of malice" (i.e. John's striking his wife Lucy on her deathbed) causes his rapid demise and resulting downfall. In many ways John Pearson resembles the tragic hero of a Greek tragedy, complete with a fatal flaw (his weakness for women) and tragic downfall (his death by trainwreck).

The novel's two main characters are modeled closely on Hurston's own parents. Lucy's deathbed scene is very similar to Hurston's mother's death (as described by Hurston later in her autobiography *Dust Tracks on a Road*). The novel is not completely autobiographical, however, for Hurston made extensive use of her growing knowledge of folklore. She also displays her remarkable facility with language, a power most often displayed in John Pearson's poetic sermons, although his sermon at the end of the novel was lifted almost completely from Hurston's field notes on a sermon given by the Rev. C.C. Lovelace on May 3, 1929, in Eau Gallie, Florida. Originally dedicated to such Negro preachers, whom Hurston called (in the manuscript version of *Jonah's Gourd Vine*) "the only real Negro poets in America," the novel was ultimately dedicated to Bob Wunsch, the English professor at Rollins College, who had helped Hurston stage *From Sun to Sun*. In the dedication Hurston calls him "one of the long-wingded angels right round the throne."

For Further Reading:

Beilke, Debra. " 'Yowin' and Jawin': Humor and the Performance of Identity in Zora Neale Hurston's *Jonah's Gourd Vine*." *Southern Quarterly* 36.3 (1998): 21–33.

Brown, Alan. " 'De Beast' Within: The Role of Nature in *Jonah's Gourd Vine*." In *Zora in Florida*. Ed. Steve Glassman and Kathryn Lee Seidel. Orlando: U of Central Florida P, 1991. 76–85.

Ciuba, Gary. "The Worm against the Word: The Hermeneutical Challenge in Hurston's *Jonah's Gourd Vine*." *African American Review* 34.1 (2000): 119–33.

Jones, Kirkland C. "Folk Humor as Comic Relief in Hurston's *Jonah's Gourd Vine*." *Zora Neale Hurston Forum* 1.1 (1986): 26–31.

Sundquist, Eric J. " 'The Drum with the Man Skin': *Jonah's Gourd Vine*." In *The Hammers of Creation: Folk Culture in Modern African-American Fiction*. Athens: U of Georgia P, 1992. 49–91. Reprinted in *Zora Neale Hurston: Critical Perspectives Past and Present*. Ed. Henry Louis Gates Jr. and K.A. Appiah. New York: Amistad Press, 1993. 13–15.

Armetta Jones.

Mules. Eatonville friend of Zora's with whom she stays on her folklore collecting trip. She is married to Ellis Jones. Her nickname is Mett.

Carrie Jones.

Mules. Woman from Pierce, Florida, who explains how she wards off bad luck by turning her stocking inside out.

Charlie Jones.

Eyes. Young man who flirts with Daisy Blunt and other young women in town.

Mules. Eatonville man who tells the tale of "How the Church Came to Be Split Up" and sings the song "John Henry"; it is he who suggests that Zora go to Polk County to collect folktales.

Clara Jones.

Mules. Jack Oscar Jones's wife, who defends her husband's knowledge of lovemaking.

Delia Jones.

"Sweat." Sykes Jones's abused wife, who is deathly afraid of snakes; she works as a washerwoman to support her unfaithful, abusive husband of fifteen years and in the end gets revenge.

Effie Jones.

Color. Young mulatto girl from Jacksonville whose lighter skin color sparks Emmaline Beasely's jealousy; Emmaline's boyfriend, John Turner, ultimately dances with Effie instead of Emmaline.

Ellis Jones.
Mules. Eatonville man who tells the tales of "How the Brother Was Called to Preach" and "How the Preacher Made Them Bow Down." He is married to Armetta Jones.

Sister Ida Jones.
Bone. Methodist woman who attends Jim Weston's trial.

Jack Oscar Jones.
Mules. Eatonville man who recites the song poem "Sue, Sal and That Pretty Johnson Gal." He is married to Clara Jones.

Pinkie Jones.
"Muttsy." Naive young girl from Eatonville who moves to Harlem seeking work. There she rooms at Ma Turner's disreputable boarding house, where she becomes the object of Muttsy Owens's obsessive advances and runs away. Two weeks later he finds her and she marries him.

Richard Jones.
Mules. Man who discusses love at the storytelling session in Eatonville.

Sim Jones.
Eyes. Eatonville resident who criticizes Joe Starks behind his back for forcing Henry Pitts to leave town.

Sykes Jones.
"Anthology." He is mentioned as coming from a crap-shooting family.
Bone. At Joe Clarke's store he says that Will Cody's "wife" is another man's wife; he is also a would-be witness at the trial.
"Contention." He brags about winning a soda cracker eating contest.
"Sweat." Delia Jones's lazy, abusive, unfaithful husband, who is killed by the snake he hid to kill Delia.

Joshua.
"Fire and Cloud." Moses' successor as leader of the Israelites who will lead the people into the land of Canaan after Moses' death.

Moses. Young teenaged Hebrew boy who is the first to offer to work for Moses when he returns to Egypt to lead the Israelites to freedom; he first becomes head military trainer of the younger boys and then military leader of all the Israelites. Later he leads the Israelites to victory in their battle with the Amelakites. He follows Moses halfway up Mt. Sinai while Moses gets the Ten Commandments. After Moses' death he becomes leader of the Israelites and leads them into the promised land.

Journeys.
The process of going on a journey provides the narrative underpinning of several of Hurston's works.

Dust. Even as a child Hurston had dreamed of going on journeys.

Eyes. Janie feels that she has been preparing all her life for a journey. Much of the novel's narrative structure parallels her journey (both the physical movement from place to place and the emotional changes she navigates her way through as she moves from one relationship to another on her journey of self-discovery).

Moses. Led by Moses, the Israelites wander around in the wilderness for forty years before arriving at their destination: the promised land.

Aunt Judy.
Moses. Old Hebrew woman whom Miriam criticizes for following after Moses' wife Zipporah.

July.
"High John." Slave whom High John de Conquer takes with him on his journey through heaven and hell in search of a song.

Uncle July.
"Cock Robin." A'nt Dooby's husband and the narrator of the real story of Cock Robin.

⇥⧗⇤ **K** ⇥⧗⇤

Jeff Kanty.
"Spunk." Joe Kanty's father, who attends Spunk Banks's wake to gloat over the body of his son's killer.

Joe Kanty.
"Spunk." Cuckolded husband whose wife Lena is cheating on him with Spunk Banks. Although reluctant to confront the two, Joe finally acts, prompting Spunk to shoot him. But Joe gets his revenge, coming back as a bob-cat to haunt the two.

Lena Kanty.
"Spunk." Joe Kanty's unfaithful wife, who cheats on him with Spunk Banks. Her plans to marry Spunk following Joe's death are thwarted by Joe's revenge.

Stella Kanty.
"John Redding." John Redding's wife, the daughter of a neighbor. Like John's mother, she is opposed to John's travel plans.

Belinda Kelsey.

Seraph. Joe and Dessie's youngest girl, who is about the same age as Kenny Meserve; as a child, she innocently stands on her head for the passengers on the train while wearing no panties.

Bubber Kelsey.

Seraph. Joe and Dessie's oldest son, who works as a yardman for a rich Yankee; he gives 3-year-old Angie Meserve a mango, which turns out to cause a fight between her and her 7-year-old brother Earl.

Dessie Kelsey.

Seraph. Joe Kelsey's wife, who first helps Jim Meserve keep his house when he is a bachelor and then helps Joe's wife Arvay, first in Sawley and then in Citrabelle. Dessie also acts as midwife for the delivery of Arvay's three babies.

Janie Kelsey.

Seraph. Jeff Kelsey's wife, who moves with him onto the Meserve place after Jim Meserve leaves his wife Arvay.

Jeff Kelsey.

Seraph. Jeff and Dessie Kelsey's third son, who works for Jim Meserve in the grove after his father quits looking after it; he later saves Jim from a gigantic rattlesnake and blames Arvay for not trying to save her husband first.

Joe Kelsey.

Seraph. Favorite Negro whom Jim Meserve works with in the turpentine business in Sawley and then partners with in a moonshine enterprise in Citrabelle after Jim invites Joe and his family to move there to help him manage his orange grove. Joe's partnership with Jim ends when Jim's wife Arvay grows jealous over Joe's influence, prompting Jim to sell his interest in the still. Joe is the one who teaches Kenny Meserve to play the guitar; later Arvay sends him to New York to look after Kenny.

George Kemp.

Seraph. Unlucky fisherman whose story Stumpy tells Jim Meserve; unlike most fisherman, George had saved his money only to be hit by heart disease and a shrewish wife; to keep her from inheriting his hardearned cash, on his deathbed he had given away all he owned.

Janie Mae Killicks.
Eyes. (See also Janie)

Logan Killicks.
Eyes. Janie's first husband; Nanny forces Janie to marry him after she catches Janie kissing Johnny Taylor under the pear tree. Logan is older, but he has sixty acres on the big road and, thus, from Nanny's perspective, can offer Janie security. Janie never falls in love with him and eventually leaves him for Joe Starks.

Laura Lee Kimble.
"Conscience." Forty-nine-year-old maid arrested for attacking a loan shark when he attempts to repossess her employer's furniture prematurely.

Tom Kimble.
"Conscience." Laura Lee Kimble's deceased husband, twelve years her senior, whose death three months earlier had prompted Laura's employer to take out a loan to pay for his funeral.

✳ L ✳

Lacey.
Vine. Young girl who is an acquaintance of John Buddy's.

Lakes.
Eyes. Hurston mentions many lakes, such as Lake Sebelius outside of Eatonville and Lake Okeechobee, where Janie and Tea Cake live on the muck. The description of the power of the rising lake during the hurricane is epic.

Mules. Marie Leveau would rise out of Lake Pontchartrain during the Midsummer's Eve feast, walk on its waters, and nine days later walk back into the lake's waters.

"Uncle Monday." Uncle Monday is supposed to have arisen out of the lake.

Pomp Lamar.
Vine. New hoe hand on Alf Pearson's place who marries Mehaley Grant.

Mr. Laurence.
Eyes. White man who, along with Captain Eaton, donated the original 50 acres of land for the settlement of Eatonville.

Leafy.
Eyes. Nanny's daughter by Marse Robert; she is raped by her school teacher when she is only 17 and runs off shortly after giving birth to Janie.

Bennie Lee.
Mules. Shug Lee's contentious stepbrother who gets drunk while they are telling tales.

Shug Lee.
Mules. Eatonville woman who tells the tale of "The Quickest Trick"; she is Bennie Lee's stepsister and has a falling out with him over their parents' inheritance.

Maggie Lemmons.
Color. Contestant from Palatka whose dance partner is Senator Lewis.

Hiram Lester.
"Anthology." Single man who had attended Tuskegee Institute.
"Black Death." Man paralyzed while working in his orange grove by one of Old Man Morgan's curses.
"Contention." Man who brags about killing a bear.
Mules. Mayor of Eatonville who greets Zora on her return home to collect folktales.

Mamie Lester.
Vine. Ex-prostitute who had come to Sanford penniless and been aided by John Pearson, yet she refuses to write him back after his fall from the pulpit of Zion Hope Baptist.

Marie Leveau.
Mules. Legendary New Orleans "queen of conjure" who had lived and died in the French Quarter. Many of the hoodoo doctors Hurston met claimed to have studied under her or even to be related to her.

Ada Lewis.
"Contention." Della Lewis's daughter, whose character is impugned by Sister Taylor during the trial.

Della Lewis.

"Black Death." Woman on whom Old Man Morgan put a loveless curse; although she has married seven times, none of her husbands has stayed more than twenty-eight days.

Bone. Baptist woman who argues with Mrs. Lucy Taylor at the trial over her daughter Ada Lewis's character.

"Contention." Baptist woman who takes offense at Brother Stringer's effrontery.

"Sweat." Owner of the boarding house where Bertha lodges with her rent paid by Sykes Jones.

Senator Lewis.

Color. Contestant from Palatka whose dance partner is Maggie Lemmons.

'Lias.

Eyes. Bahamian boy who offers Tea Cake and Janie a ride out of the Everglades to escape the coming hurricane; unfortunately, Tea Cake refuses the offer.

Light.

Eyes. Joe Starks's first act as mayor is to purchase a streetlight for Eatonville; Janie talks to Tea Cake, who has given her the sunrise so she doesn't regret the sunset: "If you kin see de light at daybreak, you don't keer if you die at dusk"; at the end of the novel Tea Cake is portrayed in an image of light.

"Light." Isis seems "drenched in light" because she is so full of life.

Joe Lindsay.

"Anthology." Biggest liar in Eatonville, according to Lum Boger.

Bone. Baptist man who finds the mule bone that becomes the object of the trial.

"Contention." Baptist man; although the smallest man in Eatonville, he is the biggest braggart; he feigns to fight Joe Clarke.

Eyes. Man who disapproves of Tony Robbins's lenient treatment of his wife and advocates physical violence.

"Sweat." One of the men sitting on Joe Clarke's porch; he comments on how hardworking Delia Jones is.

"Uncle Monday." First person in town to see Uncle Monday, who seems to walk across the lake as if walking on water.

Vine. Joe supports John Pearson's claim that John and Lucy weren't dancing when they led the grand march but admires their style.

Listening.
Eyes. Pheoby's "hungry" listening enables Janie to tell her story; Nanny's listening and hearing Johnny Taylor talking to Janie before he kisses her instigates Janie's journey toward self-discovery.

Lizzimore.
"Anthology." Blind musician who plays the organ and guitar for the grand march.

Old Man Lizzimore.
Color. Older man who escorts Effie Jones to a table at the dance contest.

Alain Locke.
Hurston's influential philosophy professor at Howard University, who served as a judge for the 1925 *Opportunity* short story competition in which Hurston won second place for "Spunk," which Locke then included in his groundbreaking anthology *The New Negro.*

Rev. Long.
"Contention." Baptist church pastor who acts as the prosecutor in the trial; he proves Jim Weston's guilt through references to the Bible.

Lou Lillian.
Color. Emmaline Beasely's illegitimate mulatto daughter, who dies at the end of the play.

Little Ida.
Mules. Woman who doubts Ellis Jones's story about a mule calling a man to preach.

"The Lives of Barney Turk."
Hurston's novel about the adventures of a white Florida man who travels to Central America and then moves to Hollywood, paralleling

Hurston's own travels in the 1940s. Although Hurston worked on the book for a year, it was rejected by Scribner's in 1950.

Love.

Love is a very powerful force in Hurston's work, a force with the power to heal and to destroy. She portrays love through a variety of relationships.

Eyes. Compared to her first two marriages, Janie's relationship with Tea Cake is a "love game." Janie compares love to the sea, which is constantly moving and changing, gaining its shape from the shore it meets, with every shore being unique.

The marital relationships presented in "Sweat" and "The Gilded Six-Bits" illustrate the range of forgiveness and revenge possible in marriages.

"Gaul." Herodias's lifelong love for Antipas is proved when she chooses to join him in exile in Gaul rather than stay in Rome.

Seraph. Jim Merserve tells his wife Arvay that love requires a person to risk everything: "It ain't really love when you gamble with your stuff out the window"; after the incident with the snake in which Arvay fails to act to save him, Jim tells her that he wants "a knowing and a doing love." Finally, at the end of the book Arvay seems ready to give him that kind of total commitment.

"Uncle Monday." Tangled relationships send people to Uncle Monday for help.

Vine. John Pearson's love for Lucy Potts is genuine, although he ultimately betrays it. He is, thus, unhappy until he finds Sally Lovelace at the end of the novel.

Oscar Lovelace.

Vine. Sally's first husband, who left her well-provided for when he died, but who would not allow her to go fishing on the pond while he was alive.

Sally Lovelace.

Vine. Prosperous 48-year-old Plant City widow who becomes John Pearson's third wife. He lives happily with her the last year of his life.

Sister Lucas.

Bone. Methodist woman who argues with Hambo at the trial.

Lucy.

Dust, Mules. Polk County woman who becomes jealous of Hurston's contact with her boyfriend Slim and attacks Hurston. Luckily, Big Sweet, Hurston's friend and protector, steps in and saves her.

Lum.

Eyes. Clerk at Joe Starks's store; he finds Matt Bonner's mule dead on its back with its feet sticking up.

✣ M ✣

Magnolia Flower.
"Magnolia." Daughter of Bentley and Swift Deer, who can curse men with her eyes; she is the apple of her father's eye until she falls in love with a light-skinned school teacher named John. After she steals the key from her father to free John, she runs away with him. This action kills her father, who dies of a heart attack. Forty-seven years later, the two lovers return and sit by the babbling brook.

"Magnolia Flower."
A happier version of *Romeo and Juliet* set in Florida on the banks of the St. John [*sic*] River, the story begins as a folk tale told by the river to a babbling brook. Two young lovers, Magnolia Flower and John, are forbidden to marry by her father, Bentley. A runaway slave who has become prosperous outside the white world by wielding his power ruthlessly over his black and Indian workers, Bentley opposes the marriage because of John's mixed blood. Eventually the two lovers manage to escape north together before Bentley can hang John. Their escape, and especially his daughter's betrayal, bring on Bentley's heart attack and death. Years later the two lovers return and sit

by the babbling brook, which has just been told their tale by the river.

Mah Honey.
Mules. Man from Pierce, Florida, who makes light of Good Bread's threat and taunts her as she leaves. He prefers Mack Ford's storytelling.

Malthrace.
"Gaul," "Veil." Antipas's Samaritan mother.

Mandolin.
"Book." Young man from Standard Bottom, Georgia, who journeys to Harlem and becomes a man of the world; he changes his name to Panic.

Marriage.
Having failed in her own two marriages, Hurston might have been embittered by the experience. But she presents a whole range of married relationships in her works, not all bad ones.

Eyes. Janie experiences three very different marriages. Her first marriage to Logan Killicks is a loveless marriage arranged for her security by her dying grandmother. Her second marriage is her attempt to escape the first marriage and build a relationship with a man on an equal footing. Joe Starks, however, cannot accept Janie as an equal. As soon as Janie realizes the futility of trying to communicate with Joe on equal terms, the marriage falters and ultimately dies. Only her final marriage to Tea Cake Woods is a marriage of equal partners, which Janie enters willfully and completely.

"Magnolia." Magnolia Flower and John's marriage endures for forty-seven years.

"Muttsy." Muttsy and Pinkie's obsessive love affair and subsequent marriage quickly dissipates when Muttsy returns to his gambling lifestyle.

Seraph. Arvay Henson and Jim Meserve's marriage manages to persevere over twenty years.

"Six-Bits." This sentimental view of marriage depicts the reconciliation of Joe and Missie May Banks even after Missie May's infidelity.

"Sweat." An abusive relationship ends in the husband's death by snakebite when Delia Jones gets her revenge on her husband Sykes.

Marse Robert.
Eyes. Nanny's white master, who fathers her daughter Leafy; therefore, he is also Janie's grandfather.

Ruth Marshall.
Mules. Woman who jokes about Jack Oscar Jones's knowledge of love at the storytelling session in Eatonville.

Joe Martin.
Mules. Polk County man and member of the swamp-gang who goes on the fishing trip; he backs up Cliff Ulmer's story about the ugliest man in the world.

Mary Ella.
Bone. Young Baptist girl who teases the Methodist children for not having window panes in their church.

Charlotte Mason.
Hurston's patroness with whom she signed a contract on December 8, 1927, which gave Mason complete ownership of the folklore materials Hurston collected, and control over their publication, in exchange for a $200/month stipend. Hurston paid tribute to Mason in the introduction to *Mules and Men*, saying that she "backed my falling in a hearty way, in a spiritual way, and in addition, financed the whole expedition in the manner of the Great Soul that she is. The world's most gallant woman." At first the relationship was cordial (Hurston called Mason "Godmother" and Mason underwrote the performance of *The Great Day*), but tensions developed as Mason attempted to control Hurston's publication of her research findings. Eventually, Hurston broke off the relationship in 1932. Mason, who was also Langston Hughes's patroness, was memorialized by Hughes as Dora Ellsworth in *Ways of White Folks.*

Old Massa.
"High John." Slave owner outwitted by High John de Conquer.

Master.
"Possum." John's white master, who comes to John's cabin and discovers John's theft of his pig.

Matilda.
Bone. Sassy young girl who defies Marshall Lum Boger.

Mayrella.
Eyes. Schoolmate of Janie's who makes fun of her for living behind the white folks' house and who excludes her from their schoolyard games.

Ruby McCollum.
African American woman who shot and killed Dr. C. Leroy Adams, a wealthy white physician and state senator, in Live Oak, Florida on August 3, 1952; McCollum had been Adams's mistress for six years and had born him a daughter, but Ruby had finally refused to have sex with the doctor in his office and shot him; the racial aspects of the case and its salacious subject matter made the subsequent trial sensational; between October 1952 and January 1953, Hurston wrote several articles about the trial (which resulted in Ruby's being found guilty and sentenced to death) for the *Pittsburgh Courier,* followed by a series of articles on Ruby's life, which appeared from February 28 through May 2, 1953.

Mr. McDuffy.
"Anthology." Man whom Elijah Mosely asks to stop beating his wife until McDuffy explains the violence as a contest of wills.

Mrs. McDuffy.
"Anthology." Woman who shouts in church, even though her husband beats her for it when they get home.

Mentu.
Moses. Old stableman who teaches Moses how to ride and becomes his mentor.

Jim Merchant.
"Anthology." Good-natured man who cures his wife's spells by "accidentally" dropping turpentine in her eye; this same incident appeared later in *Seraph on the Suwanee,* where Jim Meserve "cures" Arvay Henson's fainting fits.
"Sweat." One of the men sitting on Joe Clarke's porch; Jim's wife had once been approached by Sykes Jones and promptly rebuffed.

Lena Marchant.
"Black Death." Woman driven crazy by one of Old Man Morgan's curses.

Sam Merchant.
"Uncle Monday." Hunter who claims to see Uncle Monday's transformation from an alligator into a man.

Angeline ("Angie") Meserve.
Seraph. Arvay and Jim Meserve's second child, born healthy January 7, 1909; Angie quickly becomes her father's favorite; when she grows up she elopes with Hatton Howland.

Arvay Henson Meserve.
Seraph. See Arvay Henson.

Earl David Meserve.
Seraph. Arvay and Jim Meserve's firstborn son; born July 26, 1906, he is mentally handicapped and virtually ignored by his father; Arvay takes up for him, however, and despite his growing antisocial and violent behavior, she defends him; eventually his mental problem gets worse with the onslaught of puberty and manifests itself as some sort of psycho-sexual repression; after he attacks a neighbor girl, he is hunted down and shot.

Jim Meserve.
Seraph. Arvay Henson's husband, who tames her and battles with her during their long marriage. Despite his aristocratic background, Jim works as a woodsman and orange grove manager, moonshiner, and fisherman over the course of the novel. Eventually he manages to work his way into prosperity.

Kenny Meserve.
Seraph. Born James Kenneth Meserve, Kenny is his father's namesake and the third child of Arvay and Jim Meserve; a precocious child whose temperament matches his father's, he becomes increasingly interested in music; he eventually goes to the University of Florida in Gainesville, where he is drum major of the marching band; he later joins a jazz band and becomes a success in New York.

Annie Nathan Meyer.
White novelist and one of the founders of Barnard College, who arranged for Hurston to get a scholarship to attend the college as its first African American student in the fall of 1925. Hurston dedicated *Mules and Men* to "My Dear Friend, Mrs. Annie Nathan Meyer, who hauled the mud to make me but loves me just the same."

Carl Middleton.
Seraph. Young, handsome pastor of Day Spring Baptist Church in Sawley, Florida with whom Arvay Henson is infatuated; after he marries Arvay's sister Lorraine, Arvay begins to have spells until she is cured by Jim Meserve; years later Carl has grown older and moved to smaller churches. He and Lorraine have five children and fall into a Snopes-like poverty. At the end of the book Arvay learns that Carl had loved her but had been tricked into marrying Lorraine.

Lorraine Henson Middleton.
Seraph. See Lorraine Henson.

Migrant workers.
Eyes. Hurston describes the condition and plight of migrant workers who pick string beans and tomatoes and cut cane around Lake Okeechobee.

Skint Miller.
"Spunk." Man who helps Elijah Mosley get Spunk Banks off the circle saw after Spunk's fatal injury.

Teets Miller.
Bone. Village vamp and old girlfriend of Dave Carter's; she now goes with Albert Johnson.

Tes' Miller.
"Spunk." Sawmill worker who is cut up by circle saw and replaced almost immediately by Spunk Banks.

Artie Mimms.
"Bridge." Luke Mimms's 22-year-old son, who falls in love with his father's young wife Vangie.

Artie Mimms.
Vine. Older man and established farmer with sixty acres and two mules to whom Emmeline Potts has promised her daughter Lucy when Lucy turns 16.

Bubber Mimms.
Mules. Eatonville man who plays the guitar for Charlie Jones to sing for Zora on her last night of collecting folklore in Eatonville.

Cap'n Mimms.
Vine. White farmer to whom Ned Crittenden binds over John Buddy. During slavery days, Mimms was a sadistic overseer and had risen in social standing by marrying Miss Pinckney after her father died in the war, thus gaining control of over one thousand acres.

Fred Mimms.
"John Redding." Eye witness to the flood and the bridge's collapse, who recounts the story of the storm to Alfred, Matty, and Stella Redding. Fred is the first to spot John Redding's body floating in the water.

Luke Mimms.
"Bridge." Fifty-eight-year-old father of Artie Mimms and husband of Vangie, who dies at the end of the story when he realizes that his son loves his young wife.

Vangie Mimms.
"Bridge." Luke Mimms's young, beautiful 22-year-old wife, who falls in love with her stepson Artie.

Miriam.
Moses. Moses' (alleged) Hebrew sister, who watches over him and reports that the Princess Royal has rescued him from the Nile; she later becomes a chief priestess and becomes jealous of Moses' power; she suggests making the golden calf. Struck with leprosy by Moses, she finally begs him to allow her to die.

Miriamne.
"Veil." Herod's Asamonean son who, along with his brother Alexander, had plotted to murder their father and was executed.

Miscegenation.

In her fiction Hurston reveals the multiracial heritage of African Americans, along with a critique of their sometimes derogatory attitudes towards their own racial makeup.

Color. The conflict of the story revolves around intraracial prejudice related to variations in the darkness of skin color.

Eyes. Nanny comments that black folks are "branches without roots"; in Janie's case she is the granddaughter of Nanny's white master.

First. Ham's marriage with Eve is miscegenetic.

"Magnolia." Here the mixing is between black and Indian races.

Vine. Amy Crittenden calls her race a "mingled people," for she knows that her son John Buddy is of mixed heritage (probably the son of Alf Pearson).

Old Miss.

"High John." Wife of Old Massa, who, like her husband, is fooled by High John de Conquer's act.

Mistis.

Eyes. Marse Robert's white wife, who threatens Nanny after seeing that her daughter Leafy is half-white; Mistis's threats prompt Nanny to run away to prevent Leafy's being sold off to another plantation.

Steve Mixon.

Eyes. Man for whom Janie cuts a hunk of chewing tobacco incorrectly, thus prompting Joe's castigation of Janie and her finally lashing back at him verbally.

Monanga.

Spears. King of the Luallaba tribe, who refuses to give in to the Wahehes. His full name is Monanga Wa Bibau Biki.

Money.

Few characters in Hurston's fiction have much money, yet most seem to make their way through life quite well without it. When money does become an issue, however, it can cause conflict.

Eyes. Janie has $200 pinned inside her shirt when she runs off with Tea Cake, but she doesn't tell him; he finds the money and uses it.

After he wins money gambling, Tea Cake tells Janie to put her $200 back in the bank and tells her that they will live off what he makes.

Seraph. Jim Meserve's financial success, or more particularly his lack of honesty in telling his wife Arvay about his moonshining business, adversely affects his marriage.

"Six-Bits." The specious nature of Otis Slemmons's gilded coins and their falsity sharply contrast the genuine love that Joe and Missie May Banks share despite their meager material possessions.

Vine. John Pearson soon learns that his monetary status greatly affects the way others treat him, having left town in poverty and disgrace and returned in triumph driving a new Cadillac.

Monoko.
Spears. Chief of the Wahehes, a tribe that attacks the Luallabas and is defeated. His full name is Monoko Mwa Nkoi.

Columbus Montgomery.
Mules. Eatonville man who suggests leaving the toe-party in Wood Bridge when the food runs out.

Becky Moore.
"Anthology." Unwed mother of eleven children whom the other mothers in town won't let their children play with.

Jerry Moore.
Mules. Man whose wife Eulalia puts a hoodoo spell on to get him to marry someone else.

Old Man Morgan.
"Black Death." Very dark-skinned and powerful hoodoo man who lives alone in a two-room hut down by Lake Blue Sink.

B. Moseley.
Mules. Eatonville man who is sitting on the porch playing cards when Zora arrives in town to collect folktales. It is his duty to put out the street lights.

James Moseley.
Mules. Eatonville man who tells the tale of the "Witness of the Johnstown Flood in Heaven"; he invites Zora to the toe-party in Wood Bridge.

Mathilda Moseley.
Mules. Eatonville woman who tells the story of "Why Women Always Take Advantage of Men."

Elijah Mosely.
"Anthology." Man who spins tall tales; he asks Mr. McDuffy about his wife-beating and Mrs. McDuffy about her shouting in church.
Bone. Methodist who sits on Joe Clarke's porch; he is Frank Warrick's card partner.
"Contention." Methodist who brags about fighting with a white man.
"Spunk." Key figure who witnesses Spunk Banks walking off with Lena Kanty and teases Joe Kanty about his wife's behavior. Later Elijah relates the story of Joe's coming back as a bob-cat to haunt Spunk. At the end of the story, it is Elijah who helps get Spunk off the saw and who hears Spunk accusing Joe of pushing him. (His last name is spelled "Mosley" in this story.)
"Sweat." One of the men sitting on Joe Clarke's porch; he comments on the effect of Sykes Jones's beatings on his wife Delia Jones.

Mattie Mosely.
Vine. Eatonville woman who runs up the street announcing Lucy Pearson's death.

Sam Mosely.
Vine. Second most prosperous resident of Eatonville whom John Pearson defeats for mayor by a vote of 17–3. Sam's wagon brings Lucy Pearson to Eatonville and his wagon carries her body away.

Moses.
"Fire and Cloud." Leader of Israelites for forty years who talks to a lizard on his last day of life; he sees a vision of the land of Canaan before he dies.
Moses. (Alleged) son of Hebrews Amram and Jochebed, who is "adopted" by Princess Royal (his probable Egyptian mother), daugh-

ter of Pharaoh; he rises to become commander-in-chief of Egypt's armies and leads the Hebrews out of the land of Egypt.

Mules. Hurston describes Moses in her book of folklore as the "first man who ever learned God's power-compelling words."

Moses, Man of the Mountain.

Hurston's narrative appropriation of the Moses legend into a folklore-filled, allegorical satire of the fate of African Americans in mid-twentieth century America, *Moses, Man of the Mountain* deals with issues of power, leadership, and racial purity. Hurston transforms the figure of Moses from a Hebrew to an Egyptian of African heritage. She also weaves into the story elements of hoodoo and magic, giving Moses supernatural powers and identifying him with the voodoo god Damballa, who is associated with a snake, as is Moses with his rod of power. Hurston's satire of the Hebrew people, reluctant to follow Moses' leadership and fearful of freedom, conveys her views of common black folk in their petty jealousies and suspicion of the success of others.

Published in November 1939 to mixed reviews, the novel had been in Hurston's mind for a long time. In 1934 she published the short story "The Fire and the Cloud," essentially an early version of Moses' death at the end of the novel, but she worked on the novel intermittently over the next five years.

For Further Reading:

Caron, Timothy P. " 'Tell Ole Pharoah to Let My People Go': Communal Deliverance In Zora Neale Hurston's *Moses, Man of the Mountain*." *Southern Quarterly* 36.3 (1998): 47–60. Reprinted in *Struggles Over the Word: Race and Religion in O'Connor, Faulkner, Hurston, and Wright*." Macon: Mercer UP, 2000. 82–111.

Clariett, Kathleen. "The African Face of Moses: Liberator, Lawgiver, and Leader in Zora Neale Hurston's *Moses, Man of the Mountain*." *Zora Neale Hurston Forum* 11 (1997): 36–44.

Morris, Robert J. "Zora Neale Hurston's Ambitious Enigma: *Moses, Man of the Mountain*." *CLA Journal* 40.3 (1997): 305–35.

Sheffey, Ruthe T. "Zora Neale Hurston's *Moses, Man of the Mountain*: A Fictionalized Manifesto on the Imperatives of Black Leadership." *CLA Journal* 29.2 (1985): 206–20. Reprinted in *Trajectory: Fueling the Future and Preserving the African-American Past: Essays in Criticism (1962–1986)*. Baltimore: Morgan State UP, 1989. 165–81; and

Critical Essays on Zora Neale Hurston. Ed. Gloria L. Cronin. New York: G.K. Hall, 1998. 154–64.

Lulu Moses.
Eyes. Gossipy Eatonville woman who talks about Janie when she returns to town.

Moss.
"Sweat." One of the men sitting on Joe Clarke's porch; he comments on Sykes Jones's worthlessness.

Deacon Moss.
Vine. Churchmember of Zion Hope Baptist who is convinced after hearing John Pearson's prayer that John has been called to preach.

Joe Nathan Moss.
"Uncle Monday." Young man jilted by Mary Ella Shaw. His mother goes to Uncle Monday to place a curse on Mary Ella.

Lige Moss.
Eyes. Eatonville resident who derides Tony Taylor's speechmaking abilities; he also debates Sam Watson over philosophical questions such as which is superior—nature or caution.

"Mother Catherine."
Story of Hurston's trip to visit a hoodoo priestess; published initially in Nancy Cunard's anthology *Negro* in 1934.

Mother Catherine.
"Mother Catherine." New Orleans hoodoo priestess who conducts services and lives in a compound called "The Manger." Hurston spent two weeks with her.

Mother Seal.
"Mother Catherine." Mother Catherine's other name.

Motor Boat.
Eyes. Bahamian friend of Tea Cake's on the muck; he is one of the men involved in the fight at Mrs. Turner's. Later he flees the hurricane with Janie and Tea Cake, but remains behind in a house in the

wake of the flood; miraculously Motor Boat survives when the house floats away to higher ground while he sleeps.

Mourning.

Eyes. Janie mourns for only a short time after Joe Starks's death; she doesn't think mourning should last any longer than the grief. By contrast Janie mourns much more deeply for Tea Cake; she doesn't even dress up for his funeral, just wearing overalls.

Vine. John Pearson's mourning for his wife Lucy is short lived, but he comes to learn the error of his ways during his marriage to Hattie Tyson. Later at the end of the novel, John's death is mourned by the whole town in an elaborate funeral service.

Mrs. Doctor.

One of Hurston's unpublished (and unfinished) novels, whose characters are upper-class African Americans. After Lippincott rejected the project in September 1945, Hurston dropped it, leaving it only two-thirds finished.

Muck-Boy.

Eyes. Young man who joins the singing as the group of migrant workers who have decided to remain behind to weather the storm attempt to bolster their spirits.

Mule Bone.

Three act play written in collaboration with Langston Hughes in 1930, but which later became the cause for the end of Hurston's friendship with Hughes after they fell out over plans Hurston made to produce the play in 1931 without Hughes's knowledge. In his autobiography, *The Big Sea* (1940), Hughes admitted that the story and dialogue of the play were essentially Hurston's, while his major contribution was structural. Although Act III of the play was eventually published in 1964, the play was not published in its entirety until 1991.

In Act I, the town of Eatonville is presented in all its Saturday glory, with men playing cards on the porch of Joe Clarke's store, children playing games in the street, and everyone telling tales. The plot really starts with the arrival of Jim Weston and Dave Carter, two friends who are both interested in the same girl, the beautiful Daisy Taylor. At first all goes well. Jim and Dave play music and everyone dances. But with Daisy's arrival the competition between the two heats up, and eventually a fight breaks out. During the uproar Jim grabs a mule bone that happens to be lying around and hits Dave over the head. For this "assault" he is promptly arrested, jailed, and the trial set for Monday.

Act II then recounts the actual trial, although the real action occurs before the trial even starts. For this sleepy little town, the trial is a major social event. Additional interest derives from the religious rivalry that the trial has set up between the Methodists, who back Jim Weston, and the Baptists, who support Dave Carter. At the trial, held in the Baptist church, the two factions nearly cause havoc as they speak out against each other. Finally, Joe Clarke, who acts as judge, settles them down and the trial commences. Jim's defense rests on the assertion that he is innocent of assault because a mule bone is not a weapon. Dave's counsel, the Baptist minister, Elder Childers, however, uses biblical evidence to prove that the jawbone of an ass was used to slay 3,000 in the Old Testament. That indisputable evidence convinces Clarke, who finds Jim guilty and, for his sentence, orders him out of town for a period of two years.

In Act III, the shortest act of the play, Jim is walking down the railroad tracks on his way out of town when Daisy catches up with him. Concerned for his well-being and now more interested in him romantically, Daisy implores him to stay and live with her. Just then, however, Dave shows up and makes his case for Daisy to live with him. For a while the two men play the dozens competing to see who can promise Daisy the most, but when it becomes clear that what Daisy actually wants is someone to work hard and support her, they decide that their friendship (and their freedom) is more important than any woman. So the rejected Daisy leaves in a huff, and the two men, now fast friends once more, walk back into town together.

For Further Reading:

Boyd, Lisa. "The Folk, the Blues, and the Problems of *Mule Bone*." *Langston Hughes Review* 13.1 (1994–95): 33–44.

Gates, Henry Louis, Jr. "The Tragedy of Negro Life." In Zora Neale Hurston and Langston Hughes's *Mule Bone*. New York: Harper & Row, 1991. 5–24.

"The Mule Bone Controversy." In Zora Neale Hurston and Langston Hughes's *Mule Bone*. New York: Harper & Row, 1991. 157–280. Contains narrative accounts of the controversy from books by Lang-

ston Hughes, Robert Hemenway, and Arnold Rampersad, as well as
correspondence to and from Hurston, Hughes, and others related to
the events.

Rosenberg, Rachel A. "Looking for Zora's *Mule Bone*: The Battle for Artistic
Authority in the Hurston-Hughes Collaboration." *Modernism/Mo-
dernity* 6.2 (1999): 79–105.

Sheffey, Ruthe T. "Zora Hurston and Langston Hughes's 'Mule Bone': An
Authentic Folk Comedy and the Compromised Tradition." Re-
printed in *Trajectory: Fueling the Future and Preserving the African-
American Past: Essays in Criticism (1962–1986)*. Baltimore: Morgan
State UP, 1989. 211–31.

Mules.

The mule, that most ubiquitous of southern beasts of burden, turns
up frequently in Hurston's fiction. Hurston emphasizes the animal's
lowly status, hard work, and stubborn endurance.

"Contention," *Bone*. This trial turns on the question of whether
or not a mule bone can be a weapon.

Eyes. Nanny says black women are the "mule of the world." Matt
Bonner's yellow mule is the source of many jokes in the town. The
mule's death is the occasion of a big dragging out and mule funeral.

Mules. Hurston relates two folktales involving mules: "Why They
Always Use Rawhide on a Mule" and "The Talking Mule."

Mules and Men.

Hurston's first anthropological work based on her folklore collecting travels through the South between 1927 and 1929 (with some
further work in 1931–32) in which she turns "the spy-glass of Anthropology" on African American folk culture. Although she completed the book in Eatonville during the summer of 1932, she could
not find a publisher until 1934. The publisher, Bertram Lippincott,
suggested that Hurston add more about her research on hoodoo,
which had appeared in a 1931 article for the *Journal of American
Folklore*. So Hurston revised the book that summer, and it was published in October 1935 to good reviews.

Franz Boas, Hurston's mentor and professor of anthropology at
Barnard, wrote the book's introduction, noting Hurston's "contribution to our knowledge of the true inner life of the Negro." Hurston dedicated the book to Annie Nathan Meyer, who had helped

her get into Barnard. In the dedication Hurston says that Meyer "hauled the mud to make me but loves me just the same."

Divided into two sections, the book first recounts Hurston's exploits as she gathers and shares seventy African American folktales, the first group from Eatonville and the rest from Polk County. In Part II she moves to Louisiana, where she meets five different hoodoo doctors. The book ends with several African American folksongs that Hurston collected, as well as a listing of hoodoo formulae, ingredients, and potions.

Perhaps the most interesting aspect of the book is the narrator, Hurston herself in fictionalized form. This structure, which became an increasingly important element in the book the longer Hurston waited for a publisher and the more she revised it, transforms the book from a strictly nonfictional anthropological study of folklore to a genuinely narrative format. In fact Hurston felt free to telescope the timeframe of her expeditions for the sake of narrative, even adding folktales that she had heard long before her collecting expeditions. The final result, although not as strictly scientific as anthropologists might like, is a much more interesting and readable account of the folktales.

For Further Reading:

Boxwell, D.A. " 'Sis Cat' as Ethnographer: Self-Presentation and Self-Inscription in Zora Neale Hurston's *Mules and Men*." *African American Review* 26.4 (1992): 605–17.

Bush, Roland E. "Narrative Strategy and Purpose in Zora Neale Hurston's *Mules and Men*." *Zora Neale Hurston Forum* 8.2 (1994): 14–24.

Dolby-Stahl, Sandra. "Literary Objectives: Hurston's Use of Personal Narrative in *Mules and Men*." *Western Folklore* 51.1 (1992): 51–63. Reprinted in *Critical Essays on Zora Neale Hurston*. Ed. Gloria L. Cronin. New York: G.K. Hall, 1998. 43–52.

Domina, Lynn. " 'Protection in My Mouf': Self, Voice, and Community in Zora Neale Hurston's *Dust Tracks on a Road* and *Mules and Men*." *African American Review* 31.2 (1997): 197–209.

Dorst, John. "Rereading *Mules and Men*: Toward the Death of the Ethnographer." *Cultural Anthropology* 2.3 (1987): 305–18.

Faulkner, Howard J. "*Mules and Men*: Fiction as Folklore." *CLA Journal* 34.3 (1991): 331–39.

Harris, Trudier. "Africanizing the Audience: Hurston's Transformation of White Folks in *Mules and Men*." *Zora Neale Hurston Forum* 8.1 (1993): 43–58.

Harris, Trudier. "Performing Personae and Southern Hospitality: Zora
    Neale Hurston in *Mules and Men*." In *The Power of the Porch: The
    Storyteller's Craft in Zora Neale Hurston, Gloria Naylor, and Randall
    Kenan*. Athens: U of Georgia P, 1996. 1–50.
Hemmingway, Beulah S. "Through the Prism of Africanity: A Preliminary
    Investigation of Zora Neale Hurston's *Mules and Men*." In *Zora in
    Florida*. Ed. Steve Glassman and Kathryn Lee Seidel. Orlando: U of
    Central Florida P, 1991. 38–45.
Meisenhelder, Susan. "Conflict and Resistance in Zora Neale Hurston's
    Mules and Men." *Journal of American Folklore* 109.433 (1996):
    267–88.
Preu, Dana McKinnon. "A Literary Reading of *Mules and Men*, Part I." In
    Zora in Florida. Ed. Steve Glassman and Kathryn Lee Seidel. Or-
    lando: U of Central Florida P, 1991. 46–61.
Wainwright, Mary Katherine. "Subversive Female Folk Tellers in *Mules and
    Men*." In *Zora in Florida*. Ed. Steve Glassman and Kathryn Lee Sei-
    del. Gainesville: U of Florida P, 1991. 62–75.
Wall, Cheryl. "*Mules and Men* and Women: Zora Neale Hurston's Strategies
    of Narration and Visions of Female Empowerment." *Black American
    Literature Forum* 23.4 (1989): 661–80. Repinted in *Critical Essays
    on Zora Neale Hurston*. Ed. Gloria L. Cronin. New York: G.K. Hall,
    1998. 53–70.

Sister Murchison.

Mules. Woman who comes to Rev. Father Joe Watson to get rid
of her mother-in-law.

Music.

Music plays an integral role in almost all of Hurston's works, especially those related to the folklore that she collected. In fact, *Mules
and Men* and *Tell My Horse*, her two anthropological works, both
include appendices of folk songs.

Color, Spears. Singing and dancing are integral parts of these Hurston plays, as well as her musical revues—*The Great Day, From Sun
to Sun*, and *Singing Steel.*

Eyes. Tea Cake sings whenever he is around Janie. Tea Cake plays
guitar. People break into song in times of celebration, such as the
lighting of the lamp.

"High John." The slaves go to heaven in search of song to endure
a harsh master.

"Muttsy." Ma Turner's place rocks with songs and blues piano playing.

Seraph. Arvay and Jim Meserve are serenaded on their wedding night by Joe Kelsey and the other Negroes. Kenny Meserve's interest in music and appropriation of Negro blues guitar and piano playing are influenced by Joe Kelsey. Kenny had gotten his talent from his mother Arvay. He becomes a success in a band and travels to New York.

"Muttsy."

A cautionary tale of a naive young girl from Eatonville who moves to Harlem. There she boards at a disreputable boarding house and encounters many unsavory characters. Eventually, Pinkie becomes the object of many advances, but finally she becomes the target of a gambler, Muttsy Owens, who becomes obsessed with the girl's beauty and innocence. When Pinkie runs away, Muttsy searches for her and finds her and marries her two weeks later. Although he promises her to reform his life, his reformation is brief. Soon after their marriage he is once again gambling. After winning a second place award in the second *Opportunity* contest in 1926, the story was published in the magazine's August 1926 issue.

"My Most Humiliating Jim Crow Experience."

Published in the June 1944 *Negro Digest*, this short personal essay is an example of one of Hurston's more open criticisms of white society. After relating her account of the degrading 1931 experience of being examined in a closet by a white medical specialist in New York, Hurston closes with a condemnation of the madness of Anglo-Saxon civilization.

⊁⊰ N ⊁⊰

Nadab.
Moses. One of Moses' oldest sons, who is killed for leading the revolt that led to the building of the golden calf.

Nanny.
Eyes. Janie's grandmother, who raises her after Janie's mother deserts her. Nanny, having endured the loss of her freedom during slavery, forces Janie to marry Logan Killicks for security. Three and a half months later Nanny dies, leaving Janie alone.

Narrative techniques.
Hurston employs a variety of narrative techniques in her works.
Eyes. Pheoby helps Janie tell her story; Nanny says she has "saved de text" of her story for Janie to tell. Hurston utilizes indirect discourse to allow her, as narrator, to comment on Janie's telling of her own story.
Moses. Hurston reinvents the Moses story in terms of an African American escape motif.
Mules. Revisions of this book brought about the increasing importance of Hurston as narrator.

Seraph. Hurston uses a fairly straightforward traditional narrative stance.

Vine. Hurston incorporates both folklore and autobiography into this novel, as well as a sermon that she recorded during one of her anthropological research trips.

Ned.
"Light." Dog whose chin Joel Watts puts shaving cream on.

The New Negro.
This groundbreaking 1925 anthology of African American writing (edited by Alain Locke) included Hurston's story "Spunk."

Miss Nellie.
Eyes. White woman who is the mother of the Washburns' four grandchildren (although it's not clear whether she is their daughter or daughter-in-law). She and the children return to live with them after her husband dies.

Nero.
"Gaul." Roman emperor who succeeds Caligula; he stays at Antipas's inn in Lyons and offers to restore Antipas to his kingship, although Antipas declines his offer.

"Niggerati."
Self-deprecating term coined by Hurston, Langston Hughes, and Wallace Thurman (from the Italian "literati") to name the group of younger African American writers and artists during the Harlem Renaissance. Zora proclaimed herself queen of this group and hosted many parties for them and their supporters at her apartment.

Enoch Nixon.
Color. Contestant from Daytona whose dance partner is Janie Bradley.

Sister Doll Nixon.
Bone. Methodist wife of Willie Nixon and would-be witness at the trial; she stands up to Joe Clarke at the trial and disparages him for his treatment of his wife.

Steve Nixon.
Mules. Eatonville man who holds a class meeting at St. Lawrence Church.

Willie Nixon.
Bone. Lounger at Joe Clarke's store who joins the discussion of what should be done to Mrs. Jake Roberts; a Methodist, he incurs Hambo's wrath when he hangs his coat on the lamp at the trial in the Baptist church.

Noah.
First. Biblical patriarch who in his drunkenness curses his son Ham with blackness.

Mrs. Noah.
First. Noah's wife, who implores him to revoke his curse on their son Ham.

Peter Noble.
Mules. Polk County man and member of the swamp-gang who goes on the fishing trip; he asks Eugene Oliver to tell the story "Praying for Rain."

Notasulga.
Alabama town where Hurston was born on January 7, 1891.
Vine. John Pearson goes to Notasulga to work for Alf Pearson; there he goes to school and meets Lucy Potts.

"Now You Cookin' with Gas."
Unedited version of "Story in Harlem Slang," which includes a reference to the killing of a white policeman. It was not published until *The Complete Stories* in 1995.

Nun.
Moses. Hebrew man charged by Moses with the duty of retrieving Joseph's bones from his tomb as the Israelites leave Egypt.

Nunkie.
Bone. Child who tries to lick Rev. Simms's child's candy stick.

Nunkie.

Eyes. Flirtatious young girl who works in the fields with Tea Cake and Janie; Nunkie provokes Janie's jealousy when she flirts with Tea Cake.

Nunkie.

Mules. Man who is reading the cards at the Pine Mill the night of the big fight.

Nunkie.

Vine. Stablehand on Alf Pearson's plantation. He urges on John Pearson and Duke when they are about to fight at the barbecue.

✳ O ✳

"The Ocoee Riot."
Hurston's uncharacteristically incendiary account of a racial incident in Ocoee, Florida (a town near Eatonville) on election day in
November 1920. Negroes were prevented from voting and, when
they resisted, a mob of whites from a neighboring town turned up
and provoked further violence, ultimately resulting in the lynching of
a black farmer, July Perry.

Eugene Oliver.
Mules. Polk County man and member of the swamp-gang who
goes on the fishing trip and tells the tales of "Massa and the Bear,"
"What Smelled Worse," "Praying for Rain," "You Think I'm Gointer
Pay You But I Ain't," and "How Brer 'Gator Got His Tongue Worn
Out."

Orrie.
Seraph. Miss Hessie's grandson, whom she sends to carry the groceries Arvay Meserve had brought.

Mrs. Rufus Osgood.
Married name of Hurston's patron. (See Charlotte Mason)

Muttsy Owens.
"Muttsy." Gambler who falls hopelessly in love with Pinkie Jones and pursues her obsessively until she agrees to marry him. Not long afterward, however, he reverts back to his old habits.

Brother Owl.
"Cock Robin." Character who asks who killed Cock Robin; he decides that whoever pays for the funeral can parade Cock Robin's body.

<h1 style="text-align:center">⊁⊱ P ⊰⊀</h1>

Past.

Just as the past is never past for Faulkner, the past continues to influence the lives of Hurston's characters.

Eyes. Janie's entire story is a story of the past, which she understands much better now that she has "been to the horizon and back." With both the experience of the past under her belt and the context that such experience brings, she can then relate her life's story to her friend Pheoby Watson.

Seraph. Arvay Henson reevaluates her past relationship with her husband Jim and decides to set out on a new course with him at the end of the novel.

Vine. John Pearson begins to think more about the past (and his relationship with Lucy) when his marriage to Hattie Tyson starts falling apart.

Deacon Tracy Patton.

Vine. Timid deacon of Zion Hope Baptist Church who lacks the courage to speak out against Rev. John Pearson at the first meeting called to oppose Pearson.

Ora Patton.
Vine. Brazen young girl from Sanford who lures John Pearson into giving her a ride in his new Cadillac, resulting in his last infidelity and, ultimately, his death.

Pearson.
Eyes. Along with Hambo, he is in charge of barbecuing the three hogs for the celebration of lighting the street lamp.

Alf Pearson.
Vine. Wealthy white plantation owner (Massa Alf Pearson), who owned Amy Crittenden during slavery and possibly fathered her son John. Pearson employs John (who takes the name Pearson as a son would) and takes him under his wing. Mist' Alf gives John more and more responsibility on the plantation and helps him when John gets in trouble. Also a judge, he arranges for John to be released into his custody and then gives him $50 so that he can get out of town before the patrollers catch him.

Alfred Pearson.
Vine. White son of Alf Pearson; Alf gives John Pearson his son's hand-me-down clothes to wear while Alfred is studying abroad in Paris.

Emmeline Pearson.
Vine. John and Lucy's oldest daughter. She cooks batter cakes for Lucy just before Lucy dies.

Hezekiah Pearson.
Vine. John and Lucy Pearson's oldest son. Lucy sends him for help when she goes into labor while John is away. He stays in Jacksonville to hear his girlfriend sing in church and thus misses being at his mother's bedside when she dies.

Ike Pearson.
"Contention." Man who brags about killing a six-foot rattlesnake.

Isis "Isie" Pearson.
Vine. John and Lucy Pearson's youngest daughter, to whom Lucy gives instructions on her deathbed and to whom Lucy leaves her

feather bed. Isis's bout of typhoid prompts John Pearson's flight away from Eatonville and into the arms of Hattie Tyson.

John Pearson.
Vine. John and Lucy Pearson's second son. Rev. Pearson pulls a knife on John when he tries to keep Hattie Tyson out of the feather bed that his mother had given to his sister Isis. John attends school in Jacksonville.

Lucy Pearson.
Vine. See Lucy Potts.

Mrs. Pearson.
Eyes. Rev. Pearson's wife.

Rev. John Pearson.
Eyes, Vine. Larger than life protagonist of *Jonah's Gourd Vine*, John Pearson was modeled after Hurston's father, John Hurston, who was also a preacher. John Pearson, the Jonah of the book's title, rises from obscurity and poverty to the heights of success as minister, mayor, and state moderator only to become increasingly arrogant the more successful he becomes. His pride and his fatal flaw of infidelity lead to his ultimate downfall and then his death when he is hit by a train.

For Further Reading:

Daniel, Walter C. "Zora Neale Hurston's John Pearson: Saint and Sinner." In *Images of the Preacher in Afro-American Literature.* Washington, DC: UP of America, 1981: 83–109.

Cy Perkins.
Vine. White justice of the peace in Notasulga, Alabama, who agrees not to hold court until after Lucy Pearson has had a chance to talk to Judge Alf Pearson on her husband John's behalf.

"The 'Pet Negro' System."
Hurston's article, published in the March 1943 *American Mercury*, analyzes the sociological phenomenon of racial interactions and class structures in the South. Although originally part of *Dust Tracks on a Road*, it was edited out to make the book less controversial.

Pheemy.
Vine. Amy Crittenden's mother and John Pearson's grandmother, who looks after John when he first arrives at the Pearson plantation. She breaks up the fight between John and Duke at the barbecue. She also helps deliver the first three of Lucy and John's children.

Philip.
"Gaul." Governor of Batania and Trachopitis, and Antipas's half-brother, to whom Antipas's stepdaughter Salome is betrothed.

Photographs.
Eyes. The first time that Janie realizes that she is black (and thus different from the white Washburn children) is when she sees the picture of the children taken by a traveling photographer.

Phrony.
Vine. Fourteen-year-old girl interested in John Buddy who becomes jealous of his involvement with Mehaley. She dances with John's brother Zeke at the barbecue.

Anatol Pierre.
Mules. Middle-aged Catholic octoroon who claims kinship to Marie Leveau and whose temple is the most elaborate of any of the hoodoo doctors with whom Hurston worked; she studied with him for four months.

Sister Pierson.
"Anthology." Woman who gives Mrs. Tony Roberts some collard greens.

Pontius Pilate.
"Gaul." Roman governor whom Antipas plots to assassinate; however, Antipas is caught and exiled to Gaul.
"Veil." Roman governor who abuses the people of Palestine and prompts Antipas's opposition.

Massa Pinckney.
Vine. White owner of large Alabama plantation who dies in the Civil War.

Miss Pinckney.
Vine. White daughter of Massa Pinckney, who, after her father's death, marries the overseer Cap'n Mimms.

Sister Pindar.
Vine. Member of Zion Hope Baptist Church who is unimpressed by Rev. Felton Cozy's trial sermon, noting its lack of a biblical text.

Miz Pendleton.
"Cock Robin." White woman whom Uncle July overhears reading the story of the bird Cock Robin.

Emma Lou Pittman.
"Uncle Monday." Woman who sees Uncle Monday with his arm all mangled and his face torn up before he magically recuperates.

Edna Pitts.
Mules. Wood Bridge woman at whose house the toe-party is held.

Bootsie Pitts.
Bone. Town vamp and old girlfriend of Jim Weston's; her new beau is Jimmy Cox.

Handy Pitts.
Mules. Polk County man and member of the swamp-gang who goes on the fishing trip; he spars verbally with Tush Hawg about mean bosses.

Hawley Pitts.
Seraph. Ugliest white man in the county, whom Jim Meserve fights and then makes up with in the "Battle of the Horse's Behind" after Hawley bullies Pearly Snead. Later Hawley is the one who brings the news that Earl Meserve has been located in the Big Swamp.

Henry Pitts.
Eyes. Eatonville resident forced to leave town by Joe Starks after he is caught with a wagon load of Joe's ribbon cane.

Mr. Pitts.
Mules. Man who jokes with Zora and breaks the ice for her at the Pine Mill dance.

Sister Katie Pitts.
Bone. Baptist woman who suggests that they pray before the trial starts; she later testifies against Jim Weston on Dave Carter's behalf; her mule tears up Mrs. Mattie Clarke's tomato vines and threatens to kick Marshall Lum Boger.

Plates.
Eyes. Nanny begs Janie, "Put me down easy, Janie. Ah'm a cracked plate." Janie tells Pheoby that she doesn't have any use for an empty plate after she finishes off the mulatto rice.

Playing the dozens.
Eyes. African American game of verbal exchanges in which participants swap insults to see who can best the other.
Vine. Mehaley and Phrony play the dozens in competing over John Buddy's attentions when he first arrives.

Brother Poke.
"Contention." Baptist court observer who sides with Dave Carter.

Polk County.
Musical comedy revue based on folk material Hurston had collected; Hurston wrote the play in New York in the spring of 1944, along with Dorothy Waring, a white writer, whose husband, Stephen Kelen d'Oxylion, was supposed to act as the play's producer. During the writing of the play, Hurston clashed with Waring over artistic issues, but they eventually finished the play, although it was never produced.

Porches.
Porches act as a central gathering place for the townspeople of Hurston's stories. The porch serves both as communal social space and as communal storytelling space.
"Contention." The men talking on the porch brag about their exploits.
Eyes. Joe Stark talks to the townsfolk from the porch of his house.

Seraph. Arvay Meserve's sleeping porch gives her a sense of belonging.

Chuck Portlock.
Vine. White night rider who asks Alf Pearson about John Pearson's whereabouts the day after John has left town.

" 'Possum or Pig?"
Slave tale from "High John de Conquer" in which the slave's wit enables him to outsmart his master and saves him in the end. It was first published in *Forum* in September 1926.

Aaron Potts.
Vine. Lucy Potts's younger brother, who is ordered by their mother to go cut peach switches so that she can whip Lucy on her wedding day. Lucy refuses to take the beating.

Bud Potts.
Vine. Lucy Potts's older brother, who leads the choir at Macedonia Baptist Church, but who later takes her bed away from her as payment for a debt. John Pearson beats him up for this affront and Bud has him arrested for assault, thus prompting John's leaving Notasulga and moving to Florida.

Sister Cal'line Potts.
"Anthology." Longsuffering wife of Mitchell Potts, who puts up with his infidelity in silence until one day she kills him with an ax.

Emmeline Potts.
Vine. Lucy Potts's overbearing mother, who does not approve of her daughter's decision to marry poor John Pearson.

Grandma Potts.
"Light." Isis Watts's maternal grandmother who gets a "shave."

Lucy Potts.
"Black Death." Woman cursed with the bloody flux by Old Man Morgan.
Vine. Named after Hurston's mother, Lucy Potts is the longsuffering wife of the novel's protagonist, John Pearson. She marries John

Pearson on her birthday (December 31) when she is only 15. They are married twenty-two years, ten in Notasulga and twelve in Eatonville, during which time Lucy bears him seven children. Lucy's death, when she is only 37, presages the end of John's rise to success and precipitates the breakup of their family.

Lucy Ann Potts.
Hurston's mother's maiden name. (See also Lucy Hurston)

Mitch Potts.
"John Redding." Victim of conjuring spell who has been flat on his back for six months.

Mitchell Potts.
"Anthology." Unfaithful husband whose wife endures his infidelity only so long and finally kills him with an ax.

Richard Potts.
Vine. Lucy Potts's prosperous father. He is married to Emmeline. He sympathizes with John and Lucy, allowing John to escort his daughter home from church and inviting him to stay for dinner. Later he supports Lucy in her decision to marry John.

Prayer.
Moses. Moses' prayers are direct communication with God, giving him supernatural and magical powers.

Seraph. As if she were a heathen, Arvay Henson prays to the sun to make her third child a boy.

Vine. John Buddy's first prayer for cleansing (after his encounter with Mehaley) occurs in church when he arrives ahead of everyone else. The sound of his prayer convinces him that he should pray in church again. Emmeline Potts prays a humorous prayer about keeping John and Lucy five feet apart while they are courting. John's prayer in church following his near drowning in the Alabama River convinces Deacon Moss that John has been called to preach.

Mr. Prescott.
Eyes. District attorney who prosecutes Janie for Tea Cake's death. He quiets Sop-de-Bottom when he tries to speak during the trial.

Jim Presley.
Mules. Polk County man and member of the swamp-gang who goes on the fishing trip and tells the tales of "De Reason Niggers Is Working so Hard," "How the 'Gator Got His Mouth," and "How the Cat Got Nine Lives"; he plays guitar at the Pine Hill dance for Zora to sing "John Henry."

Albert Price III.
Hurston's second husband, a 23-year-old WPA worker, whom she married on June 27, 1939, in Fernandina Beach, Florida, but then promptly left to take a job at the North Carolina College for Negroes. The next year she filed for divorce, although they briefly reconciled before she left him again. Their divorce was not finally granted until November 9, 1943.

Puah.
Moses. Hebrew midwife who assists Jochebed at Moses' birth.

✳️ Q ✳️

Queen of Sheba.
Mules. Ethiopian queen who knows hoodoo; she gets thirsty and visits Solomon, whom she gives her talking ring.

⁕ R ⁕

Mr. Rabbit.
"Anthology." Rabbit who is Mr. Dog's rival for Miss Nancy Coon's heart; he outwits Mr. Dog by splitting Mr. Dog's tongue so that he can't sing.

Race.
Hurston's work is at once all about race and at the same time beyond race. While her fictional world acknowledges some of the racial issues, prejudices, and restrictions of her day, she does not allow polemics to obscure her real focus on her characters' lives.

Color. Emmaline Beasely's color prejudice causes her to lose the man she loves, John Turner, not once but twice.

Eyes. Janie's acceptance of diversity contrasts with Mrs. Turner's colorstruck attitudes towards darker skinned Negroes. But following the hurricane black and white corpses are treated very differently during burial. Similarly, whites and blacks are treated differently in the courtroom during Janie's trial.

"Magnolia." Bentley is guilty of reverse prejudice in his opposition to Magnolia Flower's marriage to John, a man of mixed blood.

"White Publishers," "Democracy," "Pet Negro," "Jim Crow."

Hurston's sometimes paradoxical, even contradictory mix of conservative and libertarian views on the race issues of her day are presented in these articles.

Rachel.
Moses. Hur's wife, who spreads the story over the whole village after Jochebed tells her about Moses' being rescued by the Princess.

Rain-Bringer.
Mules. Hurston's hoodoo name, given to her by Luke Turner after her sixty-nine-hour initiation ceremony.

Rape.
Although never presented by Hurston in its full graphic violence, rape is, nevertheless, presented as a violent exertion of male power over a weaker, defenseless female.

Eyes. Leafy, Janie's mother, is raped by the school teacher, just as Nanny had earlier been raped by her master.

Seraph. Jim Meserve rapes Arvay Henson under the mulberry tree to make her his own before eloping with her.

Alfred Redding.
"John Redding." John Redding's father, who encourages John's dreams of travel; after John dies, it is Alfred who orders that his son's body be allowed to float up the river to the sea.

John Redding.
"John Redding." Titular protagonist, who is a 10-year-old dreamer at the start of the story; he goes to school, marries Stella Kanty, and settles down, but he never loses his desire to travel. He finally gets his wish when he drowns in a flood. John's father allows his body to continue floating up the river to the sea, thus fulfilling John's lifelong dream.

Matty Redding.
"John Redding." John Redding's overprotective mother, who uses guilt to keep her son from traveling as he wants to do.

Stella (Kanty) Redding.
"John Redding." John Redding's wife. (See also Stella Kanty)

Redmond.
Eyes. According to the tall tale, Matt Bonner's yellow mule tired of Redmond's long-winded prayer and went inside the Baptist church and broke up the meeting.

Religious rivalry.
"Contention," *Bone.* Baptists and Methodists square off at the trial of Jim Weston, each group supporting their own member. Dave Carter, the plaintiff, is supported by the Baptists; Jim, the defendant, is supported by the Methodists.

Revenge.
"Black Death." With the help of conjure, many acts of revenge are completed.
"Spunk." Joe Kanty returns as a bobcat and haunts Spunk Banks, finally pushing him onto a circle saw and killing him for stealing his wife.
"Sweat." Delia Jones's revenge on her abusive and unfaithful husband Sykes takes the form of a rattlesnake.
Vine. Hattie Tyson seeks revenge against Rev. John Pearson by divorcing him, hopefully causing him to lose his church.

Officer Richardson.
Mules. Polk County man and member of the swamp-gang who goes on the fishing trip; he spars verbally with Blue Baby about ugly men.

Will Richardson.
Mules. Polk County man and member of the swamp-gang who tells a "Deer Hunting Story."

"The Rise of Begging Joints."
Hurston's article, first published in the March 1945 *American Mercury,* condemning the substandard Negro academies that offered inferior educations and false promises to their students; according to Hurston, these institutions seem to exist for the sole purpose of enriching the bureaucrats who run them; rather than supporting them, she urges benefactors to do some research into which schools are really educating their students and to give money to these schools.

The River.
"Magnolia." Narrator of the story who tells the tale of Magnolia Flower and John to the brook.

Rivers.
"John Redding." The St. John [*sic*] River floods and carries John Redding away.
"Magnolia." The river and the brook are characters in this story.
Moses. Moses is put into the Nile River as a baby to save his life.
Vine. John Buddy crosses the Big Creek to start his new life. He carries Lucy over the creek. When John falls in the Alabama River after the bridge collapses, his "baptism" changes him and prompts him to begin his new life as a preacher.

Roads.
Eyes. Joe has a road put in in front of his store; Janie considers walking down the road to escape.

Tony Robbins.
Eyes. Longsuffering husband of Mrs. Tony; he humors his troublesome wife because he loves her.

Mrs. Tony Robbins.
Eyes. Tony Robbin's wife, who shames him by begging food from Joe Starks and then putting on a show when he gives her too little.

Mrs. Jake Roberts.
Bone. Woman who pesters Joe Clarke and other townspeople for food.

Tony Roberts.
"Anthology." Name of Tony Robbins in "The Eatonville Anthology."

Mrs. Tony Roberts.
"Anthology." Name of Mrs. Tony Robbins in "The Eatonville Anthology."

Willie Roberts.
Mules. Polk County man who goes on the fishing trip and tells the tale of "Shooting Up Hill."

George Robinson.
"Light." White cattleman who rides past the Watts' gate.

Jim Robinson.
"Light." White cattleman who rides past the Watts' gate; he gives Isis Watts a short ride on his horse.

Lee Robinson.
Mules. Eatonville man who leads the church in singing an old spiritual.

Rachael Roe.
Mules. Young woman, jilted by her lover of three years, John Doe, who seeks Kitty Brown's help in first cursing and then removing the curse from her lover when he returns to her.

Roxy.
Vine. Horse John Pearson is riding when he falls into the Alabama River.

Princess Royal.
Moses. Pharaoh's daughter, who rescues the baby Moses from the Nile and then adopts him.

Ruel.
Moses. Jethro's ceremonial, priestly name.

✳ S ✳

Sack Daddy.
Mules. Polk County man who goes on the fishing trip and gloats over John's besting Ole Massa. He spent five years in jail for murder after his luck changed when he killed a cat.

St. Prompt Succor.
"Mother Catherine." Assistant to Mother Catherine.

Salome.
"Veil." Beautiful daughter of Herod and Herodias, who dances the dance of the seven veils for Antipas; she is named after her great-grandmother.
"Gaul." After gaining John the Baptist's head for her mother, she gives up dancing.

Salome.
"Veil." King Herod the Great's sister and most trusted adviser; Herodias's grandmother.

Sam.
Color. Effie Jones's old boyfriend, whose absence leaves Effie available for John Turner to dance with after his breakup with Emmaline Beasely.

Mrs. Samuels.
Eyes. Widowed landlady who rents Janie and Tea Cake a room in Jacksonville; she gives Janie coffee while Janie waits for Tea Cake to return.

Sapelo.
Seraph. Negro captain of the *Rosalie Eye.*

Sister Scale.
Vine. Member of Zion Hope Baptist Church who seems willing to give Rev. Felton Cozy's sermon a chance to compare with John Pearson's.

School.
Hurston, herself determined to further her own education despite her age, encourages education in her fiction.
Vine. John Pearson attends school for the first time in Notasulga. Later his children all attend school, an indication of the value that he places on education. Lucy encourages her daughter Isis to continue her education as much as possible.

Oscar Scott.
Eyes. Eatonville resident who criticizes Joe Starks behind his back.

Seeds.
Eyes. The only item Janie brings home to Eatonville with her after Tea Cake's death is some seeds that he had been going to plant.

Self.
Eyes. The search for self is an integral issue in this work. Janie is looking for her self throughout her life. After Joe's death she looks in the mirror for the girl she thought she was and discovers a woman. But the other aspect of this issue is a splitting of self. Joe's control over her beats her down and prompts her to break into two halves, a public and a private self. At his funeral she shows the public self to

the world, a widow with a stone face, but inside the private self is coming alive for the first time. Only after she experiences freedom with Tea Cake does Janie find her true self.

Seraph. Arvay Henson's search for self leads her to confront her past and then to move forward into the future in the arms of her husband Jim Meserve. (See also Identity.)

For Further Reading:

Bobb, June D. "Taking a Stand on High Ground: The Recreated Self in *Their Eyes Were Watching God.*" *Zora Neale Hurston Forum* 2.1 (1987): 1–7.

Chinn, Nancy. "Like Love, 'A Moving Thing': Janie's Search for Self and God in *Their Eyes Were Watching God.*" *South Atlantic Review* 60.1 (1995): 77–95.

Dawson, Emma J. Waters. "Redemption Through Redemption of the Self in *Their Eyes Were Watching God* and *The Color Purple.*" In *Alice Walker and Zora Neale Hurston: The Common Bond.* Ed. Lillie P. Howard. Westport, CT: Greenwood Press, 1993. 69–82.

Seminoles.

Eyes. The Seminoles who live in the Everglades know to leave at the first sign of the coming hurricane.

Semmie.

Vine. Young classmate of John Pearson's whose mother is jealous of Lucy Potts's academic accomplishments and threatens to take her daughter out of school.

Seraph on the Suwanee.

After J.B. Lippincott rejected Hurston's plans for two projects, on April 15, 1947, she signed a contract with Scribner's (which was influenced by the recommendation of one of its best-selling authors, Marjorie Kinnan Rawlings), to produce a novel on life in Florida. The novel, at different times titled *The Sign of the Sun, Sang the Suwanee in the Spring, The Queen of the Golden Hand, Angel in the Bed, Lady Angel with Her Man, Seraph with a Man on Hand, So Said the Sea, Good Morning Sun,* and *Seraph on the Suwanee River,* marked a major departure for Hurston out of black folklife into the mainstream white culture. It was a conscious decision to try to widen her reading audience and to make an artistic statement that a writer, black or white, had no boundaries constraining his or her choice of subject matter.

Hurston had been planning an expedition to look for a fabled "lost city," so in May 1947 she left for Honduras. Between May and November Hurston wrote the early versions of *Seraph*, but when she submitted the manuscript for publication, Scribner's asked her to make further revisions, which she completed during the first months of 1948 with the help of editor Burroughs Mitchell. The novel, published in October 1948, was dedicated to Marjorie Kinnan Rawlings and Mrs. Spessard L. Holland (wife of the governor of Florida).

The novel starts out as a white trash version of *Taming of the Shrew*. Arvay Henson, embittered after her older sister Lorraine had stolen the attentions of and married the local Baptist minister, Carl Middleton, resists all subsequent attempts to court her until handsome, cocky, and resourceful Jim Meserve arrives in Sawley, Florida, the small north Florida town where the novel is set.

Slowly, patiently, but determinedly, Jim persists and ultimately Arvay acquiesces to Jim's suit. To make sure that Arvay understands that he is in charge, even before they marry, Jim goes so far as to take her forcefully while they are together under the large mulberry tree behind her parents' house. Strangely, Arvay does not seem to mind the rape, but over the next few years conflicts do develop between the two lovers as Arvay pits her will against Jim's.

The first conflict arises with the birth of their first child, Earl, whose mental handicap causes Jim to distance himself emotionally. Jim's distance only increases Arvay's devotion to her child. Two other normal children, a daughter—Angeline "Angie" and a son—James Kenneth "Kenny," are born to the family after they move south to Citrabelle, where Jim prospers as an orange grower and, unbeknownst at first to Arvay, as a moonshiner. Much of Jim's prosperity comes as the result of help from Joe Kelsey, the black turpentine chipper with whom Jim had worked in Sawley who moves to Citrabelle with his family to help Jim with the grove and the still.

When Arvay discovers the real source of the family's prosperity, she blames Joe Kelsey for bringing Jim down to his level and ultimately drives the man away. To replace Joe, Jim hires a Portuguese family, the Corregios, to help with the grove. But the Corregios' oldest daughter has a destablizing effect on Earl, who has aged and is obviously mentally unbalanced. Despite Jim's pleas to allow him to institutionalize Earl, Arvay refuses. Instead she sends him back to

Sawley to live with her aging mother. The emotional rift between Jim and Arvay widens further.

Unable to stand being away from her son, eventually Arvay journeys to Sawley and brings Earl home. But disaster strikes when the psychically deranged Earl attacks the Corregio girl and then flees into the swamp, where he is hunted down and shot. Arvay is devastated by the loss of her son.

After Earl's death, Jim tries to reconcile with Arvay, and for a time they grow closer. Years pass and the couple's other two children grow up. Kenny becomes interested in music and goes off to college. Angie marries a young man from the north who becomes successful as a real estate developer. Jim's attempts to persuade Arvay to relate to him on a deeper level, however, fail and the relationship stagnates, often degenerating into episodes of forced sexual encounters in which he feels that Arvay is always holding something of herself back from him.

The crowning blow to the relationship comes one day in the grove when Jim catches a huge rattlesnake that begins to wrap itself around his body. Although he cries out for Arvay's assistance, she is so paralyzed by fear that she cannot help Jim. Jim almost dies before Joe Kelsey's son Jeff arrives to extricate the snake off him. Convinced that Arvay's behavior proves that she does not have the kind of "knowing and doing love" that he wants in a marriage, Jim tells Arvay that he is leaving her, although he assures her that he will take her back if he ever sees "signs of [her] coming to be the woman [he] married [her] for."

Over the next several months Jim spends most of his time on the two fishing boats that he has bought and runs with the help of Alfred Corregio. Now home by herself most of the time, Arvay feels increasingly alone. One day a telegram arrives from Sawley announcing that her mother is dying. Arvay rushes home and there realizes how wrong she has been in her treatment of Jim. Standing under the same mulberry tree where he had taken her so forcefully years earlier, she realizes what a difference Jim has made in her life.

So Arvay returns home with a new attitude. She goes to the coast, locates Jim's boat, and goes to sea with him. There on the ocean she finds what she has been looking for all along in his arms.

In writing this "white" novel, Hurston tackled more than issues of race; she dealt more deeply than she ever had before with issues related to sexual politics, gender roles, and marriage. Ironically, the sexual scenes in *Seraph* were used against her when she was falsely accused of molesting a young boy in New York and arrested on September 13, 1948. The next month the *Baltimore Afro-American*, a leading black newspaper, published an inaccurate and sensationalized version of the case, just a week after the novel's publication. Although initial sales of the book were good, Hurston was so devastated and demoralized by the controversy that she did not feel up to promoting the book. Ultimately, despite relatively good reviews, sales suffered. (The case against Hurston was not dropped until March 1949.)

For Further Reading:

Coleman, Ancilla. "Mythological Structure and Psychological Significance in Hurston's *Seraph on the Suwanee.*" *Publications of the Mississippi Philological Association* (1988): 21–27.

Dubek, Laura. "The Social Geography of Race in Hurston's *Seraph on the Suwanee.*" *African American Review* 30.3 (1996): 341–51.

Howard, Lillie. "*Seraph on the Suwanee.*" Reprinted in *Zora Neale Hurston: Critical Perspectives Past and Present.* Ed. Henry Louis Gates Jr. and K.A. Appiah. New York: Amistad Press, 1993. 267–79.

Marsh-Lockett, Carol P. "What Ever Happened to Jochebed? Motherhood as Marginality in Zora Neale Hurston's *Seraph on the Suwanee.*" In *Southern Mothers: Fact and Fictions in Southern Women's Writing.* Ed. Nagueyalti Warren and Sally Wolff. Baton Rouge: Louisiana State UP, 1999. 100–110.

Meisenhelder, Susan. "Hurston's Critique of White Culture in *Seraph on the Suwanee.*" In *All About Zora.* Ed. Alice Morgan Grant. Winter Park, FL: Four-G, 1991. 79–92.

Tate, Claudia. "Hitting 'A Straight Lick with a Crooked Stick': *Seraph on the Suwanee*, Zora Neale Hurston's Whiteface Novel." In *The Psychoanalysis of Race.* Ed. Christopher Lane. New York: Columbia UP, 1998. 380–94.

Tate, Claudia. "Mourning, Humor, and Reparation: Detecting the Joke in *Seraph on the Suwanee*, by Zora Neale Hurston." In *Psychoanalysis and Black Novels.* New York: Oxford UP, 1998. 148–77.

Sermons.

Eyes. Nanny tells Janie that she has always desired to preach "a great sermon about colored women sittin' on high." With her coming death, however, she passes the mantle of that task on to Janie, who fulfills her grandmother's wish by telling her life story to her friend Pheoby Watson.

Vine. Hurston had originally planned to dedicate *Jonah's Gourd Vine* to Negro preachers, whom she considered the true poets of their race. So John Pearson's sermons are homage to their oratory skill. He preaches several sermons, including his most powerful sermon, his final sermon on the betrayal of friends.

"The Seventh Veil."

One of Hurston's biblical stories, "The Seventh Veil" is a retrospective prequel to the story of Salome's dancing the dance of the seven veils and asking for the head of John the Baptist as her reward. Hurston concentrates on the familial intrigues of the Judaean royal family and the relationship between Antipas and Herodias, tensions and conflicts in whose marriage ultimately precipitate John's death. The story remained unpublished until it appeared in *The Complete Stories of Zora Neale Hurston* in 1995.

Sewell.

"Anthology." Baldheaded loner who moves so frequently that his chickens supposedly lie down and cross their legs to be tied every time he walks into his yard.

Sewell.

"Light." White driver who stops for Isis Watts.

Soddy Sewell.

Mules. Man who attends the toe-party in Wood Bridge.

Big Willie Sewell.

Mules. Man who wants to dance with more than one girl at the toe-party in Wood Bridge.

Sex.

Hurston's portrayal of sex is rather explicit for her day and time. She reveals this human longing in both its most beautiful and bestial forms.

Eyes. Janie and Tea Cake have steamy "makeup sex" after the misunderstanding about Nunkie.

Seraph. Jim Meserve's rape of Arvay and subsequent sexual encounters in *Seraph* make this book one of her most explicit. In chapter 19, Jim's sexual control over Arvay borders on the sado-masochistic, yet it seems to keep her steady; he commands her to stand before him naked and not to move until he tells her to.

"Slanguage." Hurston's original glossary for her "Story in Harlem Slang" included several sexually explicit terms.

Vine. John Pearson's initiation into sex with Mehaley begins a series of affairs with various women that he continues even after his marriage to Lucy Potts.

Horace Sharp.

Mules. Man from Pierce, Florida (in Polk County), who tells the story "All These Are Mine."

Mary Ella Shaw.

"Uncle Monday." Young woman who jilts Joe Nathan Moss the day before their wedding when she sees Caddie Brewton. Cursed by Uncle Monday, she can never keep a man longer than twenty-eight days, even though she eventually has four husbands, numerous lovers, and eight children.

Herbert Sheen.

Hurston's first husband, who was from Decatur, Illinois; like Zora, he was a minister's son; they met at Howard University, where he was a medical student. On May 19, 1927, they were married in St. Augustine, Florida, but the relationship lasted less than a year due to separations required by Zora's travels and Sheen's studies. They were not officially divorced, however, until July 7, 1931.

Shelby.

Eyes. White playmate of young Janie and oldest of the Washburns' grandsons; he tells the photographer to take the picture of the children.

Mist' Shelby.

Vine. White farmer Ned Crittenden binds himself over to after he has to leave Beasley's place for stealing one of his cows. Shelby insists on John Buddy's return as a condition of Ned's employment, thus prompting John's first return from over the Big Creek.

Shem.

First. Noah's first-born son, who (along with his brother Japheth) is jealous of Noah's favoritism toward their younger brother Ham; Shem and Japheth cover their drunken father after Ham laughs at his nakedness, hoping that Noah will now favor them. But after Noah curses Ham, they implore him to revoke his curse.

Mrs. Shem.

First. Shem's wife, who reproves Ham for not bringing anything to sacrifice; jealous of Noah's favoritism of Ham over his other sons, she urges Shem and Japheth to wake their father and tell him about Ham's shameful deed; later, however, she implores Noah to revoke his terrible curse on Ham.

Ships.

Eyes.   In the opening of *Their Eyes Were Watching God*, Hurston uses images of ships coming and going to the horizon, just as Janie has done in her life.

"John Redding." John Redding floats ships made of leaves and sticks up river when he is a child.

Seraph. All the fishing boats that Jim Meserve and Arvay Henson see inspire them to seek and find the freedom of the sea in their own lives.

Shorty.

"Muttsy." One of the men at Ma Turner's who expresses interest in Pinkie Jones.

Mrs. Rachel Silas.

Mules. Woman from Sanford, Florida, whom Zora asks where to find a hoodoo doctor.

Dr. Simmons.

Eyes. White doctor on the muck who treats Tea Cake's rabies and later testifies at Janie's trial.

Rev. Simms.

Bone. Methodist minister and Joe Clarke's rival for power in town; he acts as Jim Weston's defense attorney.

"Contention." Methodist minister who aspires to be mayor; he acts as defense attorney for Jim Weston during the trial.

Singing Steel.

Version of *The Great Day* and *From Sun to Sun* presented in Chicago on November 23 and 24, 1934.

Otis D. Slemmons.

"Six-Bits." Ostentatious man from Chicago with a mouth full of gold teeth and gold jewelry; he opens up an ice cream parlor and seduces Missie May Banks with his false promises and gilded money. He is caught *in flagrante delicto* and run out of town by Missie May's husband, Joe Banks.

Capt. Dutch Smith.

Seraph. Captain of the *Savannah,* who is sad over losing a man overboard on his previous fishing trip.

Gussie Smith.

"Book." Neighbor's daughter whom Mandolin's father wants him to marry.

Snakes.

Every garden of Eden has its snake; so too do many of Hurston's stories. The snakes represent tangible fears and the embodiment of evil power.

Moses. Moses goes to Koptos and outwits the deathless snake guarding the book of Thoth; later he has a contest with Pharaoh's priests and turns his rod into a snake and then back again.

Mules. In the book's "Hoodoo" section, Hurston tells of the legendary hoodoo doctor Marie Leveau, whose rattlesnake always accompanies her; it even sings. Later Luke Turner wraps the snake's skin around his shoulders when he wants power. In the book's "Folklore" section, Jim Allen tells the story of how the snake got its poison.

Seraph. Jim Meserve catches a rattlesnake, but cannot control it and is almost killed while his wife Arvay watches without helping; he is finally saved by Jeff Kelsey, not Arvay, whom he soon leaves. This scene is reminiscent of Eve's temptation in the Garden of Eden.

"Sweat." Delia Jones fears snakes; she gets revenge on her abusive husband with a rattlesnake.

"Uncle Monday." The singing stone possessed by Uncle Monday is guarded by a deadly snake who lives in the depths of the lake.

Vine. John Pearson kills a moccasin in the stream that Lucy Potts has to cross.

Pearly Snead.
Seraph. Cuckolded Citrabelle man whom Hawley Pitts tries to goad into a fight, only to be defended by Jim Meserve.

Solomon.
Mules. King of Israel who learns wisdom from the Queen of Sheba, who gives him her magic talking ring.

Songahatchee.
Vine. The Big Creek that John Buddy crosses when he leaves his family and goes to Notasulga.

Sop-de-Bottom.
Eyes. Migrant worker who plays cards and loses to Ed Dockery; Sop tells Tea Cake that he will boycott Mrs. Turner's restaurant due to her anti-Negro attitudes. Later he sets off the fight at her place when he refuses to give up his seat to Coodemay. He tries to speak against Janie at the trial but is silenced by the white prosecutor, Mr. Prescott. Eventually he forgives Janie and helps run off Mrs. Turner's brother.

Sosius.
"Gaul." Roman general and Herod the Great's ally in his war against Antigonus.

Spears.
This short two-act play set in Africa was first published in 1926 in *X-Ray*, the yearbook of the Zeta Phi Beta sorority at Howard University. It won honorable mention in the first *Opportunity* contest in 1925.

Sister Speckled-Hen.
"Cock Robin." Character who holds a big fish fry and barbecue that diverts the crowd's attention away from Cock Robin's funeral parade, prompting them to leave his body for the white folks to bury.

Speeches.
Eyes. Joe Starks has a fondness for making speeches, yet he refuses to let Janie speak at the welcoming. After Joe frees the mule, however, Janie makes a speech.

Spider.
Vine. Lucy Pearson watches the progress of a spider down a wall as her death approaches, reminiscent of Jonathan Edwards's spider hanging over the pit of hell.

Spittoons.
Eyes. Joe Starks's fancy brass spittoon and Janie's flowered one set them apart from the rest of the town.

"Spunk."
A story of marital infidelity, superstition, violence, and revenge, "Spunk" relates the tale of Spunk Banks' cuckolding of Joe Kanty by stealing his wife Stella. When Joe confronts Spunk, Spunk shoots him in self-defense, but Joe gets his revenge by returning in the form of a bobcat and causing Spunk's bloody death on a circle saw. The story won second place in the first *Opportunity* contest in 1925 and was published in *Opportunity* in June 1925; the same year it was included in Alain Locke's groundbreaking anthology, *The New Negro.*

For Further Reading:

Eisen, Kurt. "Blues Speaking Women: Performing Cultural Change in *Spunk* and *Ma Rainey's Black Bottom.*" *Text & Presentation* 14 (1993): 21–26.

Hale, David G. "Hurston's 'Spunk' and *Hamlet.*" *Studies in Short Fiction* 30.3 (1993): 397–98.

Peter Stagg.
Mules. Man who attends the toe-party in Wood Bridge.

Gabriel "Gabe" Staggers.
Mules. Minnie Foster's boyfriend on whom she has Kitty Brown place multiple love charms.

Harriet Staggers.
Mules. Three-year-old girl who is the smallest girl in the "Chirck, mah Chick, mah Craney crow" game the children are playing in the street on Zora's last day in Eatonville.

Janie Starks.
Eyes. Janie's name while she is married to Joe Starks. (See also Janie.)

Joe Starks.
Eyes. Janie's second husband; "a citified, stylish dressed man" who promises Janie to make her a lady; a self-assured promoter from Georgia, he builds a store in Eatonville and becomes mayor of the town. Janie's nickname for him is Jody, but their relationship deteriorates as Joe attempts to exert more and more control over Janie. When he dies, he is called "The Little Emperor of the cross-roads."

Dick Sterrett.
Eyes. Friend of Coodemay's who backs him up in the drunken fight at Mrs. Turner's; he comes back on Monday and pays Mrs. Turner $5 for damages.

Stew Beef.
Eyes. One of the men involved in the fight at Mrs. Turner's; he also plays the drums. He helps chase off Mrs. Turner's brother.

Jim Stone.
Eyes. Man who agrees with Joe Lindsay's negative appraisal of Tony Robbin's lenient treatment of his troublesome wife.

Pearl Stone.
Eyes. Eatonville woman who talks about Janie after she returns to town; she resents Janie for not stopping to tell everyone where she's been.

Storms.
Eyes. The hurricane destroys everything on the muck and also Janie and Tea Cake's lives.
"John Redding." The flood carries away the bridge, killing John Redding.

"Story in Harlem Slang."
Edited version of "Now You Cookin' with Gas." At the end of the story is a glossary of Harlem slang. The story was first published in the July 1942 issue of *American Mercury.*

Brother Stringer.
"Contention." Methodist man who arrives late to the trial and causes a stir by putting his coat on an empty lamp bracket.

Dr. Strong.
Mules. Popular New Orleans hoodoo doctor who lives on Urquhart St. He advises Mrs. Grant to draw her enemy's "wine" (blood) to counteract her curse.

Stumpy.
Seraph. First mate on the *Angeline* when Jim Meserve takes over as captain; Stumpy borrows $10 from Jim after telling him the story of fisherman George Kemp.

Stylus.
Howard University literary club's magazine, sponsored by Alain Locke and Montgomery Gregory. "John Redding Goes to Sea," Hurston's first published story, was published in *Stylus* in May 1921.

Mrs. Sumpkins.
Eatonville woman who is watching with the others when Janie returns to town; she offers to walk over to Janie's with Pheoby, but Pheoby declines her offer.

Sun.
The sun acts as a power source and an inspiration in Hurston's fiction.
Eyes. Janie views the sun as the creation of a new day. Later she describes Tea Cake as the "son of Evening Sun."

Seraph. Arvay Meserve prays to the sun that her third child will be a boy. At the end of the novel the sun comes up over the ocean, signaling a new beginning for Arvay and Jim Meserve.

Aunt Shady Anne Sutton.
"High John." Old woman born two years after slavery who tells about the power of High John de Conquer.

"Sweat."
Hurston's oft-anthologized story of the marital strife between Delia and Sykes Jones, a conflict which ultimately results in Sykes's death by snakebite (as contrived by Delia). The story was one of Hurston's two contributions to *Fire!!* (1926) (the other was her play *Color Struck*). The story can be interpreted as a revenge tale of a victimized wife driven to violence and retribution or as a morality tale in which the "victim" becomes as evil as her oppressor by adopting his methods and using them against him.

For Further Reading:

Green, Suzanne D. "Fear, Freedom and the Perils of Ethnicity: Otherness in Kate Chopin's 'Beyond the Bayou' and Zora Neale Hurston's 'Sweat.' " *Southern Studies* 5.3–4 (1994): 105–24.

Hurd, Myles Raymond. "What Goes Around Comes Around: Characterization, Climax, and Closure in Hurston's 'Sweat.' " *Langston Hughes Review* 12.2 (1993): 7–15.

Seidel, Kathryn Lee. "The Artist in the Kitchen: The Economics of Creativity in Hurston's 'Sweat.' " In *Zora in Florida.* Ed. Steve Glassman and Kathryn Lee Seidel. Orlando: U of Central Florida P, 1991. 110–20. Reprinted in *Zora Neale Hurston: "Sweat."* Ed. Cheryl A. Wall. New Brunswick, NJ: Rutgers UP, 1997. 169–81.

Wall, Cheryl A., ed. *Zora Neale Hurston: "Sweat."* New Brunswick, NJ: Rutgers UP, 1997.

Sweet Back.
"Gas," "Harlem Slang." Harlem pimp and a friend of Jelly's, whom he meets on the street and asks for money; they spar verbally over their sexual prowess with women. In "Gas," he claims to have killed a white policeman in Georgia, a detail that was edited out of "Harlem Slang" when it was published in *American Mercury* in 1942.

Swift Deer.
"Magnolia." Bentley's Cherokee wife and the mother of Magnolia Flower; Bentley's affection for Swift Deer fades as his ambition grows.

⤞ T ⤝

"The Tablets of the Law."
Excerpt from *Moses, Man of the Mountain* recounting Moses' coming down from Mt. Sinai with the Ten Commandments only to find that, in his absence, the Hebrews have built a golden calf to worship; the story culminates with Moses' return up the mountain to receive the laws from God again; the story was first printed by Doubleday in *The Word Lives On: A Treasury of Spiritual Fiction* in 1951. It was included in *The Complete Stories* in 1995.

Beulah Tansill.
Vine. Member of Zion Hope Baptist Church who disapproves of John Pearson.

Tante Celestine.
Mules. Woman who borrows nickels from her neighbor to put a curse on her.

Tante Lida.
Mules. Levi Conway's housekeeper, who calls a conjure woman to find out what's wrong with Levi.

Ta-Phar.

Moses. Pharaoh's son and Crown Prince of Egypt, who becomes Moses' rival and then nemesis when he succeeds his father as Pharaoh; as Pharaoh he stubbornly refuses to accede to Moses' demand to let the Hebrews leave Egypt until after the final plague kills the firstborn of Egypt.

Fred Tate.

Vine. Conspirator (with Hattie Tyson and Aleck Harris) to overthrow John Pearson as pastor by publicly chastising him for his involvement with Sister Berry.

Coon Taylor.

"Anthology." Thief who knocks Joe Clarke over the head with a watermelon by mistake; later Coon is caught stealing sugar cane and forced to leave town for three months.

Daisy Taylor.

"Anthology." Dark, pigeon-toed town vamp who wears shingle nails to keep her hair down and who flirts with married men; after an affair with Albert Crooms, Crooms's wife Laura attacks Daisy with an ax handle and she moves away to Orlando.

Daisy Taylor.

Bone. Young Methodist woman who is courted by both Jim Weston and Dave Carter; they fight over her, Jim is tried and convicted, but then the two friends make up and abandon Daisy. She is also called Daisy Bailey in Act I and Daisy Blunt in Act II.

Emma Taylor.

"Black Death." Woman whose teeth fall out after she is cursed by Old Man Morgan.

Johnny Taylor.

Eyes. The first boy to kiss Janie; when Nanny sees the kiss, she determines to marry Janie off to Logan Killicks for Janie's own protection.

Miss Lucy Taylor.
Color. Contestant from St. Augustine who is Ned Coles's dance partner.

Mrs. Lucy Taylor.
Bone. Tony Taylor's bossy wife; she argues with Sister Lewis at the trial over disparaging remarks made about her character and about Sister Lewis's daughter Ada. Much to Mrs. Taylor's dismay, Joe Clarke will not allow her to testify since she left the store before the fight started. (cf. Sister Taylor)

Sam Taylor.
"Contention." Sister Taylor's husband, whom the sheriff had had to force to marry her. (cf. Tony Taylor)

Sister Taylor.
"Contention." Methodist woman who tries to fight Della Lewis during the trial for making disparaging remarks about her. (cf. Mrs. Lucy Taylor)

Tony Taylor.
Bone. Methodist man who can't stay to talk because his wife has finished buying groceries. The sheriff had had to force Tony to marry her. (cf. Sam Taylor)
Eyes. Eatonville resident who attempts to make a speech welcoming Joe and Janie to the town but is ridiculed for his exaggeration; he later nominates Joe Starks as mayor.

Teadi.
Eyes. Pretty young girl whom the boys all want to buy treats for.

Tell My Horse.
Hurston's second and less successful anthropological work, commercially and artistically, was based on research that she gathered thanks to a Guggenheim Fellowship in trips to Jamaica (April to September 1936) and to Haiti (September 1936 to March 1937 and May to September 1937).

The first part of the book describes Hurston's time in Jamaica, during which she studied the Maroons, descendents of slaves who had fought fiercely to win their freedom. Hurston finally earned their trust enough to be taken on a ritual wild boar hunt, which culminated in a celebratory barbecue. In the final chapter of this section, Hurston comments on the overt chauvinism of Jamaican society. Noting the lowly position of women in the society, Hurston describes American women, by contrast, as "Miss America, World's champion woman."

Part II is an odd (and often historically inaccurate) account of Hurston's views on Haitian history, politics, and several political personalities. Recounting the violence and turmoil of Haiti's internal politics and troubled history, she naively asserts the United States' benevolence in intervening in Haiti and too often accepts as fact, unquestioningly, what she is told.

By far the most interesting section of the book is Part III, which relates Hurston's findings on voodoo practices in Haiti. After outlining the voodoo pantheon of gods, Hurston recounts stories about (and some actual encounters with) voodoo priests called houngans. She also writes of an actual encounter with a zombie (Felicia Felix Mentor) and provides detailed descriptions of several different voodoo ceremonies. Thus, despite its flaws, the book does finally succeed at least in treating voodoo anthropologically as a serious religion.

Following a severe bout with a "violent gastric disturbance," Hurston cut short her second trip to Haiti and returned to Florida. There, between February and March 1938, she wrote *Tell My Horse*, which was published in October 1938 and which she dedicated to Carl Van Vechten, whom she called "God's image of a friend."

For Further Reading:

Bush, Roland. " 'Ethnographic Subjectivity' and Zora Neale Hurston's *Tell My Horse*." *Zora Neale Hurston Forum* 5.2 (1991): 11–18.

Fischer-Hornung, Dorothea. "An Island Occupied: The U.S. Marine Occupation of Haiti in Zora Neale Hurston's *Tell My Horse* and Katherine Dunham's *Island Possessed*." In *Holding Their Own: Perspectives on the Multi-Ethnic Literature of the United States.* Ed. Dorothea Fischer-Hornung and Heiki Raphael-Hernandez. Stauffenburg, Germany: Tubingen, 2000. 153–68.

Menke, Pamela Glenn. " 'The Lips of Books': Hurston's *Tell My Horse* and *Their Eyes Were Watching God* as Metalingual Texts." *The Literary Griot* 4.1–2 (1992): 75–99.

Trefzer, Annette. "Possessing the Self: Caribbean Identities in Zora Neale Hurston's *Tell My Horse*." *African American Review* 34.2 (2000): 299–312.

"The Ten Commandments of Charm."

Satiric decalogue of advice on how a woman can keep a man's interest through flattery, restraint, and coquetry. This piece was first published in 1925 in *X-Ray*, the yearbook of the Zeta Phi Beta sorority at Howard University.

Texas Red.

Mules. Slightly drunk tenor who sings "Ol' Pal, Why Don't You Answer Me" and annoys Big Sweet during the card game.

Their Eyes Were Watching God.

Often cited as Hurston's masterpiece, *Their Eyes Were Watching God* is considered by many to be the prototypical African American feminist novel. It recounts the story of Janie, who returns to Eatonville following a journey to the horizon and back, to tell the story of her life to her best friend, Pheoby Watson. The novel's circular, retrospective structure allows Janie to narrate both the literal account of her life (childhood, loss of innocence, three marriages, etc.) and the development of her self, as well as her growing awareness of that self, which, now that the experience is in the past, she can relate to her friend as she reflects back on how and when these developmental changes occurred in her life.

Written in Haiti in the fall of 1936 in just seven weeks, *Their Eyes Were Watching God* grew out of Hurston's feelings about the ending of a love affair with a younger West Indian man in New York. The man, whom Hurston identified only as P.M.P. in her autobiography *Dust Tracks on a Road*, had been a member of the cast of *The Great Day*, a college graduate, and an intellectual. Hurston loved him deeply and felt that she had finally found someone who was her equal in every way. Yet over the next years friction developed between the two of them over Hurston's career, resulting in their breakup. So, as she writes in *Dust Tracks*, although "the plot was far from the circumstances, [she] tried to embalm all the tenderness of [her] passion for him in *Their Eyes Were Watching God*." P.M.P. became the inspiration for, although not the embodiment of, Tea Cake, Janie's third husband and the only man to accept her for her true self in the novel. Thus, in her fiction, Hurston was able to translate the failure of her private experience with the man she loved into a successful relationship in her fictionalized account.

When the novel was published on September 18, 1937, it was well received by most reviewers, with the notable exception of African American reviewers, most notably Alain Locke, whose review in *Opportunity* bemoaned the book's "oversimplification," and Richard Wright, whose review in *New Masses* condemned Hurston's "minstrel technique" aimed at satisfying only her white audience. Hurston got her revenge, however. In her review of Wright's book of short stories, *Uncle Tom's Children*, for the April 2, 1938, *Saturday Review*, she called the book "a book about hatreds" with "not one act of understanding [or] sympathy . . . in the entire work." At the end of her review, she dismisses Wright's attitude as communistic—"the solution of the Party—state responsibility for everything and individual responsibility for nothing, not even feeding one's self."

For Further Reading:

Awkward, Michael. " 'The inaudible voice of it all': Silence, Voice, and Action in *Their Eyes Were Watching God.*" In *Inspiriting Influences: Tradition, Revision, and Afro-American Women's Novels.* New York: Columbia UP, 1989. 15–56; and *Studies in Black American Literature, Vol. 3: Black Feminist Criticism and Critical Theory.* Ed. Joe Weixlmann and Houston A. Baker, Jr. Greenwood, FL: Penkevill Publishing, 1988. 57–109.

Awkward, Michael, ed. *New Essays on* Their Eyes Were Watching God. Cambridge: Cambridge UP, 1990.

Bloom, Harold, ed. *Modern Critical Interpretations: Zora Neale Hurston's* Their Eyes Were Watching God. New York: Chelsea House, 1987.

Brigham, Cathy. "The Talking Frame of Zora Neale Hurston's Talking Book: Storytelling as Dialectic in *Their Eyes Were Watching God.*" *CLA Journal* 37.4 (1994): 402–19.

Daniel, Janice. " 'De understandin' to go 'long wid it': Realism and Romance in *Their Eyes Were Watching God.*" *Southern Literary Journal* 24.1 (1991): 66–76.

Ford, Sarah. "Necessary Chaos in Hurston's *Their Eyes Were Watching God.*" *CLA Journal* 43.4 (2000): 407–19.

Goodwyn, Floyd. "Nature Imagery in *Their Eyes Were Watching God.*" *Publications of the Mississippi Philological Association* (1990): 90–96.

Holloway, Karla F.C. "Holy Heat: Rituals of the Spirit in Zora Neale Hurston's *Their Eyes Were Watching God.*" *Religion and Literature* 23.3 (1991): 127–41.

Kubitschek, Missy Dehn. " 'Save de Text': History, Storytelling, and the Female Quest in *Their Eyes Were Watching God.*" In *Claiming the Heritage: African-American Women Novelists and History.* Jackson: UP of Mississippi, 1991. 52–68.

Marks, Donald R. "Sex, Violence, and Organic Consciousness in Zora Neale Hurston's *Their Eyes Were Watching God.*" *Black American Literature Forum* 19.4 (1985): 152–57.

Thelma.
Mules. Young Polk County woman who marries Cliffert Ulmer.

Floyd Thomas.
Mules. Polk County man who goes on the fishing trip and tells the tale of "How God Made Butterflies."

George Thomas.
Mules. Eatonville man who is playing cards on the porch when Zora arrives to collect folktales. He sings with Georgia Burke at the toe-party in Wood Bridge.

Hoyt Thomas.
Vine. Eatonville resident who tries to take the pillow from underneath Lucy Pearson's head to ease her death but is stopped by Isis, who is acting on her mother's instructions.

Sister Boyt Thomas.
Bone. Young Methodist woman in her thirties who, after reading the notice of Jim Weston's trial, prepares supper ahead of time so she can attend.

Walter Thomas.
"Anthology." Man hanging out at Joe Clarke's store who urges Laura Crooms to fight Daisy Taylor.

Bone. Methodist man who hangs out on the porch of Joe Clarke's store; he is Lum Boger's card partner.

"Contention." Methodist man who brags about chinning the bar twenty times.

Eyes. One of the men who tease Matt Bonner about his mule; Joe Starks also catches him touching Janie's hair unbeknownst to her; he urges Sam Watson and Lige Moss on in their battle of wits.

"Sweat." One of the men sitting on Joe Clarke's porch; he comments on how pretty Delia Sykes had been when Sykes Jones first married her.

Vine. Walter teases John Pearson about his wife making his fortune.

Clardia Thornton.
Mules. Woman from Magazine Point, Alabama, who attends the Pine Mill dance and tells Zora how another woman took her husband away from her.

Wallace Thurman.
Co-editor, along with Hurston and Langston Hughes, of the first and only edition of *Fire!!* in November 1926; Thurman paid tribute to Hurston's wit and energetic personality in the form of the character Sweetie Mae Carr in his 1932 novel *Infants of the Spring.*

Tiberius.
"Gaul." Stepson of Augustus Caesar; Antipas had renamed the Sea of Galilee after Tiberius.

Tibernius.
"Veil." Roman emperor who had once imprisoned Antipas for his lack of morals.

Tipo Tipo.
Spears. Monanga's servant.

Tippy.
"Anthology." Sykes Jones's thin, thieving, egg-sucking dog, who withstands all attempts to kill him.

Titty-Nipple.
Seraph. Mate on the *Arvay Henson,* who helps head shrimp.

Fritz Toomer.
Seraph. Captain of the *Ramos;* he is the son of the boat's owner.

Mary Toomer.
Seraph. Wife of the shipowner, who runs the business office; she invites Arvay Meserve inside to wait for Jim.

Toothsome.
"Book." Man who leaves Harlem and returns home to Standard Bottom, Georgia; his stories of life in Harlem persuade Mandolin to travel north.

Too-Sweet.
Vine. Fellow worker at the tie camp who loves to hear John Pearson's stories.

Trains.
Trains represent power, escape, dreams, freedom, and opportunity in Hurston's works. Many Negros ride the train to begin new lives in the North.
"Anthology." Old Man Anderson's encounter with the train proves too much for him.
Eyes. Joe Starks and Janie arrive in Eatonville by train; Janie leaves on the train to meet Tea Cake in Jacksonville.
Mules. Arthur Hopkins relates a tale of a goat that flagged down a train.
Seraph. Kenny Meserve is fascinated by trains and has Belinda Kelsey stand on her head to entertain the passengers one day; unfortunately, she has no panties on.
Vine. John Pearson is fascinated by the power of the first train he sees in Notasulga. Of his first train ride on his trip to Florida, he thinks: "To him nothing in the world ever quite equalled that first ride on a train." At the end of the book, ironically, John is killed when his car is struck by a train.

Trees.
Trees prove highly symbolic of growth, change, and insight in Hurston's work and serve as settings for important events in her characters' lives.
Eyes. Janie has her first vision of love and gets kissed by Johnny Taylor under a blossoming pear tree; when Joe Starks walks into her life, she is dreaming under an oak tree.
Seraph. Jim Meserve and Arvay Henson walk under a mulberry tree in her backyard after he proposes; then shortly before their wedding day, Jim rapes her under the mulberry tree but she feels a "pain remorseless sweet." Years later Arvay returns home after her mother's death and goes back to look at the tree and realizes that it was here that "in violent ecstasy, had begun her real life."
Vine. John Pearson and Lucy Potts meet at a tree by the creek and there John proposes.

Trials.
Hurston's characters have their fair share of legal battles to endure. The justice system, however, usually produces a just, if sometimes humorous, verdict.

"Conscience." Laura Lee Kimble's trial exonerates her for being loyal to her mistress.

"Contention," *Bone.* Jim Weston's trial for hitting Dave Carter with the mule bone ends quite differently in the two stories.

Eyes. Janie's trial for Tea Cake's death ends in a just verdict.

"Spunk." Spunk Banks is cleared by virtue of self-defense for the murder of Joe Kanty.

Vine. John Pearson and Hattie Tyson's divorce trial ends anticlimactically when John refuses to contest her claim.

Mrs. Tully.
Eyes. According to one of the tales told about Matt Bonner's yellow mule, she is run off the croquet ground by the mule.

Tunk.
"High John." Slave whom High John de Conquer takes with him on his journey through heaven and hell in search of a song.

Ike Turk.
Vine. Moonshiner from whom Ned Crittenden buys his liquor.

Pinkie Turk.
"Bridge." Young girl interested in Artie Mimms.

Baby-face Turl.
Mules. Man from Pierce, Florida who wants to hear no tales about witches.

Deacon Turl.
Vine. Deacon at Zion Hope Baptist Church who agrees with Deacon Moss's flattering assessment of John Pearson's prayers.

Minnie Turl.
Vine. Young girl on Pearson plantation who plays hide and seek with John and the other children.

Deacon Turner.
Vine. Deacon from Pilgrim Rest Baptist Church in Plant City who wants John Pearson to preach a revival meeting.

John Turner.
Color. Light-skinned man who escorts Emmaline Beasely to the cake walk dance contest, but then falls out with her over her jealousy of lighter skinned women; following the death of his wife twenty years later, he returns to ask Emmaline to marry him; when he realizes how color struck she still is, however, he leaves.

Luke Turner.
Mules. The sixth hoodoo doctor with whom Hurston studies (for five months). At first he refuses to take Hurston on as a pupil, but her persistence wears him down. Eventually he is so impressed with Zora's progress that he offers to let her take over his business, but she refuses. He tells her stories about Marie Leveau, whose nephew he claims to be, and wears Marie's snake's skin around his shoulders when he wants power.

Ma Turner.
"Muttsy." A former madam named "Forty-dollars-Kate," she now runs a boarding house and juke joint; she encourages Pinkie Jones's developing relationship with Muttsy Owens.

Mr. Turner.
Eyes. Mrs. Turner's ineffectual, henpecked husband.

Mrs. Turner.
Eyes. Colorstruck woman who befriends Janie because she thinks Janie's light skin makes her superior to other blacks; she tries to interest Janie in her brother, prompting Tea Cake's antipathy and ultimate revenge when he wrecks her restaurant during a fight. The mother of six children, Mrs. Turner has lost all but the youngest, a useless 20-year-old son, who is described as the "last stroke of exhausted nature."

Ole Man Turner.
"Muttsy." Ma Turner's lazy husband, who attempts to "educate" young Pinkie Jones about big city ways.

Tush Hawg.
Mules. Polk County man and member of the swamp-gang who goes on the fishing trip; he spars verbally with Handy Pitts about mean bosses.

Annie Tyler.
Eyes. Fifty-two-year-old widow who squanders her money on young men; she sells her house in Eatonville and runs off to Tampa with Who Flung, who takes her money and abandons her; she returns to Eatonville a broken woman and goes off to her daughter's house in Ocala to die. Janie sees her as an object lesson during her doubting times about Tea Cake.

Coon Tyler.
Vine. Worker at the tie camp who hassles John Pearson. After Coon steals the ash-cake John has made for his brother Zeke, John beats him up soundly. He becomes John's constant rival at the camp, but he can hold only one ax to John's two.

Hattie Tyson.
Vine. Woman of low character from Oviedo who has an affair with John Pearson while his wife Lucy is still living. She uses the hoodoo charms of Aunt Dangie Dewoe to help her capture John's attention. Then within three months of Lucy's death she convinces John to marry her. They are married for seven unhappy years. When he discovers that she has been casting spells on him, he beats her. So she sues him for divorce, but John does not contest it.

⁂ U ⁂

Uledi.
Spears. Bravest of the Luallaba warriors, who falls in love with Zaida.

Cliffert "Cliff" Ulmer.
Mules. Young Polk County man (and Jim Allen's grandson), who goes on the fishing trip and tells the tales of "Ole Massa and John Who Wanted to Go to Heaven," "What the Rabbit Learned," "Why We Have Gophers," "Strength Test Between Jack and the Devil," and "Why the Waves Have Whitecaps"; he informs Hurston that the reason people are not talking to her when she first arrives in Loughman, Florida, is that they think she is a detective or a revenue officer.

Uncle Monday.
"Uncle Monday." Conjure doctor whom people know very little about even though he has lived in the town for forty years. He seemed to walk on water out of the lake when he first appeared to Joe Lindsay in the late 1880s. He possesses mysterious powers to regenerate injured body parts and claims to have been dead for many

years. He is believed to possess a mythical singing stone that allows
him to know everything without being told.

"Uncle Monday."

Short story recounting the amazing powers of hoodoo doctor Uncle Monday. It was first published in Nancy Cunard's anthology *Negro* in 1934.

"Under the Bridge."

This early Hurston short story, recounting a love triangle between
a father, son, and his second (and much younger) wife, was first published in 1925 in *X-Ray*, the yearbook of the Zeta Phi Beta sorority
at Howard University.

⋈ V ⋈

Carl Van Vechten.
Wealthy white novelist (author of *Nigger Heaven*), critic, patron of
the arts, and mentor of Hurston and other Harlem Renaissance writers, whose integrated parties were all the rage in New York in the
mid-1920s. Hurston mentions Van Vechten in her story "Book of
Harlem" as the "Chief of the Niggerati." Van Vechten also mediated
(unsuccessfully) the feud between Hurston and Langston Hughes
over the production of their collaboratively written play *Mule Bone*.

Vanderpools.
Eyes. Owners of a big white house, which is compared to Joe
Starks's house.

Vent Vogel.
Spears. Monoko's servant, who brings his master's terms of surren-
der to the Luallabas.

Ole Man Vickers.
Eyes. Bootlegger from Pahokee; Coodemay and Dick Sterrett offer
to buy liquor from him for the men who fight at Mrs. Turner's as a
peace offering.

Violence.

Violence is an integral part of many of the settings of Hurston's stories. Men fight for honor, for money, for self-defense, and for revenge.

Dust. Hurston fought bitterly with her stepmother.

Eyes. Tea Cake is cut during a fight with Double Ugly. Wife beating is common. The fight at Mrs. Turner's place gets out of hand and wrecks her restaurant.

Mules, Dust. The fight between Lucy and Big Sweet saves Hurston's skin and allows her to make a quick escape.

Seraph. Jim Meserve fights several times during the novel, but the most violent incident is his son Earl's violent death by gunfire, following his attack on a young girl.

"Spunk." Joe Kanty's death is followed by Spunk Banks's death on the saw.

"Sweat." Delia Jones revenges the abuse her husband inflicts on her with a snakebite.

Vine. John Buddy fights Coon Tyler at the tie camp to establish his reputation. John Pearson beats his wife Lucy once and his second wife, Hattie Tyson, on multiple occasions.

Voice.

Eyes. Janie feels that Joe Starks's big voice drowns out all others.

Vine. John Pearson's commanding voice is the primary reason for the great impact of his prayers and sermons.

King Volstead.

"Book." King of Hokum during the great drought.

Pere Voltaire.

Mules. Man who puts a curse on Levi Conway.

Voodoo.

Voodoo is the white name for hoodoo, the supernatural blend of magic and religion practiced in Africa and brought to America. (See also Hoodoo)

✴ W ✴

Waganga.
Spears. Luallaba medicine man, who prepares the tribe's warriors for battle against the Wahehes.

Ella Wall.
Mules. Vampish woman from Mulberry, Florida, who tries to move in on Big Sweet's man, Joe Williard.

War Pete.
Vine. Conjure man who lives up near Palatka; Deacon Harris encourages Hattie Tyson to consult him following the death of Aunt Dangie Dewoe.

Frank Warrick.
Bone. Man who brags about killing a huge snake; he is Lige Mosely's card partner.

Mis' Washburn.
Eyes. A white woman who befriends Nanny, hires her as housekeeper, and allows her to live behind their house with Janie. She helps

Nanny to buy a place of her own and also helps with Janie's wedding to Logan Killicks.

Mr. Washburn.
Eyes. White man who is Mrs. Washburn's husband.

Water.
Eyes. Water takes on an elemental force in the images of rising water during the hurricane; later Tea Cake has an aversion to water due to his rabies.

"John Redding." The St. John [*sic*] River is the source of John's death and his ultimate freedom.

Moses. The Nile River and the Red Sea are waters used by Moses in his attempt to free the Israelites from bondage.

Watson.
"Contention." Man who lends Brazzle his two horses to drag his mule's carcass out of town.

Deacon Watson.
Vine. One of the group of deacons from Zion Hope Baptist Church who call John Pearson to account for his hasty marriage to Hattie Tyson so soon after his first wife Lucy's death.

Rev. Father Joe Watson.
Mules. Hoodoo doctor nicknamed "The Frizzly Rooster" for his ability to remove curses; Hurston became his pupil.

Mary Watson.
Mules. Rev. Father Joe Watson's wife, who continually threatens to leave him because of his repeated infidelities yet stays on as his assistant out of fear of his powers.

Nelse Watson.
Vine. Wrestling opponent from another tie camp whom John Pearson pins to win his first wrestling match. He and Deacon Hoffman run after John Pearson when he walks out of the church following his final sermon at Zion Hope Baptist.

Pheoby Watson.
Eyes. Janie's best friend who, after listening to Janie tell her story, says that she feels she has "done growed ten feet higher from jus' listenin' tuh you, Janie." She is married to Sam Watson.

Sam Watson.
Eyes. Pheoby's good-natured husband, who has little use for the gossips of the town; he and Lige Moss participate in philosophical debates, such as the question of whether Nature or Caution is more powerful in regulating one's life.

Sister Watson.
Vine. Member of Zion Hope Baptist Church who is unimpressed by Rev. Felton Cozy's trial sermon. She defends Rev. John Pearson against Hattie Tyson's allegations at the church meeting following Pearson's divorce from Hattie.

Isis ("Isie") Watts.
"Light." Precocious 11-year-old girl who hangs around the gate of her house waiting for excitement; she winds up riding off to entertain a passing carload of whites.

Joel Watts.
"Light." Isis's older brother, who helps her "shave" their grandmother.

John Watts.
"Light." Widowed father of Isis and Joel Watts.

Weddings.
Eyes. Janie's wedding to Logan Killicks is fixed by Nanny and Mrs. Washburn.
Vine. John and Lucy's wedding is the source of conflict between Lucy and her mother, although her father finally drives her to the church. Pomp Lamar and Mehaley Grant's wedding almost doesn't take place, first because Mehaley holds out in hopes that John Pearson will leave Lucy for her and then because Pomp arrives late to the ceremony.

Wesley.
Color. John Turner's old friend who tells him where he can find Emmaline Beasely when John returns to Jacksonville to see her, twenty years after their breakup.

Jim Weston.
Bone. Methodist guitar player and rival for Daisy Taylor's hand; he is tried for hitting Dave Carter with a mule bone, but the two friends make up in the end.

"Contention." Methodist and bully, who steals Joe Clarke's hens and Dave Carter's turkey; he is tried in court and then run out of town.

Eyes. Young man who tries to impress Daisy Blunt and win her attention over Charlie Jones.

"What White Publishers Won't Print."
Hurston's article, first published in April 1950 *Negro Digest,* which promotes the need to understand minorities, derides the public's adherence to old stereotypes, and asserts the essential humanity of all human beings. Noting that differences are often perceived as bad by the majority of the public, Hurston urges publishes to print stories focused on the average Negro, not the "exceptional" or the "quaint," thus portraying the totality of Negro life.

Elder Wheeler.
Vine. Preacher who finally gives in to Woody Grant's stubbornness and allows him to perform the marriage ceremony of his daughter Mehaley to Pomp Lamar.

Bishop Whipple.
Eyes. Owner of big white house, the color of which Joe Starks's house resembles.

Larkins White.
Mules. Polk County man and member of the swamp-gang who goes on the fishing trip and tells the tales of "From Pine to Pine Mr. Pinkney," "God an' de Devil in de Cemetery," "Kill the White Folks," "How the Possum Lost the Hair Off His Tail," and "Tall Hunting Story."

Sister White.
Vine. Member of Zion Hope Baptist Church who brings ginger-bread and melon-rind preserves to John Pearson after he quits the pulpit of the church. She and Sister Carey encourage him to return to the pulpit, but he declines.

Mrs. Viney White.
Mules. Neighbor of Mrs. Rachel Silas, who also shares her views on hoodoo with Hurston.

Who Flung.
Eyes. Young scoundrel who convinces Annie Tyler to sell her house and run off to Tampa with him, where he takes her money and abandons her, leaving her broken and penniless.
Mules. Man at the card game with whom Nunkie wants to pick a fight.

Lillie Wilcox.
"Black Death." Woman whose blood dries up after Old Man Morgan puts a curse on her by burying some of her fingernail clippings with lizard's feet.

Joe Wiley.
Mules. Polk County man and member of the swamp-gang who goes on the fishing trip and tells several stories: "Big Talk," "The Fortune Teller," " 'Member Youse a Nigger," "Man and the Catfish," "How Brer Dog Lost His Beautiful Voice," and "Why They Always Use Rawhide on a Mule."

Frankie Williams.
Mules. Mrs. Williams's 4-year-old daughter, whom she rocks to sleep singing "Mister Frog."

Mrs. Williams.
Mules. Frankie Williams's mother.

Robert Williams.
Mules. Eatonville man who tells the tale of "How to Write a Letter."

Sister Williams.
Vine. Member of Zion Hope Baptist Church who talks to Rev. Felton Cozy at church on the morning he arrives to listen to John Pearson preach before preaching his trial sermon that night in an attempt to replace Pearson as pastor.

Joe Williard.
Mules. Polk County man and member of the swamp-gang who goes on the fishing trip and who calls figures for the dance at Pine Hill; he shacks up with Big Sweet.

Willie.
Bone. Young Methodist boy who teases the Baptist children.

Dick Willie.
Mules. Shack-rouser at Loughman, Florida, sawmill camp whose job it is to sing and wake the men up to make sure they get to work on time.

Wife-beating.
See Domestic violence.

"The Woman in Gaul"
One of the manuscripts almost destroyed in a fire just days after Hurston's death, "The Woman in Gaul" retells the biblical story of the death of John the Baptist from the perspective of Herodias, Salome's mother. In the story, Hurston focuses on the political intrigues of the day and the marital conflict between Antipas and Herodias. The story remained unpublished until it appeared in *The Complete Stories: Zora Neale Hurston* in 1995.

Janie Woods.
Eyes. Janie's name while she is married to Teacake Woods. (See also Janie)

Vergible "Tea Cake" Woods.
Eyes. Twelve years younger than Janie, Tea Cake becomes Janie's third husband. A gambler, he takes Janie "on the muck" to work the fields down in the Everglades. He gives her a freedom that none of her other husbands had, yet he is still jealous of her. After he is bitten

by a rabid dog during a hurricane, he contracts rabies, goes out of his mind, and attempts to shoot Janie. Luckily, she shoots him first, albeit reluctantly. To show her love for him, she gives him a lavish funeral.

⋇ X, Y, Z ⋇

X-Ray.
Yearbook of the Zeta Phi Beta sorority at Howard University, which published some of Hurston's early works: "Under the Bridge," "The Ten Commandments of Charm," and *Spears*.

Zaida.
Spears. Monanga's beautiful daughter, who, like Pocahontas, offers her own life to save the man she loves, Uledi.

Zeppo.
Moses. Jethro's cousin who stops sponging on Jethro after Moses sends a plague of frogs on Zeppo.

Zipporah.
Moses. Jethro's oldest daughter, who becomes Moses' wife.

Appendix

**ZORA NEALE HURSTON MANUSCRIPTS AND
RESEARCH MATERIALS**

Rare Book and Manuscript Library
Columbia University
535 West 114th Street
615 Butler Library
New York, NY 10027

Contents:

1. ZNH to Helen Worden Erskine, 1947–51
2. ZNH to Frederick Woltman, 22 Feb. 1951
3. Carbon copy of Hurston's essay "Back to the Middle Ages or How to Become a Peasant in the United States"
4. Carbon copy of Hurston's essay "The Lost Keys of Glory," with corrections in her own hand

Special Collections
Fisk University Library
Nashville, TN 37208

Contents:

1. 1 folder containing grant applications in the Rosenwald Fund Papers
2. ms. of "Black Death" in the Johnson Papers

Department of Special Collections
208 Smathers Library
University of Florida
Gainesville, FL 32611

Contents:

A. Manuscripts

    1. *Herod the Great* (with some burn damage)

    2. *Seraph on the Suwanee*

    3. "The Elusive Goal—Brotherhood of Mankind"

    4. "The Enemy—Unique Personal Experience"

    5. "Unique Personal Experience"

    6. "Florida's Migrant Farm Worker"

    7. "The Migrant Worker in Florida"

    8. "The Woman in Gaul"

    9. "The Seventh Veil"

    10. "The South Was Had"

    11. "Take for Instance Spessard Holland"

    12. "The Fiery Chariot" (drama)

    13. "First Version of Folklore"

    14. "Go Gator and Muddy the Waters, Florida Writers' Project"

    15. "Cuban Music"

    16. "Art and Such," 13 Jan. 1938

    17. "Cross City: Turpentine Camp," Aug. 1939

    18. "At the Camp Meetin'," poem

    19. "Reading the Deck," poem

B. Correspondence

  The Collection includes nearly 200 letters to, from, and about Hurston from 1926 to 1960. Most of them are from the 1950s. There are also a few additional letters to and from Marjorie Kinnan Rawlings (located in the Marjorie Kinnan Rawlings Collection), Tracy L'Engle (located in the Tracy L'Engle Angas Collection), and Mary Holland (located in the P.K. Yonge Florida History Collection).

C. Photographs

The Collection includes over 40 photographs of and related to Hurston at almost all ages. The largest group of them was presented to the Collection by Stetson Kennedy in 1990. Five of the photos were taken by Carl Van Vechten.

The Collection also includes miscellaneous papers, reprints of published articles by and about Hurston and her work, and copies of playbills of some of the dramatic and musical productions produced by Hurston.

Moorland-Spingarn Research Center
Howard University
500 Howard Place, NW
Washington, DC 20059

Contents:

In the Arthur Spingarn Papers:
   1. Correspondence regarding the *Mule Bone* controversy
In the Georgia Douglas Johnson Papers:
   1. ZNH to GDJ, 18 July 1925
In the Glenn Carrington Papers:
   1. Photograph of Hurston, 1927
In the Alain Locke Papers:

   A. Writings

      1. "All Day Long," incomplete

      2. "Barracoon," drafts and typescripts, 1931

      3. "Black Death"

      4. "The Bone of Contention"

      5. "From Sun to Sun"

      6. "Joe Wiley of Magazine Point," 1928

      7. Untitled short story

   B. Correspondence

      1. Alain Locke, 1927–43

      2. Charlotte Osgood Mason, 1928–33

      3. Notes and drafts of letters from Locke to Hurston, 1930–32

      4. Contracts and expense statements between Hurston, Charlotte Osgood Mason, and Forbes Randolph, 1927, 1931–32

      5. Review of *Dust Tracks on a Road*

      6. Locke's notes on Hurston

Library of Congress
101 Independence Ave., S.E.
Washington, DC 20540–4680

Contents:

Manuscript Division
1. *Cold Keener, a Revue*
2. *De Turkey and de Law*, a comedy in 3 acts
3. *Spunk*, a play in 3 acts
4. "Poker," a sketch
5. "Lawing and Jawing," a sketch
6. "Woofing," a sketch
7. "Forty Yards," a skit
8. *Plantation Play*, three authentic folk dances from the deep South, by Josephine Van Dolzen Pease, with melodies, adapted from unpublished material collected by ZNH
9. *Mule Bone*, a comedy of Negro life in 3 acts, by Langston Hughes and Zora [sic] Hurston (Copyrighted by Hughes 22 Jan. 1931.)

In the Franz Boas Papers:
1. 13 letters from ZNH to FB from 29 Mar. 1927 to Apr. 1940
2. 16 letters from FB to ZNH from 24 Mar. 1927 to 1 Apr. 1935
3. ZNH to Otto Klineberg 22 Oct. 1929
4. The Julius Rosenwald Fund to ZNH 19 Dec. 1935

In the Countee Cullen Papers:
1. ZNH to CC 11 Mar. 1926
2. ZNH to CC 5 Mar. 1943

In the Margaret Mead Papers:
1. MM to ZNH 20 May 1940
2. ZNH to Jane Belo 3 Dec. 1938
3. ZNH to JB 20 Mar. 1940
4. ZNH to JB 2 May 1940
5. ZNH to JB 1 Oct. 1944
6. ZNH to JB and Frank Tannenbaum 14 Oct. 1944
7. ZNH to JB and FT 18 Oct. 1944
8. ZNH and Norman Chalfin to JB 20 May 1940

9. ms. of "Ritualistic Expression from the Lips of the Communicants of the Seventh Day Church of God, Beaufort, South Carolina"

10. 5 photos of ZNH in folder "Jane Belo Photos—Portrait File"

In the NAACP Papers (Group I):

Letters to and from Walter White

1. WW to ZNH 7 Apr. 1932
2. WW to ZNH 31 May 1932
3. WW to ZNH 4 June 1932
4. WW to ZNH 7 June 1932
5. ZNH to WW 6 June 1932 (telegram)
6. ZNH to WW 15 June 1932
7. WW to ZNH 17 June 1932
8. ZNH to WW, n.d.
9. WW to ZNH 9 Aug. 1932
10. ZNH to WW 8 Mar. 1934
11. WW to ZNH 14 Mar. 1934
12. ZNH to WW 23 July 1934
13. WW to ZNH 27 July 1934
14. WW to ZNH 22 Mar. 1935
15. ZNH to WW 24 Oct. 1935
16. WW to ZNH 28 Oct. 1935
17. WW to ZNH 27 Mar. 1936

In the Lawrence Spivak Papers:

1. "You Don't Know Us Negroes"

In the Carter G. Woodson Papers:
1. ZNH to CGW, n.d.

In the W.P.A. Federal Writers' Project:

1. "Negro Folk Tales"
2. "Negro Legends"
3. "Negro Religious Customs
4. "Negro Folk Customs and Folk Lore"
5. "Eatonville (When You Look at It)"
6. "The Sanctified Church"
7. "Negro Work Songs"

Music Division

    1. *Meet the Mama*, a musical play

Rare Book and Special Collections Division

    1. *Polk County*, a comedy of Negro life on a sawmill camp with authentic Negro music, in 3 acts (Text by ZNH and Dorothy Waring.)

Archive of Folk Culture

    1. 18 discs of songs, stories, and instrumentals recorded in Florida and Georgia during the summer of 1935 by Mary Elizabeth Barnicle, Alan Lomax, and ZNH (AFS 370–387)

    2. 3 American Negro children's songs and explanation, sung and spoken by ZNH. Recorded in Petionville, Haiti, 21 Dec. 1936. (AFS 1879 A1–3)

        A1: "Bluebird"

        A2: "Bama, Bama"

        A3: "There Stands a Bluebird," with explanation

    3. 6 discs with 18 songs, stories, and explanations sung and spoken by ZNH. Recorded in Jacksonville, Florida 18 June 1939. (AFS 3135–3136; 3137B-3139; 3144B)

AFS 3135

        A: "Gonna See My Long-Haired Babe"

        B1: "Let's Shake It"

        B2: "Dat Old Black Gal"

        AFS 3136

        A: "Shove It Over"

        B: "Mule on the Mount"

        AFS 3137

        B1: "Georgia Skin"

        B2: Let the Deal Go Down"

        AFS 3138

        A1: "Uncle Bud"

        A2: "Oh, the Buford Boat Done Come"

        B1: "Ever Been Down"

        B2: "Halimuhfack"

        AFS 3139

        A1: "Tampa"

> A2: "Po' Gal"
>
> B1: "Mama Don't Want No Peas, No Rice"
>
> B2: "Crow Dance"
>
> AFS 3144
>
> B1: "Wake Up, Jacob"
>
> B2: "Oh, Mr. Brown"
>
> B3: "Tilly, Lend Me Your Pigeon"
>
> B4: "Evelina"

4. 1 disc containing 6 songs sung by a choir sponsored by the Rollins College Folklore Group led by Hurston. Recorded at National Folk Festival in Washington, DC on 6 May 1938. (AFS 9845)

> A1: "Can't You Line It"
>
> A2: "Mule on de Mount"
>
> A3: "Dat Old Black Gal"
>
> A4: "Oh Lula, Oh Gal"
>
> A5: "Somebody's Knockin' at My Door"
>
> A6: Unidentified song

5. Taped interview with Mary Elizabeth Barnicle recorded in Townsend, TN Jan.-Feb. 1977, in which Barnicle discusses her 1935 folklore gathering expedition with ZNH and Alan Lomax. (AFS 19, 536A)

Motion Picture, Broadcasting and Recorded Sound Division

1. "Hurston, Zora Neale." Silent film footage taken by ZNH in the field ca. 1927–29. (VBF 3411)

2. Interview of ZNH by Mary Margaret McBride on WEAF Radio on 25 Jan. 1943. (RWC 6858B)

Prints and Photographs Division

1. Biographical File—photo of ZNH outside city building in hat

2. Alan Lomax Collection—5 photos of ZNH in Florida during 1935

3. Carl Van Vechten Photographs—1938 photo of ZNH wearing a hat

Schomburg Center for Research in Black Culture
New York Public Library
515 Malcolm X Blvd.
New York, NY 10037–1801

Contents:

1. ms. of *Jonah's Gourd Vine*
2. "The Conversion of Man," a short story
3. Correspondence with William Clifford and Lawrence Jordan
4. 9 poems

Harry Ransom Humanities Research Center
University of Texas at Austin
P.O. Box 7219
Austin, TX 78713–7219

Contents:

Letters from Zora Neale Hurston to Fannie Hurst:

1926 Christmas card

5 Nov. 1932

8 Mar. 1934

10 Jan. 1936

29 Feb. 1936

13 Apr. 1936

3 July 1936

22 Jan. 1937

15 Oct. 1937

5 Nov. 1937

10 Feb. 1939

30 Jan. 1940

6 Feb. 1940

4 Aug. 1940

10 Feb. 1949

2 undated letters (probably 1925 or 1926) and another from 1949

Letters to and pertaining to Zora Neale Hurston:

13 Nov. 1931, Hurst's secretary to ZNH

29 Nov. 1933, Guggenheim Memorial Foundation to Hurst

1 Dec. 1933, Hurst to Guggenheim Memorial Foundation

13 Jan. 1935, Annie Nathan Meyer to Hurst

14 Jan. 1935, Hurst to Annie Nathan Meyer
23 Jan. 1935, Hurst to ZNH

1 May 1935, Annie Nathan Meyer to Hurst

6 May 1935, Hurst to Annie Nathan Meyer

7 May 1935, Annie Nathan Meyer to Hurst

7 May 1935, Women's University Club to Hurst

13 May 1935, Hurst to Annie Nathan Meyer

6 Dec. 1935, Hurst to Mr. Walsh, John Day Co.

9 Dec. 1935, Guggenheim Memorial Foundation to Hurst

no date, Hurst to Guggenheim Memorial Foundation

6 Mar. 1936, Hurst to ZNH

12 Mar. 1936, Hurst to ZNH

14 July 1936, Hurst to ZNH

no date, A.S. Scott of *Atlanta Daily World* to Hurst

9 Dec. 1936, Hurst to A.S. Scott

26 Jan. 1937, Hurst to ZNH

21 Sept. 1937, Christopher Morley to ZNH

23 Dec. 1937, Hurst to ZNH

27 Jan. 1940, Hurst to ZNH

12 Feb. 1940, Hurst to ZNH

19 Aug. 1940, Hurst to ZNH

Several letters from Carl Van Vechten to Fannie Hurst which mention ZNH

**The Beinecke Rare Book and Manuscript Library
Yale University Library
P.O. Box 208240
New Haven, CT 06520–8240**

Contents:

Zora Neale Hurston Collection

A. Correspondence

    1. Ruby Harmon, 26 Mar. 1934

    2. Harold Jackman, 1933, 1944

    3. Carl Van Vechten, 14 Nov. 1930

    4. Barrett H. Clark to Carl Van Vechten, 1931

    5. Langston Hughes to Carl Van Vechten, 1931

    6. Theatre Guild to Carl Van Vechten, 1931

B. Writings

    1. "Are We Citizens," fragment, ts carbon

    2. "Book of Harlem," ts carbon

3. "The Chick with One Hen," ts carbon, corrected

4. *Dust Tracks on a Road*, holograph ms., chapter drafts, ts carbon, corrected, setting ts, with printers notes

5. "The Emperor Effaces Himself," ts carbon

6. "Harlem Slanguage," ts carbon

7. *Moses, Man of the Mountain*, holograph ms.

8. "Mule Bone," Act One, mimeograph

9. "Now You Cookin' With Gas," 2 versions (one incomplete), ts carbon

10. *Tell My Horse*, holograph ms., with ts additions and rewrites, notes and misc. pages

11. *Their Eyes Were Watching God*, holograph ms.

Bibliography

PRIMARY BIBLIOGRAPHY

Books by Zora Neale Hurston

Dust Tracks on a Road. Philadelphia: J.B. Lippincott, 1942. Reprint, with Introduction by Darwin Turner, New York: Arno Press, 1969; Introduction by Larry Neal, New York: J.B. Lippincott, 1971; Urbana: U of Illinois P, 1984; and New York: Harper & Row, 1990; and in *Zora Neale Hurston: Folklore, Memoirs, and Other Writings*. New York: Library of America, 1995. 557–808. Manuscript in James Weldon Johnson Memorial Collection, Collection of American Literature, Beinecke Rare Book and Manuscript Library, Yale University.

Go Gator and Muddy the Water: Writings by Zora Neale Hurston from the Federal Writers' Project. Ed. Pamela Bordelon. New York: W.W. Norton, 1999.

I Love Myself When I Am Laughing . . . and Then Again When I Am Looking Mean and Impressive: A Zora Neale Hurston Reader. Ed. Alice Walker. Old Westbury, NY: Feminist Press, 1979.

Jonah's Gourd Vine. Philadelphia: J.B. Lippincott, 1934. Reprint, with Introduction by Larry Neal, Philadelphia: J.B. Lippincott, 1971; New York: Harper and Row, 1990; and in *Zora Neale Hurston: Novels and Short Stories*. New York: Library of America, 1995. 1–168. Manuscript in Schomburg Collection, New York Public Library.

Moses, Man of the Mountain. Philadelphia: J.B. Lippincott, 1939. Reprint, Chatham, NJ: Chatham Bookseller, 1974; New York: Harper & Row, 1991; and in *Zora Neale Hurston: Novels and Short Stories*. New York: Library of America, 1995. 335–595. Manuscript in James Weldon Johnson Memorial Collection, Collection of American Literature, Beinecke Rare Book and Manuscript Library, Yale University.

Mules and Men. Philadelphia: J.B. Lippincott, 1935. Reprint, New York: Negro Universities Press, 1969; Introduction by Darwin Turner, New York: Harper and Row, 1970; New York: Harper and Row, 1991; and in *Zora Neale Hurston: Folklore, Memoirs, and Other Writings*. New York: Library of America, 1995. 1–267.

The Sanctified Church. Foreword by Toni Cade Bambara. Berkeley: Turtle Island, 1981. Reprint, New York: Marlowe, 1997.

Seraph on the Suwanee. New York: Charles Scribner's Sons, 1948. Reprint, Ann Arbor, MI: University Microfilms, 1971; New York: AMS Press, 1974; New York: Harper & Row, 1991; and in *Zora Neale Hurston: Novels and Short Stories*. New York: Library of America, 1995. 597–920. Manuscript in Hurston Collection, Rare Books and Manuscripts, University of Florida Library.

Spunk: The Selected Stories of Zora Neale Hurston. Berkeley: Turtle Island, 1985.

Tell My Horse. Philadelphia: J.B. Lippincott, 1938. Reprint, New York: Harper and Row, 1990; and in *Zora Neale Hurston: Folklore, Memoirs, and Other Writings*. New York: Library of America, 1995. 269–555. Manuscript in James Weldon Johnson Memorial Collection, Collection of American Literature, Beinecke Rare Book and Manuscript Library, Yale University.

Their Eyes Were Watching God. Philadelphia, J.B. Lippincott, 1937. Reprint, Greenwich, CT: Fawcett Publications, 1965; New York: Negro Universities Press, 1969; Urbana: U of Illinois P, 1978; New York: Harper & Row, 1990; and in *Zora Neale Hurston: Novels and Short Stories*. New York: Library of America, 1995. 173–333. Manuscript in James Weldon Johnson Memorial Collection, Collection of American Literature, Beinecke Rare Book and Manuscript Library, Yale University.

Zora Neale Hurston: Folklore, Memoirs, and Other Writings. New York: Library of America, 1995.

Zora Neale Hurston: Novels and Short Stories. New York: Library of America, 1995.

Plays by Zora Neale Hurston

Color Struck: A Play. Fire!! 1 (Nov. 1926): 7–14. Reprinted in *Fire!! Devoted to Younger Negro Artists.* Nendeln, Liechtenstein: Kraus-Thomson, 1968. 7–14; *Black Female Playwrights: An Anthology of Plays Before 1950.* Ed. Kathy A. Perkins. Bloomington: Indiana UP, 1989. 89–102; *The Portable Harlem Renaissance Reader.* Ed. David Levering Lewis. New York: Viking, 1994. 699–715; and *Zora Neale Hurston, Eulalie Spence, Marita Bonner, and Others: The Prize Plays and Other One-Acts Published in Periodicals.* Ed. Henry Louis Gates Jr. New York: G.K. Hall, 1996. 79–95.

The First One. In *Ebony and Topaz: A Collectanea.* Ed. Charles S. Johnson. New York: Opportunity, National Urban League, 1927. 53–57. Reprinted in *Black Female Playwrights: An Anthology of Plays Before 1950.* Ed. Kathy A. Perkins. Bloomington: Indiana UP, 1989. 80–88; and *Zora Neale Hurston, Eulalie Spence, Marita Bonner, and Others: The Prize Plays and Other One-Acts Published in Periodicals.* Ed. Henry Louis Gates Jr. New York: G.K. Hall, 1996. 96–106.

Mule Bone (with Langston Hughes). New York: Harper & Row, 1991. Act III was originally published in *Drama Critique* (spring 1964): 103–7.

Spears. Zeta Phi Beta *X-Ray* (1926): 9–12. Reprinted in "Three by Zora Neale Hurston: Story, Essay, and Play." *Southern Quarterly* 36.3 (1998): 99–102.

Short Stories by Zora Neale Hurston

"Black Death." In *The Complete Stories: Zora Neale Hurston.* New York: HarperCollins, 1995; paperback 1996 by HarperPerennial. 202–8.

"The Bone of Contention." In *Mule Bone.* New York: Harper & Row, 1991. 27–39. Reprinted in *The Sleeper Wakes: Harlem Renaissance Stories by Women.* Ed. Marcy Knopf. New Brunswick, NJ: Rutgers UP, 1993. 240–49; *Zora Neale Hurston: Novels and Short Stories.* New York: Library of America, 1995. 968–78; and *The Complete Stories: Zora Neale Hurston.* New York: HarperCollins, 1995; paperback 1996 by HarperPerennial. 209–20.

"Book of Harlem." In *Spunk: The Selected Stories of Zora Neale Hurston.* Berkeley: Turtle Island, 1985. 75–81. Reprinted in *Zora Neale Hurston: Novels and Short Stories.* New York: Library of America, 1995. 979–84; and *The Complete Stories: Zora Neale Hurston.* New York: HarperCollins, 1995; paperback 1996 by HarperPerennial. 221–26.

"Cock Robin Beale Street." *Southern Literary Messenger* (July 1941): 321–
23. Reprinted in *Spunk: The Selected Stories of Zora Neale Hurston.*
Berkeley: Turtle Island, 1985. 69–74; and *The Complete Stories: Zora
Neale Hurston.* New York: HarperCollins, 1995; paperback 1996 by
HarperPerennial. 122–26.

"The Conscience of the Court." *Saturday Evening Post,* 18 Mar. 1950. 22–
23+. Reprinted in *The Saturday Evening Post Stories, 1950.* New
York: Random House, 1950. 16–30; *Florida Stories.* Ed. Kevin
McCarthy. Gainesville: U of Florida P, 1989. 83–98; and *The Complete Stories: Zora Neale Hurston.* New York: HarperCollins, 1995;
paperback 1996 by HarperPerennial. 162–77.

"Drenched in Light." *Opportunity* 2 (Dec. 1924): 371–74. Reprinted in
*Readings from Negro Authors, for Schools and Colleges, with a Bibli-
ography of Negro Literature.* Ed. Otelia Cromwell, Lorenzo Dow
Turner, and Eva B. Dykes. New York: Harcourt, Brace, 1931. 112–
20; *Within Our Gates: Selections on Tolerance and the Foreign-Born
of Today.* Ed. Mary B. McLellan and Albert V. De Bonis. New York:
Harper & Brothers, 1940. 239–47. *The Portable Harlem Renaissance
Reader.* Ed. David Levering Lewis. New York: Viking, 1994. 691–
98; *Zora Neale Hurston: Novels and Short Stories.* New York: Library
of America, 1995. 940–48; and *The Complete Stories: Zora Neale
Hurston.* New York: HarperCollins, 1995; paperback 1996 by
HarperPerennial. 17–25. Reprinted under the title "Isis" in *Spunk:
The Selected Stories of Zora Neale Hurston.* Berkeley: Turtle Island,
1985. 9–18; and *The Unforgettable Heart: An Anthology of Short
Stories by African American Women, 1859–1993.* Ed. Asha Kanwar.
San Francisco: Aunt Lute Books, 1993. 111–17.

"The Eatonville Anthology." Originally published serially in the *Messenger*
8 (Sept. 1926): 261–62; (Oct. 1926): 297+; and (Nov. 1926): 332.
Reprinted in *I Love Myself When I Am Laughing . . . and Then Again
When I Am Looking Mean and Impressive: A Zora Neale Hurston
Reader.* Ed. Alice Walker. Old Westbury, NY: Feminist Press, 1971.
177–88; *The Norton Book of American Short Stories.* Ed. Peter S.
Prescott. New York: Norton, 1988. 357–67; *The Complete Stories:
Zora Neale Hurston.* New York: HarperCollins, 1995; paperback
1996 by HarperPerennial. 59–72; and *Zora Neale Hurston: Folklore,
Memoirs, and Other Writings.* New York: Library of America, 1995.
813–25.

"Escape from Pharaoh." In *The Ways of God and Men: Great Stories from
the Bible in World Literature.* Ed. Ruth Selden. New York: Stephen
Daye, 1950. 89–106. Reprinted in *The Complete Stories: Zora Neale
Hurston.* New York: HarperCollins, 1995; paperback 1996 by
HarperPerennial. 178–92.

"The Fire and the Cloud." *Challenge* (Sept. 1934): 10–14. Reprinted in *Zora Neale Hurston: Novels and Short Stories*. New York: Library of America, 1995. 997–1000; and *The Complete Stories: Zora Neale Hurston*. New York: HarperCollins, 1995; paperback 1996 by HarperPerennial. 117–21.

"The Gilded Six-Bits." *Story* (Aug. 1933): 60–70. Reprinted in *The Best Short Stories by Negro Writers; An Anthology from 1899 to the Present*. Ed. Langston Hughes. Boston: Little, Brown, 1967. 74–85; *I Love Myself When I Am Laughing . . . and Then Again When I Am Looking Mean and Impressive: A Zora Neale Hurston Reader*. Ed. Alice Walker. Old Westbury, NY: Feminist Press, 1971. 208–18; *Black Hands on a White Face: A Timepiece of Experiences in a Black and White America*. Ed. Whit Burnett. New York: Dodd, Mead, 1971. 129–43; *Black Writers of America: A Comprehensive Anthology*. Ed. Richard Barksdale and Keneth Kinnamon. New York: Macmillan, 1972. 613–18; *Spunk: The Selected Stories of Zora Neale Hurston*. Berkeley: Turtle Island, 1985. 54–68; *A Modern Southern Reader: Major Stories, Drama, Poetry, Essays, Interviews, and Reminiscences from the Twentieth-Century South*. Ed. Ben Forkner. Atlanta: Peachtree, 1986. 90–99; *Stories of the Old South*. Ed. Ben Forkner and Patrick Samway. New York: Penguin Books, 1989. 224–34; *Black American Short Stories: One Hundred Years of the Best*. Ed. John Henrik Clarke. New York: Hill and Wang, 1993. 63–74; *Calling the Wind: Twentieth Century African-American Short Stories*. Ed. Clarence Major. New York: HarperPerennial, 1993. 69–78; *Centers of the Self: Stories by Black American Women from the Nineteenth Century to the Present*. Ed. Judith A. Hamer and Martin J. Hamer. New York: Hill and Wang, 1994. 110–20; *Classic Fiction of the Harlem Renaissance*. Ed. William L. Andrews. New York: Oxford UP, 1994. 90–99; *Zora Neale Hurston: Novels and Short Stories*. New York: Library of America, 1995. 985–96; and *The Complete Stories: Zora Neale Hurston*. New York: HarperCollins, 1995; paperback 1996 by HarperPerennial. 86–98.

"Harlem Slanguage." In *The Complete Stories: Zora Neale Hurston*. New York: HarperCollins, 1995; paperback 1996 by HarperPerennial. 227–32.

"High John De Conquer." *American Mercury* (Oct. 1943): 450–58. Reprinted in *The American Mercury Reader: A Selection of Distinguished Articles, Stories, and Poems Published in* The American Mercury *during the Past Twenty Years*. Philadelphia: Blakiston, 1944. 106–12; *Mother Wit from the Laughing Barrel: Readings in the Interpretation of Afro-American Folklore*. Ed. Alan Dundes. Englewood Cliffs, NJ: Prentice Hall, 1973. 541–48; and *The Complete Stories: Zora Neale*

Hurston. New York: HarperCollins, 1995; paperback 1996 by HarperPerennial. 139–48.

"Hurricane." In *The Complete Stories: Zora Neale Hurston.* New York: HarperCollins, 1995; paperback 1996 by HarperPerennial. 149–61.

"John Redding Goes to Sea." *Stylus* 1 (May 1921): 11–22. Reprinted in *Opportunity* 4 (Jan. 1926): 16–21; *The Sleeper Wakes: Harlem Renaissance Stories by Women.* Ed. Marcy Knopf. New Brunswick, NJ: Rutgers UP, 1993. 227–39; *Zora Neale Hurston: Novels and Short Stories.* New York: Library of America, 1995. 925–39; and *The Complete Stories: Zora Neale Hurston.* New York: HarperCollins, 1995; paperback 1996 by HarperPerennial. 1–16.

"Magnolia Flower." *Spokesman.* (July 1925): 26–29. Reprinted in *The Complete Stories: Zora Neale Hurston.* New York: HarperCollins, 1995; paperback 1996 by HarperPerennial. 33–40.

"Man and the Cat-fish." In *Fish Tales: Stories from the Sea.* Ed. John Miller. Harrisburg, PA: Stackpole Books, 1993. 85–87.

"Mother Catherine." In *Negro: An Anthology.* Ed. Nancy Cunard. London: Wishart, 1934. 54–57. Reprinted in *The Complete Stories: Zora Neale Hurston.* New York: HarperCollins, 1995; paperback 1996 by HarperPerennial. 99–105; and *Zora Neale Hurston: Folklore, Memoirs, and Other Writings.* New York: Library of America, 1995. 854–60.

"Muttsy." *Opportunity* (Aug. 1926): 246–50. Reprinted in *Spunk: The Selected Stories of Zora Neale Hurston.* Berkeley: Turtle Island, 1985. 19–37; and *The Complete Stories: Zora Neale Hurston.* New York: HarperCollins, 1995; paperback 1996 by HarperPerennial. 41–56.

"Now You Cookin' with Gas." In *The Complete Stories: Zora Neale Hurston.* New York: HarperCollins, 1995; paperback 1996 by HarperPerennial. 233–41.

" 'Possum or Pig?" *Forum* (Sept. 1926): 465. Reprinted in *The Complete Stories: Zora Neale Hurston.* New York: HarperCollins, 1995; paperback 1996 by HarperPerennial. 57–58.

"The Seventh Veil." In *The Complete Stories: Zora Neale Hurston.* New York: HarperCollins, 1995; paperback 1996 by HarperPerennial. 242–60.

"Spunk." *Opportunity* (June 1925): 171–73. Reprinted in *The New Negro,* Ed. Alain Locke. New York: Albert and Charles Boni, 1925. 105–11 and in the 1992 reprint of *The New Negro,* with an introduction by Arnold Rampersad. New York: Atheneum, 1992. 105–11; *Spunk: The Selected Stories of Zora Neale Hurston.* Berkeley: Turtle Island, 1985. 1–8; *Zora Neale Hurston: Novels and Short Stories.* New York: Library of America, 1995. 949–54; *The Complete Stories: Zora Neale Hurston.* New York: HarperCollins, 1995; paperback 1996 by

HarperPerennial. 26–32; *Harlem's Glory: Black Women Writing, 1900–1950.* Cambridge, MA: Harvard UP, 1996. 233–38; and *Restless Spirits: Ghost Stories by American Women, 1872–1926.* Ed. Catherine A. Lundie. Amherst: U of Massachusetts P, 1996. 62–67.

"Story in Harlem Slang." *American Mercury* (July 1942): 84–96. Reprinted in *Mother Wit from the Laughing Barrel: Readings in the Interpretation of Afro-American Folklore.* Ed. Alan Dundes. Englewood Cliffs, NJ: Prentice-Hall, 1973. 222–29; *Spunk: The Selected Stories of Zora Neale Hurston.* Berkeley: Turtle Island, 1985. 82–89; *Zora Neale Hurston: Novels and Short Stories.* New York: Library of America, 1995. 1001–7; and *The Complete Stories: Zora Neale Hurston.* New York: HarperCollins, 1995; paperback 1996 by HarperPerennial. 127–38.

"Sweat." *Fire!!* 1 (Nov. 1926): 40–45. Reprinted in *Fire!! Devoted to Younger Negro Artists.* Nendeln, Liechtenstein: Kraus-Thomson, 1968. 40–45; *I Love Myself When I Am Laughing . . . and Then Again When I Am Looking Mean and Impressive: A Zora Neale Hurston Reader.* Ed. Alice Walker. Old Westbury, NY: Feminist Press, 1971. 197–207; *Voices from the Harlem Renaissance.* Ed. Nathan Irvin Huggins. New York: Oxford UP, 1976. 199–207; *Spunk: The Selected Stories of Zora Neale Hurston.* Berkeley: Turtle Island, 1985. 38–53; *American Women Writers: Diverse Voices in Prose Since 1845.* Ed. Eileen Barrett and Mary Cullinan. New York: St. Martin's, 1992. 342–51; *The Oxford Book of American Short Stories.* Ed. Joyce Carol Oates. New York: Oxford UP, 1992. 353–64; *Classic Fiction of the Harlem Renaissance.* Ed. William L. Andrews. New York: Oxford UP, 1994. 79–89; *The Oxford Book of Women's Writing in the United States.* Ed. Linda Wagner-Martin and Cathy N. Davidson. New York: Oxford UP, 1995. 101–10; *Zora Neale Hurston: Novels and Short Stories.* New York: Library of America, 1995. 955–67; *The Complete Stories: Zora Neale Hurston.* New York: HarperCollins, 1995; paperback 1996 by HarperPerennial. 73–85; *Zora Neale Hurston: "Sweat."* Ed. Cheryl A. Wall. New Brunswick, NJ: Rutgers UP, 1997. 25–40; and *African-American Literature: An Anthology of Nonfiction, Fiction, Poetry, and Drama.* 2nd ed. Comp. Demetrice A. Worley and Jesse Perry Jr. Lincolnwood, IL: National Textbook, 1998. 432–42.

"The Tablets of the Law." Excerpt from *Moses: Man of the Mountain,* in *The Word Lives On: A Treasury of Spiritual Fiction.* Ed. Frances Brentano. Garden City, NY: Doubleday, 1951: 7–14. Reprinted in *The Complete Stories: Zora Neale Hurston.* New York: HarperCollins, 1995; paperback 1996 by HarperPerennial. 193–201.

"Uncle Monday." In *Negro: An Anthology.* Ed. Nancy Cunard. London: Wishart, 1934. 57–61. Reprinted in *The Complete Stories: Zora Neale*

Hurston. New York: HarperCollins, 1995; paperback 1996 by HarperPerennial. 106–16; *Zora Neale Hurston: Folklore, Memoirs, and Other Writings.* New York: Library of America, 1995. 860–69; and *Go Gator and Muddy the Water: Writings by Zora Neale Hurston from the Federal Writers' Project.* Ed. Pamela Bordelon. New York: W.W. Norton, 1999. 114–18.

"Under the Bridge." Zeta Phi Beta *X-Ray* (1925): 4–5+. Reprinted in "Three by Zora Neale Hurston: Story, Essay, and Play." *Southern Quarterly* 36.3 (1998): 95–98.

"The Woman in Gaul." In *The Complete Stories: Zora Neale Hurston.* New York: HarperCollins, 1995; paperback 1996 by HarperPerennial. 261–83.

Nonfiction Articles and Essays by Zora Neale Hurston

"Art and Such." In *Reading Black, Reading Feminist: A Critical Anthology.* Ed. Henry Louis Gates Jr. New York: Meridian, 1990. 21–26. Reprinted in *Zora Neale Hurston: Folklore, Memoirs, and Other Writings.* New York: Library of America, 1995. 905–11; and *Go Gator and Muddy the Water: Writings by Zora Neale Hurston from the Federal Writers' Project.* Ed. Pamela Bordelon. New York: W.W. Norton, 1999. 139–45.

"Characteristics of Negro Expression." In *Negro: An Anthology.* Ed. Nancy Cunard. London: Wishart, 1934. 39–46. Reprinted in *Zora Neale Hurston: Folklore, Memoirs, and Other Writings.* New York: Library of America, 1995. 830–46; and *Zora Neale Hurston: "Sweat."* Ed. Cheryl A. Wall. New Brunswick, NJ: Rutgers UP, 1997. 55–71.

"Communication." *Journal of Negro History* 12 (Oct. 1927): 664–67.

"Conversions and Visions." In *Negro: An Anthology.* Ed. Nancy Cunard. London: Wishart, 1934. 47–49; and in *Zora Neale Hurston: Folklore, Memoirs, and Other Writings.* New York: Library of America, 1995. 846–51.

"Crazy for This Democracy." *Negro Digest* (Dec. 1945): 45–48. Reprinted in *I Love Myself When I Am Laughing . . . and Then Again When I Am Looking Mean and Impressive: A Zora Neale Hurston Reader.* Ed. Alice Walker. Old Westbury, NY: Feminist Press, 1971. 165–68; and *Zora Neale Hurston: Folklore, Memoirs, and Other Writings.* New York: Library of America, 1995. 945–49.

"Cudjo's Own Story of the Last African Slaver." *Journal of Negro History* 12 (Oct. 1927): 648–63.

"Dance Songs and Tales from the Bahamas." *Journal of American Folklore* 43 (July–Sept. 1930): 294–312.

"Fannie Hurst." *Saturday Review,* 9 Oct. 1937: 15–16.

"Folklore and Music." In *Zora Neale Hurston: Folklore, Memoirs, and Other Writings*. New York: Library of America, 1995. 875–94.

"Hoodoo in America." *Journal of American Folklore* 44 (Oct.-Dec. 1931): 317–418.

"How It Feels to Be Colored Me." *The World Tomorrow* 11 (May 1928): 215–16. Reprinted in *I Love Myself When I Am Laughing . . . and Then Again When I Am Looking Mean and Impressive: A Zora Neale Hurston Reader*. Ed. Alice Walker. Old Westbury, NY: Feminist Press, 1971. 152–55; *Bearing Witness: Selections from African-American Autobiography in the Twentieth Century*. Ed. Henry Louis Gates Jr. New York: Pantheon Books, 1991. 32–37; *American Women Writers: Diverse Voices in Prose Since 1845*. Ed. Eileen Barrett and Mary Cullinan. New York: St. Martin's, 1992. 351–54; *Zora Neale Hurston: Folklore, Memoirs, and Other Writings*. New York: Library of America, 1995. 826–29; and *The Norton Book of Personal Essays*. Ed. Joseph Epstein. New York: W.W. Norton, 1997. 132–36.

"The Hue and Cry about Howard University." *Messenger* (Sept. 1925): 315–19+.

"I Saw Negro Votes Peddled." *American Legion Magazine* (Nov. 1950): 12–13+. Condensed in *Negro Digest* (Sept. 1951): 77–85.

"The Last Slave Ship." *American Mercury* (Mar. 1944): 351–58. Condensed in *Negro Digest* (May 1944): 11–16.

"Lawrence of the River." *Saturday Evening Post*, 5 Sept. 1942: 18+. Condensed in *Negro Digest* (Mar. 1943): 47–49.

"Mourner's Bench, Communist Line: Why the Negro Won't Buy Communism." *American Legion Magazine* (June 1951): 14–15+.

"My Most Humiliating Jim Crow Experience." *Negro Digest* (June 1944): 25–26. Reprinted in *I Love Myself When I Am Laughing . . . and Then Again When I Am Looking Mean and Impressive: A Zora Neale Hurston Reader*. Ed. Alice Walker. Old Westbury, NY: Feminist Press, 1971. 163–64; and *Zora Neale Hurston: Folklore, Memoirs, and Other Writings*. New York: Library of America, 1995. 935–36.

"Negro Mythical Places." In *Zora Neale Hurston: Folklore, Memoirs, and Other Writings*. New York: Library of America, 1995. 894–97. Reprinted in *Go Gator and Muddy the Water: Writings by Zora Neale Hurston from the Federal Writers' Project*. Ed. Pamela Bordelon. New York: W.W. Norton, 1999. 106–111.

"A Negro Voter Sizes Up Taft." *Saturday Evening Post*, 8 Dec. 1951: 29+.

"Negroes without Self-Pity." *American Mercury* (Nov. 1943): 601–03. Reprinted in *Zora Neale Hurston: Folklore, Memoirs, and Other Writings*. New York: Library of America, 1995. 932–34.

"Now Take Noses." In *Cordially Yours*. Ed. Thomas Page Smith and George E. Harris. Philadelphia: Lippincott, 1939. 25–27.

"The Ocoee Riot." In *Zora Neale Hurston: Folklore, Memoirs, and Other Writings*. New York: Library of America, 1995. 897–901. Reprinted in *Go Gator and Muddy the Water: Writings by Zora Neale Hurston from the Federal Writers' Project*. Ed. Pamela Bordelon. New York: W.W. Norton, 1999. 146–50.

"The 'Pet Negro' System." *American Mercury* (May 1943): 593–600. Condensed in *Negro Digest* (June 1943): 37–40. Reprinted in *I Love Myself When I Am Laughing . . . and Then Again When I Am Looking Mean and Impressive: A Zora Neale Hurston Reader*. Ed. Alice Walker. Old Westbury, NY: Feminist Press, 1971. 156–62; and *Zora Neale Hurston: Folklore, Memoirs, and Other Writings*. New York: Library of America, 1995. 914–21.

"The Rise of the Begging Joints." *American Mercury* (Mar. 1945): 288–94. Condensed in *Negro Digest* as "Beware the Begging Joints." (May 1945): 27–32. Reprinted in *Zora Neale Hurston: Folklore, Memoirs, and Other Writings*. New York: Library of America, 1995. 937–44.

"The Sermon." In *Negro: An Anthology*. Ed. Nancy Cunard. London: Wishart, 1934. 50–54.

"Shouting." In *Negro: An Anthology*. Ed. Nancy Cunard. London: Wishart, 1934. 49–50; and *Zora Neale Hurston: Folklore, Memoirs, and Other Writings*. New York: Library of America, 1995. 851–54.

"Spirituals and Neo-Spirituals." In *Negro: An Anthology*. Ed. Nancy Cunard. London: Wishart, 1934. 359–61; and *Zora Neale Hurston: Folklore, Memoirs, and Other Writings*. New York: Library of America, 1995. 869–74.

"The Ten Commandments of Charm." Zeta Phi Beta *X-Ray* (1925): 22. Reprinted in "Three by Zora Neale Hurston: Story, Essay, and Play." *Southern Quarterly* 36.3 (1998): 98.

[The Trial of Ruby McCollum]. In William Bradford Huie, *Ruby McCollum: Woman in the Suwannee Jail*. New York: E.P. Dutton, 1956. 89–101.

"What White Publishers Won't Print." *Negro Digest* (Apr. 1950): 85–89. Reprinted in *I Love Myself When I Am Laughing . . . and Then Again When I Am Looking Mean and Impressive: A Zora Neale Hurston Reader*. Ed. Alice Walker. Old Westbury, NY: Feminist Press, 1971. 169–73; and *Zora Neale Hurston: Folklore, Memoirs, and Other Writings*. New York: Library of America, 1995. 950–55.

Book Reviews by Zora Neale Hurston

"At the Sound of the Conch Shell." [Rev. of *New Day* by Victor Stafford Reid]. *New York Herald Tribune Weekly Book Review*, 20 Mar. 1949: 4.

"Bible, Played by Ear in Africa." [Rev. of *How God Fix Jonah* by Lorenz Graham]. *New York Herald Tribune Weekly Book Review*, 24 Nov. 1946: 5.

"Full of Mud, Sweat and Blood." [Rev. of *God Shakes Creation* by David M. Cohn]. *New York Herald Tribune Books*, 3 Nov. 1935: 8.

"Jazz Regarded as Social Achievement." [Rev. of *Shining Trumpets* by Rudi Blesh]. *New York Herald Tribune Weekly Book Review*, 22 Dec. 1946: 8.

"Race Cannot Become Great Until It Recognizes Its Talent." *Washington Tribune*, 29 Dec. 1934.

Rev. of *Voodoo in New Orleans* by Robert Tallant. *Journal of American Folklore* 60 (Oct.-Dec. 1947): 436–38.

"Rural Schools for Negroes." [Rev. of *The Jeanes Teacher in the United States* by Lance G.E. Jones]. *New York Herald Tribune Books*, 20 Feb. 1938: 24.

"Some Fabulous Caribbean Riches Revealed." [Rev. of *The Pencil of God* by Pierre Marcelin and Philippe Thoby Marcelin]. *New York Herald Tribune Weekly Book Review*, 4 Feb. 1951: 5.

"Star-Wrassling Sons-of-the-Universe." [Rev. of *The Hurricane's Children* by Carl Carmer]. *New York Herald Tribune Books*, 26 Dec. 1937: 4.

"Stories of Conflict." [Rev. of *Uncle Tom's Children* by Richard Wright]. *Saturday Review*, 2 Apr. 1938: 32. Reprinted in *Zora Neale Hurston: Folklore, Memoirs, and Other Writings*. New York: Library of America, 1995. 912–13.

"Thirty Days among Maroons." [Rev. of *Journey to Accompong* by Karharine Dunham]. *New York Herald Tribune Weekly Book Review*, 12 Jan. 1947: 8.

"The Transplanted Negro." [Rev. of *Trinidad Village* by Melville Herskovits and Frances Herskovits]. *New York Herald Tribune Weekly Book Review*, 9 Mar. 1947: 20.

Newspaper Articles by Zora Neale Hurston

"Bare Plot in McCollum Death Trial." *Pittsburgh Courier*, 29 Nov. 1952: 1+.

"Court Order Can't Make Races Mix." *Orlando Sentinel*, 11 Aug. 1955: 10. Reprinted in *Zora Neale Hurston: Folklore, Memoirs, and Other Writings*. New York: Library of America, 1995. 956–58.

"The Farm Laborer at Home." *Fort Pierce Chronicle*, 27 Feb. 1959.

"Hoodoo and Black Magic." Column in *Fort Pierce Chronicle*, 11 July 1958–7 Aug. 1959.

"The Life Story of Mrs. Ruby J. McCollum!" Serialized in the *Pittsburgh Courier* on 28 Feb. 1953: 3; 7 Mar. 1953: 2; 14 Mar. 1953: 2; 21

Mar. 1953: 3; 28 Mar. 1953: 2; 4 Apr. 1953: 3; 11 Apr. 1953: 3; 18 Apr. 1953: 2; 25 Apr. 1953: 3; and 2 May 1953: 2.

"McCollum-Adams Trial Highlights." *Pittsburgh Courier*, 27 Dec. 1952: 4.

"Ruby Bares Her Love Life." *Pittsburgh Courier*, 3 Jan. 1953: 1+.

"Ruby McCollum Fights for Life." *Pittsburgh Courier*, 22 Nov. 1952: 15.

"Ruby's Story: Doctor's Threats, Tussle over Gun Led to Slaying." *Pittsburgh Courier*, 10 Jan. 1953: 1+.

"Ruby's Troubles Mount: Named in $100,000 Lawsuit." *Pittsburgh Courier*, 17 Jan. 1953: 1+.

"This Juvenile Delinquency." *Fort Pierce Chronicle*, 12 Dec. 1958.

"The Tripson Story." *Fort Pierce Chronicle*, 6 Feb. 1959.

"Zora's Revealing Story of Ruby's First Day in Court." *Pittsburgh Courier*, 11 Oct. 1952: 1+.

Poetry by Zora Neale Hurston

"Journey's End." *Negro World* (1922).

"Night." *Negro World* (1922).

"O Night." *Stylus* 1 (May 1921): 42.

"Passion." *Negro World* (1922).

"Poem." *Howard University Record* 16 (Feb. 1922): 236.

SELECTED SECONDARY BIBLIOGRAPHY

Books about Hurston

Awkward, Michael, ed. *New Essays on* Their Eyes Were Watching God. Cambridge: Cambridge UP, 1990.

Bloom, Harold, ed. *Modern Critical Interpretations: Zora Neale Hurston's* Their Eyes Were Watching God. New York: Chelsea House, 1987.

Bloom, Harold, ed. *Modern Critical Views: Zora Neale Hurston*. New York: Chelsea House, 1986.

Carter-Sigglow, Janet. *Making Her Way With Thunder: A Reappraisal of Zora Neale Hurston's Narrative Art*. Frankfurt: Peter Lang, 1994.

Cronin, Gloria L., ed. *Critical Essays on Zora Neale Hurston*. New York: G.K. Hall, 1998.

Davis, Rose Parkman. *Zora Neale Hurston: An Annotated Bibliography and Reference Guide*. Westport, CT: Greenwood Press, 1997.

Gates, Henry Louis, Jr., and K.A. Appiah, eds. *Zora Neale Hurston: Critical Perspectives Past and Present*. New York: Amistad Press, 1993.

Glassman, Steve, and Kathryn Lee Seidel, eds. *Zora in Florida*. Orlando: U of Central Florida P, 1991.

Grant, Alice Morgan, ed. *All About Zora: Views and Reviews by Colleagues and Scholars at the Academic Conference of the First Annual Zora Neale Hurston Festival of the Arts, January 26–27, 1990, Eatonville, Florida.* Winter Park, FL: Four-G, 1991.

Hemenway, Robert E. *Zora Neale Hurston: A Literary Biography.* Urbana: U of Illinois P, 1977.

Hill, Lynda Marion. *Social Rituals and the Verbal Art of Zora Neale Hurston.* Washington, DC: Howard UP, 1996.

Holloway, Karla F.C. *The Character of the Word: The Texts of Zora Neale Hurston.* New York: Greenwood Press, 1987.

Howard, Lillie P., ed. *Alice Walker and Zora Neale Hurston: The Common Bond.* Westport, CT: Greenwood Press, 1993.

Howard, Lillie P. *Zora Neale Hurston.* Boston: G.K. Hall, 1980.

Johnson, Yvonne. *The Voices of African American Women: The Use of Narrative and Authorial Voice in the Works of Harriet Jacobs, Zora Neale Hurston, and Alice Walker.* New York: Peter Lang, 1998.

Karanja, Ayana I. *Zora Neale Hurston: The Breath of Her Voice.* New York: Peter Lang, 1999.

Lowe, John. *Jump at the Sun: Zora Neale Hurston's Cosmic Comedy.* Urbana: U of Illinois P, 1994.

Meisenhelder, Susan Edwards. *Hitting a Straight Lick with a Crooked Stick: Race and Gender in the Work of Zora Neale Hurston.* Tuscaloosa: U of Alabama P, 1999.

Nathiri, N.Y., ed. *Zora! Zora Neale Hurston: A Woman and Her Community.* Orlando: Sentinel Communications, 1991.

Neal, Lester A. *Understanding Zora Neale Hurston's* Their Eyes Were Watching God: *A Student Casebook to Issues, Sources, and Historical Documents.* Westport, CT: Greenwood, 1999.

Newson, Adele S. *Zora Neale Hurston: A Reference Guide.* Boston: G.K. Hall, 1987.

Peters, Pearlie Mae Fisher. *The Assertive Woman in Zora Neale Hurston's Fiction, Folklore, and Drama.* New York: Garland, 1998.

Plant, Deborah G. *Every Tub Must Sit on Its Own Bottom: The Philosophy and Politics of Zora Neale Hurston.* Urbana: U of Illinois P, 1995.

Sheffey, Ruthe T., ed. *A Rainbow Round Her Shoulder: The Zora Neale Hurston Symposium Papers.* Baltimore: Morgan State UP, 1982.

Wall, Cheryl A., ed. *Zora Neale Hurston: "Sweat."* New Brunswick, NJ: Rutgers UP, 1997.

Articles and Sections of Books

Abbott, Dorothy. "Recovering Zora Neale Hurston's Work." *Frontiers: A Journal of Women Studies* 12.1 (1991): 174–81.

Abdallah, Ayana Kehema. "Privileged Identity: Representation of Subjectivity in *Their Eyes Were Watching God.*" In *Juxtapositions: The Harlem Renaissance and the Lost Generation.* Ed. Lesley Marx, Loes Nas, and Chandre Carstens. Cape Town, South Africa: University of Cape Town, 2000. 127–35.

Abel, Elizabeth. "(E)Merging Identities: The Dynamics of Female Friendship in Contemporary Fiction by Women." *Signs: Journal of Women in Culture and Society* 6 (1981): 413–35.

Abrahams, Roger D. "Negotiating Respect: Patterns of Presentation among Black Women." *Journal of American Folklore* 88 (1975): 58–80. Reprinted in *Zora Neale Hurston: "Sweat."* Ed. Cheryl A. Wall. New Brunswick, NJ: Rutgers UP, 1997. 73–106.

Adams, Amelia Marie. "Zora Neale Hurston: Native Anthropologist." In *All About Zora: Views and Reviews by Colleagues and Scholars at the Academic Conference of the First Annual Zora Neale Hurston Festival of the Arts, January 26–27, 1990, Eatonville, Florida.* Ed. Alice Morgan Grant. Winter Park, FL: Four-G, 1991. 35–42.

Albright, Angela. "Zora Neale Hurston's *Their Eyes Were Watching God* as a Blueprint for Negro Writing." *Publications of the Arkansas Philological Association* 23.1 (1997): 1–11.

Alps, Sandra. "Concepts of Selfhood in *Their Eyes Were Watching God* and *The Color Purple.*" *Pacific Review* 4 (spring 1986): 106–12.

Anderson, Ronald F. "Zora Neale Hurston's *Their Eyes Were Watching God.*" *Marjorie Kinnan Rawlings Journal of Florida Literature* 5 (1993): 87–90.

Andrews, Adrianne R. "Of Mules and Men and Men and Women: The Ritual of Talking B(l)ack." In *Language, Rhythm, and Sound: Black Popular Cultures into the Twenty-First Century.* Ed. Joseph K. Adjaye and Adrianne R. Andrews. Pittsburgh: U of Pittsburgh P, 1997. 109–20.

Angelou, Maya. Foreword to *Dust Tracks on a Road.* New York: HarperPerennial, 1991. vii–xii.

Anokye, Akua Duku. "Private Thoughts, Public Voices: Letters from Zora Neale Hurston." *Women: A Cultural Review* 7.2 (1996): 150–59.

Ashe, Bertram D. " 'Why Don't He Like My Hair?': Constructing African-American Standards of Beauty in Toni Morrison's *Song of Solomon* and Zora Neale Hurston's *Their Eyes Were Watching God.*" *African American Review* 29.4 (1995): 579–92.

Awkward, Michael. " 'The inaudible voice of it all': Silence, Voice, and Action in *Their Eyes Were Watching God.*" In *Inspiriting Influences: Tradition, Revision, and Afro-American Women's Novels.* New York: Columbia UP, 1989. 15–56; and *Studies in Black American Literature, Vol. 3: Black Feminist Criticism and Critical Theory.* Ed. Joe

Weixlmann and Houston A. Baker Jr. Greenwood, FL: Penkevill Publishing, 1988. 57–109.

Awkward, Michael. Introduction to *New Essays on* Their Eyes Were Watching God. Ed. Michael Awkward. Cambridge: Cambridge UP, 1990. 1–27.

Awkward, Michael. "Race, Gender, and the Politics of Reading." *Black American Literature Forum* 22 (1988): 13–15.

Babb, Valerie. "Women and Words: Articulating the Self in *Their Eyes Were Watching God* and *The Color Purple*." In *Alice Walker and Zora Neale Hurston: The Common Bond*. Ed. Lillie P. Howard. Westport, CT: Greenwood Press, 1993. 83–93.

Babcock, C. Merton. "A Word-List from Zora Neale Hurston." *Publication of the American Dialect Society* 40 (Nov. 1963): 1–11. Published for the Society by the University of Alabama Press.

Baker, Houston A., Jr. Section VII of chapter one, "Figurations for a New American Literary History: Archaeology, Ideology, and Afro-American Discourse." In *Blues, Ideology, and Afro-American Literature: A Vernacular Theory*. Chicago: U of Chicago P, 1984. 56–60. Reprinted as "Ideology and Narrative Form." In *Modern Critical Interpretations: Zora Neale Hurston's* Their Eyes Were Watching God. Ed. Harold Bloom. New York: Chelsea House, 1987. 35–39.

Baker, Houston, A., Jr. "Workings of the Spirit: Conjure and the Space of Black Women's Creativity." In *Workings of the Spirit: The Poetics of Afro-American Women's Writing*. Chicago: U of Chicago P, 1991. 69–101. Reprinted in *Zora Neale Hurston: Critical Perspectives Past and Present*. Ed. Henry Louis Gates Jr. and K.A. Appiah. New York: Amistad Press, 1993. 280–308.

Banks, Kimberly. "Their Eyes Were Watching White Folks as Gods: The Irony of Race Relations in Hurston's Work." *Zora Neale Hurston Forum* 11 (1997): 47+.

Barbeito, Patricia Felisa. " 'Making Generations' in Jacobs, Larsen, and Hurston: A Genealogy of Black Women's Writing." *American Literature* 70.2 (1998): 365–95.

Basu, Biman. " 'Oral Tutelage' and the Figure of Literacy: Paule Marshall's *Brown Girl, Brownstones* and Zora Neale Hurston's *Their Eyes Were Watching God*." *MELUS* 24.1 (1999): 161–76.

Batker, Carol. " 'Love Me Like I Like to Be': The Sexual Politics of Hurston's *Their Eyes Were Watching God*, the Classic Blues, and the Black Women's Club Movement." *African American Review* 32.2 (1998): 199–213.

Bauer, Margaret D. "The Sterile New South: An Intertextual Reading of *Their Eyes Were Watching God* and *Absalom, Absalom!*" *CLA Journal* 36.4 (1993): 384–405.

Baum, Rosalie Murphy. "The Shape of Hurston's Fiction." In *Zora in Florida*. Ed. Steve Glassman and Kathryn Lee Seidel. Orlando: U of Central Florida P, 1991. 94–109.

Beardslee, Karen E. "Self-Actualization in *Their Eyes Were Watching God* and *The Color Purple*." *Zora Neale Hurston Forum* 6.1 (1991).

Beilke, Debra. " 'Yowin' and Jawin': Humor and the Performance of Identity in Zora Neale Hurston's *Jonah's Gourd Vine*." *Southern Quarterly* 36.3 (1998): 21–33.

Bell, Bernard W. "The Harlem Renaissance and the Search for New Modes of Narrative." In *The Afro-American Novel and Its Tradition*. Amherst: U of Massachusetts P, 1987. 93–149. Hurston is discussed on pp. 119–28.

Benesch, Klaus. "Oral Narrative and Literary Text: Afro-American Folklore in *Their Eyes Were Watching God*." *Callaloo* 11.3 (1988): 627–35.

Berrian, Brenda F. "The Evolution of Janie from *Their Eyes Were Watching God* into Three Characters from Marita Golden's *A Woman's Place*." *Zora Neale Hurston Forum* 6.1 (1991).

Bethel, Lorraine. " 'This Infinity of Conscious Pain': Zora Neale Hurston and the Black Female Literary Tradition." In *All the Women Are White, All the Blacks Are Men, But Some of Us Are Brave: Black Women's Studies*. Ed. Gloria T. Hull, Patricia Bell Scott, and Barbara Smith. Old Westbury, NY: Feminist Press, 1982. 176–88. Reprinted in *Modern Critical Interpretations: Zora Neale Hurston's* Their Eyes Were Watching God. Ed. Harold Bloom. New York: Chelsea House, 1987. 9–17.

Birch, Eva Lennox. "Autobiography: The Art of Self-Definition." In *Black Women's Writing*. Ed. Gina Wisker. New York: St. Martin's, 1993. 127–45.

Blake, Emma L. "Zora Neale Hurston: Author and Folklorist." *Negro History Bulletin* 29 (Apr. 1966): 149–50+.

Blickle, Peter. "Reading Zora's Eyes: Vision and Perspective in Zora Neale Hurston's *Their Eyes Were Watching God*." *Zora Neale Hurston Forum* 5.1 (1990): 1–9.

Bloom, Harold, ed. "Zora Neale Hurston, c. 1891–1960." In *Black American Prose Writers of the Harlem Renaissance*. New York: Chelsea House, 1994. 78–93.

Bloom, Harold, ed. "Zora Neale Hurston." *Black American Women Fiction Writers*. New York: Chelsea House, 1995. 56–72. Reprinted in *Major Black American Writers Through the Harlem Renaissance*. Ed. Harold Bloom. New York: Chelsea House, 1995. 102–18.

Bloom, Harold, ed. "Zora Neale Hurston, c. 1891–1960." In *Women Memoirists*. Vol. 1. Philadelphia: Chelsea House, 1998. 108–21.

Boas, Franz. Preface to *Mules and Men*. Philadelphia: J.B. Lippincott, 1935.

Reprinted in *Mules and Men*. New York: HarperPerennial, 1990. xiii-xiv; and as "Preface to *Mules and Men*." In *Modern Critical Views: Zora Neale Hurston*. Ed. Harold Bloom. New York: Chelsea House, 1986. 5.

Bobb, June D. "Taking a Stand on High Ground: The Recreated Self in *Their Eyes Were Watching God*." *Zora Neale Hurston Forum* 2.1 (1987): 1–7.

Boesenberg, Eva. " 'Ah'll Tell 'Em What You Tell Me to Tell 'Em': Dialect(ic)al Speech-Presentation and Narrative Technique in *Their Eyes Were Watching God*." In *Gender—Voice—Vernacular: The Formation of Female Subjectivity in Zora Neale Hurston, Toni Morrison and Alice Walker*. Heidelberg: Universitatsverlag C. Winter, 1999. 82–104.

Boesenberg, Eva. " 'Crayon Enlargements of Life': African American Folklore in *Their Eyes Were Watching God*." In *Gender—Voice—Vernacular: The Formation of Female Subjectivity in Zora Neale Hurston, Toni Morrison and Alice Walker*. Heidelberg: Universitatsverlag C. Winter, 1999. 63–82.

Boesenberg, Eva. "Mules and Women: Sex and Gender in *Their Eyes Were Watching God*." In *Gender—Voice—Vernacular: The Formation of Female Subjectivity in Zora Neale Hurston, Toni Morrison and Alice Walker*. Heidelberg: Universitatsverlag C. Winter, 1999. 45–63.

Boesenberg, Eva. "*Their Eyes Were Watching God* as Bildungsroman." In *Gender—Voice—Vernacular: The Formation of Female Subjectivity in Zora Neale Hurston, Toni Morrison and Alice Walker*. Heidelberg: Universitatsverlag C. Winter, 1999. 27–45.

Boi, Paola. "Moses, Man of Power, Man of Knowledge: A 'Signifying' Reading of Zora Neale Hurston (Between a Laugh and a Song)." In *Women and War: The Changing Status of American Women from the 1930s to the 1950s*. Ed. Maria Diedrich and Dorothea Fischer-Hornung. New York: Berg, 1990. 107–25; and *Looking Inward, Looking Outward: From the 1930s through the 1940s*. Ed. Steve Ickringill. Amsterdam: VU UP, 1990. 136–50.

Boi, Paola. "Zora Neale Hurston's *Autobiographie Fictive*: Dark Tracks on the Canon of a Female Writer." In *The Black Columbiad: Defining Moments in African American Literature and Culture*. Ed. Werner Sollors and Maria Diedrich. Cambridge, MA: Harvard UP, 1994. 191–200.

Bond, Cynthia. "Language, Speech, and Difference in *Their Eyes Were Watching God*." In *Zora Neale Hurston: Critical Perspectives Past and Present*. Ed. Henry Louis Gates Jr. and K.A. Appiah. New York: Amistad Press, 1993. 204–17.

Bone, Robert. "Aspects of the Racial Past." In *The Negro Novel in America.* New Haven: Yale UP, 1958; rev. ed. 1965. 120–52. Hurston is discussed on pp. 126–32. Reprinted as "Ships at a Distance: The Meaning of *Their Eyes Were Watching God.*" In *Modern Critical Views: Zora Neale Hurston.* Ed. Harold Bloom. New York: Chelsea House, 1986. 15–20.

Bone, Robert. "Zora Neale Hurston." In *The Black Novelist.* Ed. Robert Hemenway. Columbus: Charles E. Merrill, 1970. 55–61.

Bordelon, Pamela. "New Tracks on *Dust Tracks*: Toward a Reassessment of the Life of Zora Neale Hurston." *African American Review* 31.1 (1997): 5–21.

Borders, Florence Edwards. "Zora Neale Hurston: Hidden Woman." *Callaloo* 2.2 (1979): 89–92.

Boudreaux, Joan S. "Identification of African Ritual in *Jonah's Gourd Vine.*" In *All About Zora.* Ed. Alice Morgan Grant. Winter Park, FL: Four-G, 1991. 51–60.

Boxwell, D.A. " 'Sis Cat' as Ethnographer: Self-Presentation and Self-Inscription in Zora Neale Hurston's *Mules and Men.*" *African American Review* 26.4 (1992): 605–17.

Boyd, Lisa. "The Folk, the Blues, and the Problems of *Mule Bone.*" *Langston Hughes Review* 13.1 (1994–95): 33–44.

Brantley, Will. "O'Connor, Porter, and Hurston on the State of the World." *Contemporary Literature* 37.1 (1996): 132–44.

Brantley, Will. "Zora Neale Hurston: The Ethics of Self-Representation." In *Feminine Sense in Southern Memoir: Smith, Glasgow, Welty, Hellman, Porter, and Hurston.* Jackson: UP of Mississippi, 1993. 185–239.

Brawley, Benjamin. "One of the New Realists." In *Modern Critical Views: Zora Neale Hurston.* Ed. Harold Bloom. New York: Chelsea House, 1986. 11–12.

Braxton, Joanne M. "Motherless Daughters and the Quest for a Place: Zora Neale Hurston and Era Bell Thompson." In *Black Women Writing Autobiography: A Tradition Within a Tradition.* Philadelphia: Temple UP, 1989. 144–80.

Bray, Rosemary. "Now Our Eyes Are Watching Her." *New York Times Book Review*, 25 Feb. 1990: 11.

Brigham, Cathy. "The Talking Frame of Zora Neale Hurston's Talking Book: Storytelling as Dialectic in *Their Eyes Were Watching God.*" *CLA Journal* 37.4 (1994): 402–19.

Brock, Sabine, and Anne Koenen. "Alice Walker in Search of Zora Neale Hurston: Rediscovering a Black Female Tradition." In *History and Tradition in Afro-American Culture.* Ed. Gunter H. Lenz. Frankfurt: Campus, 1984. 167–80.

Brockman, Kurt. "The Christian and Hoodoo: Religious Motifs in Zora Neale Hurston's *Their Eyes Were Watching God*." *Zora Neale Hurston Forum* 11 (1997): 1–9.

Brown, Alan. " 'De Beast' Within: The Role of Nature in *Jonah's Gourd Vine*." In *Zora in Florida*. Ed. Steve Glassman and Kathryn Lee Seidel. Orlando: U of Central Florida P, 1991. 76–85.

Brown, Lloyd W. "Zora Neale Hurston and the Nature of Female Perception." *Obsidian* 4.3 (1978): 39–45.

Brown, Mary Beth. "Zora Neale Hurston in the Caribbean: Women in Religion and Society." In *A Rainbow Round Her Shoulder: The Zora Neale Hurston Symposium Papers*. Ed. Ruthe T. Sheffey. Baltimore: Morgan State UP, 1982. 104–17.

Burke, Virginia M. "Zora Neale Hurston and Fannie Hurst as They Saw Each Other." *CLA Journal* 20 (June 1977): 435–47.

Burnette, R.V. "Keys to the Kingdom: The Folk Language of Zora Neale Hurston." *Zora Neale Hurston Forum* 2.1 (1987): 10–17.

Burns, Allan F. "Zora as an Anthropologist, Folklorist, Author." In *All About Zora*. Ed. Alice Morgan Grant. Winter Park, FL: Four-G, 1991. 31–34.

Bus, Heiner. "The Establishment of Community in Zora Neale Hurston's 'The Eatonville Anthology' (1926) and Rolando Hinojosa's 'Estampas del Valle' (1973)." In *European Perspectives on Hispanic Literatures of the United States*. Ed. Genevieve Fabre. Houston: Arte Publico Press, 1988. 66–81.

Bush, Roland. " 'Ethnographic Subjectivity' and Zora Neale Hurston's *Tell My Horse*." *Zora Neale Hurston Forum* 5.2 (1991): 11–18.

Bush, Roland E. "Narrative Strategy and Purpose in Zora Neale Hurston's *Mules and Men*." *Zora Neale Hurston Forum* 8.2 (1994): 14–24.

Bush, Trudy Bloser. "Transforming Vision: Alice Walker and Zora Neale Hurston." *Christian Century*, 16 Nov. 1988: 1035–39.

Byrd, James W. "Black Collectors of Black Folklore: An Update on Zora Neale Hurston and J. Mason Brewer." *Louisiana Folklore Miscellany* 6.2 (1986–87): 1–7.

Byrd, James W. "Zora Neale Hurston: A Novel Folklorist." *Tennessee Folklore Society Bulletin* 21.2 (1955): 37–41. Reprinted in *The Harlem Renaissance 1920–1940: Analysis and Assessment, 1940–1979*. Ed. Cary D. Wintz. New York: Garland, 1996. 495–99.

Byrd, Rudolph P. "Shared Orientation and Narrative Acts in *Cane*, *Their Eyes Were Watching God*, and *Meridian*." *MELUS* 17.4 (1991–92): 41–56.

Cairney, Paul. "Writings about Zora Neale Hurston's *Their Eyes Were Watching God*: 1987–1993." *Bulletin of Bibliography* 52.2 (1995): 121–32.

Callahan, Bob. Foreword to *Spunk: The Selected Stories of Zora Neale Hurston*. Berkeley: Turtle Island, 1985. ix–xiii.

Callahan, John. " 'Mah Tongue Is in Mah Friend's Mouf': The Rhetoric of Intimacy and Immensity in *Their Eyes Were Watching God*." In *Modern Critical Interpretations: Zora Neale Hurston's* Their Eyes Were Watching God. Ed. Harold Bloom. New York: Chelsea House, 1987. 87–113. Reprinted in *In the African-American Grain: The Pursuit of Voice in Twentieth-Century Black Fiction*. Urbana: U of Illinois P, 1988. 115–49.

Cantarow, Ellen. "Sex, Race and Criticism: Thoughts of a White Feminist on Kate Chopin and Zora Neale Hurston." *Radical Teacher* 9 (Sept. 1978): 30–33.

Caputi, Jane. " 'Specifying' Fannie Hurst: Langston Hughes's 'Limitations of Life,' Zora Neale Hurston's *Their Eyes Were Watching God*, and Toni Morrison's *The Bluest Eye* as 'Answers' to Hurst's *Imitation of Life*." *Black American Literature Forum* 24.4 (1990): 697–716.

Carby, Hazel. Foreward to *Seraph on the Suwanee*. New York: Harper, 1991. vii-xviii.

Carby, Hazel V. "The Politics of Fiction, Anthropology, and the Folk: Zora Neale Hurston." In *New Essays on* Their Eyes Were Watching God. Ed. Michael Awkward. Cambridge: Cambridge UP, 1990. 71–93. Reprinted in *History and Memory in African-American Culture*. Ed. Genevieve Fabre and Robert O'Meally. New York: Oxford UP, 1994. 28–44.

Caron, Timothy P. " 'Tell Ole Pharoah to Let My People Go': Communal Deliverance in Zora Neale Hurston's *Moses, Man of the Mountain*." *Southern Quarterly* 36.3 (1998): 47–60. Reprinted in *Struggles Over the Word: Race and Religion in O'Connor, Faulkner, Hurston, and Wright*." Macon: Mercer UP, 2000. 82–111.

Carr, Glynis. "Storytelling as *Bildung* in Zora Neale Hurston's *Their Eyes Were Watching God*." *CLA Journal* 31.2 (1987): 189–200.

Carr, Pat, and Lou-Ann Crouther. "Pulling in the Horizon: Death, Sacrifice, and Rabies in Zora Neale Hurston's *Their Eyes Were Watching God*." *Marjorie Kinnan Rawlings Journal of Florida Literature* 4 (1992): 51–57.

Carson, Warren J. "Hurston as Dramatist: The Florida Connection." In *Zora in Florida*. Ed. Steve Glassman and Kathryn Lee Seidel. Orlando: U of Central Florida P, 1991. 121–29.

Cassidy, Thomas. "Janie's Rage: The Dog and the Storm in *Their Eyes Were Watching God*." *CLA Journal* 36.3 (1993): 260–69.

Champion, Laurie, and Bruce A. Glasrud. "Zora Neale Hurston (1891–1960)." In *African American Authors, 1745–1945: A Bio-*

Bibliographical Critical Sourcebook. Ed. Emmanuel S. Nelson. Westport, CT: Greenwood Press, 2000. 259–69.

Charnov, Elaine S. "The Performative Visual Anthropological Films of Zora Neale Hurston." *Film Criticism* 23.1 (1998): 38–47.

Chinn, Nancy. "Like Love, 'A Moving Thing': Janie's Search for Self and God in *Their Eyes Were Watching God.*" *South Atlantic Review* 60.1 (1995): 77–95.

Chinn, Nancy, and Elizabeth E. Dunn. " 'The Ring of Singing Metal on Wood': Zora Neale Hurston's Artistry in 'The Gilded Six-Bits.' " *Mississippi Quarterly* 49.4 (1996): 775–90.

Christian, Barbara. *Black Women Novelists: The Development of a Tradition, 1892–1976.* Westport, CT: Greenwood Press, 1980. 56–61.

Ciuba, Gary. "The Worm against the Word: The Hermeneutical Challenge in Hurston's *Jonah's Gourd Vine.*" *African American Review* 34.1 (2000): 119–33.

Clariett, Kathleen. "The African Face of Moses: Liberator, Lawgiver, and Leader in Zora Neale Hurston's *Moses, Man of the Mountain.*" *Zora Neale Hurston Forum* 11 (1997): 36–44.

Clark, Jean W. "Zora Neale Hurston's *Their Eyes Were Watching God*: The Ephesian Love Mystery." *MAWA Review* 4.2 (1989): 51–54.

Classon, H. Lin. "Re-Evaluating *Color Struck*: Zora Neale Hurston and the Issue of Colorism." *Theatre Studies* 42 (1997): 5–18.

Cobb-Moore, Geneva. "Zora Neale Hurston as Local Colorist." *Southern Literary Journal* 26.2 (1994): 25–34.

Coleman, Ancilla. "Mythological Structure and Psychological Significance in Hurston's *Seraph on the Suwanee.*" *Publications of the Mississippi Philological Association* (1988): 21–27.

Collins, Derek. "The Myth and Ritual of Ezili Freda in Hurston's *Their Eyes Were Watching God.*" *Western Folklore* 55.2 (1996): 137–54.

Connor, Kimberly Rae. "Called to Preach." In *Conversions and Visions in the Writings of African-American Women.* Knoxville: U of Tennessee P, 1994. 110–69.

Cooke, Michael G. "Solitude: The Beginnings of Self-Realization in Zora Neale Hurston, Richard Wright, and Ralph Ellison." In *Afro-American Literature in the Twentieth Century: The Achievement of Intimacy.* New Haven: Yale UP, 1984. 71–109. Reprinted in *Modern Critical Views: Zora Neale Hurston.* Ed. Harold Bloom. New York: Chelsea House, 1986. 139–49.

Cooper, Jan. "Zora Neale Hurston Was Always a Southerner Too." In *The Female Tradition in Southern Literature.* Ed. Carol S. Manning. Urbana: U of Illinois P, 1993. 57–69.

Corkin, Stanley, and Phyllis Frus. "An Ex-Centric Approach to American Cultural Studies: The Interesting Case of Zora Neale Hurston as a Noncanonical Writer." *Prospects* 21 (1996): 193–228.

Cornwell, JoAnne. "Searching for Zora in Alice's Garden: Rites of Passage in Hurston's *Their Eyes Were Watching God* and Walker's *The Third Life of Grange Copeland*." In *Alice Walker and Zora Neale Hurston: The Common Bond*. Ed. Lillie P. Howard. Westport, CT: Greenwood Press, 1993. 97–107.

Crabtree, Claire. "The Confluence of Folklore, Feminism and Black Self-Determination in Zora Neale Hurston's *Their Eyes Were Watching God*." *Southern Literary Journal* 17.2 (1985): 54–66.

Cronin, Gloria L. "Going to the Far Horizon: Zora Neale Hurston and Christianity." *Literature and Belief* 15 (1995): 49–71. Reprinted as "Introduction: Going to the Far Horizon." In *Critical Essays on Zora Neale Hurston*. Ed. Gloria L. Cronin. New York: G.K. Hall, 1998. 1–29.

Crosland, Andrew. "The Text of Zora Neale Hurston: A Caution." *CLA Journal* 37.4 (1994): 420–24.

Curren, Erik D. "Should Their Eyes Have Been Watching God?: Hurston's Use of Religious Experience and Gothic Horror." *African American Review* 29.1 (1995): 17–25.

Dalgarno, Emily. "Words Walking without Masters: Ethnography and Creative Process in *Their Eyes Were Watching God*." *American Literature* 64.3 (1992): 519–41.

Dance, Daryl. "Following in Zora Neale Hurston's *Dust Tracks*: Autobiographical Notes by the Author of *Shuckin' and Jivin'*." *Journal of the Folklore Institute* 16 (1979): 120–26.

Dance, Daryl C. "Zora Neale Hurston." In *American Women Writers: Bibliographical Essays*. Ed. Maurice Duke, Jackson R. Bryer, and M. Thomas Inge. Westport, CT: Greenwood, 1983. 321–51.

Daniel, Janice. " 'De understandin' to go 'long wid it': Realism and Romance in *Their Eyes Were Watching God*." *Southern Literary Journal* 24.1 (1991): 66–76.

Daniel, Walter C. "Zora Neale Hurston's John Pearson: Saint and Sinner." In *Images of the Preacher in Afro-American Literature*. Washington, DC: UP of America, 1981. 83–109.

Davie, Sharon. "Free Mules, Talking Buzzards, and Cracked Plates: The Politics of Dislocation in *Their Eyes Were Watching God*." *PMLA* 108.3 (1993): 446–59.

Davies, Kathleen. "Zora Neale Hurston's Poetics of Embalmment: Articulating the Rage of Black Women and Narrative Self-Defense." *African American Review* 26.1 (1992): 147–59.

Davis, Arthur P. "Zora Neale Hurston." In *From the Dark Tower: Afro-*

American Writers, 1900 to 1960. Washington, DC: Howard UP, 1974. 113–20.

Davis, Jane. "*The Color Purple*: A Spiritual Descendant of Hurston's *Their Eyes Were Watching God.*" *Griot* 6.2 (1987): 79–96.

Dawson, Emma J. Waters. "Redemption Through Redemption of the Self in *Their Eyes Were Watching God* and *The Color Purple.*" In *Alice Walker and Zora Neale Hurston: The Common Bond.* Ed. Lillie P. Howard. Westport, CT: Greenwood Press, 1993. 69–82.

Dean, Lance. "Remembering and Dismembering: The Isolating Powers of Creation in *Their Eyes Were Watching God.*" *Zora Neale Hurston Forum* 7.2 (1993): 1–19.

Dearborn, Mary V. "Black Women Authors and the Harlem Renaissance." In *Pocahontas's Daughters: Gender and Ethnicity in American Culture.* New York: Oxford UP, 1986. 61–70.

Deck, Alice A. "Zora Neale Hurston." In *Epic Lives: One Hundred Black Women Who Made a Difference.* Ed. Jessie Carney Smith. Detroit: Visible Ink Press, 1993. 285–90.

Deck, Alice A. "Zora Neale Hurston, Noni Jabavu, and Cross-Disciplinary Discourse." *Black American Literature Forum* 24.2 (1990): 237–56.

Dee, Ruby. Foreword to *Their Eyes Were Watching God.* Urbana: U of Illinois P, 1991. v–xi.

Demastes, William W., ed. "Zora Neale Hurston." In *American Playwrights, 1880–1945: A Research and Production Sourcebook.* Westport, CT: Greenwood Press, 1995. 206–13.

Dickerson, Vanessa D. " 'It Takes Its Shape from de Shore It Meets': The Metamorphic God in Hurston's *Their Eyes Were Watching God.*" *LIT (Literature, Interpretation, Theory)* 2.3 (1991): 221–30.

Dixon, Melvin. "Keep me from sinking down: Zora Neale Hurston, Alice Walker, and Gayl Jones." In *Ride Out the Wilderness: Geography and Identity in Afro-American Literature.* Urbana: U of Illinois P, 1987. 83–120.

Dixon, Melvin. "Zora Neale Hurston: I'll See You When Your Troubles Get Like Mine." *Zora Neale Hurston Forum* 9.2 (1995): 13.

Dolby-Stahl, Sandra. "Literary Objectives: Hurston's Use of Personal Narrative in *Mules and Men.*" *Western Folklore* 51.1 (1992): 51–63. Reprinted in *Critical Essays on Zora Neale Hurston.* Ed. Gloria L. Cronin. New York: G.K. Hall, 1998. 43–52.

Domina, Lynn. " 'Protection in My Mouf': Self, Voice, and Community in Zora Neale Hurston's *Dust Tracks on a Road* and *Mules and Men.*" *African American Review* 31.2 (1997): 197–209.

Dominguez, Susan. "Snapshots of Twentieth-Century Writers Mary Antin, Zora Neale Hurston, Zitkala-Sa, and Anzia Yezierska. *Centennial Review* 41.3 (1997): 547–52.

Donaldson, Laura E. "Rereading Moses/Rewriting Exodus: The Postcolonial Imagination of Zora Neale Hurston." In *Decolonizing Feminisms: Race, Gender & Empire-Building*. Ed. Sidonie Smith and Julia Watson. Chapel Hill: U of North Carolina P, 1992. 102–17.

Donlon, Jocelyn Hazelwood. "Porches: Stories: Power: Spatial and Racial Intersections in Faulkner and Hurston." *Journal of American Culture* 19.4 (1996): 95–110.

Dorsey, Peter A. "The Varieties of Black Experience: Zora Neale Hurston's *Dust Tracks on a Road* and the Autobiography of Richard Wright." In *Sacred Estrangement: The Rhetoric of Conversion in Modern American Autobiography*. University Park: Pennsylvania State UP, 1993. 165–89.

Dorst, John. "Rereading *Mules and Men*: Toward the Death of the Ethnographer." *Cultural Anthropology* 2.3 (1987): 305–18.

Dove, Rita. Foreword to *Jonah's Gourd Vine*. New York: Quality Paperbacks, 1990. vii–xv.

Dubek, Laura. "The Social Geography of Race in Hurston's *Seraph on the Suwanee*." *African American Review* 30.3 (1996): 341–51.

duCille, Ann. " 'The Intricate Fabric of Feeling': Romance and Resistance in *Their Eyes Were Watching God*." *Zora Neale Hurston Forum* 4.2 (1990): 1–16. Reprinted in *All About Zora* Ed. Alice Morgan Grant. Winter Park, FL: Four-G, 1991. 93–107.

duCille, Ann. "Stoning the Romance: Passion, Patriarchy, and the Modern Marriage Plot." In *The Coupling Convention: Sex, Text, and Tradition in Black Women's Fiction*. New York: Oxford UP, 1993. 110–42.

DuPlessis, Rachel Blau. "Power, Judgment, and Narrative in a Work of Zora Neale Hurston: Feminist Cultural Studies." In *New Essays on Their Eyes Were Watching God*. Ed. Michael Awkward. Cambridge: Cambridge UP, 1990. 95–123. Reprinted in *Critical Essays on Zora Neale Hurston*. Ed. Gloria L. Cronin. New York: G.K. Hall, 1998. 79–99.

DuPlessis, Rachel Blau. *Writing Beyond the Ending: Narrative Strategies of Twentieth-Century Women Writers*. Bloomington: Indiana UP, 1985. 156–58.

Dutton, Wendy. "The Problem of Invisibility: Voodoo and Zora Neale Hurston." *Frontiers* 13.2 (1993): 131–52.

Edwards, Lee R. "Makers of Art, Makers of Life: Creativity and Community in *Sula*, *Their Eyes Were Watching God*, and *The Dollmaker*." In *Psyche as Hero: Female Heroism and Fictional Form*. Middletown, CT: Wesleyan UP, 1984. 188–235.

Eisen, Kurt. "Blues Speaking Women: Performing Cultural Change in *Spunk* and *Ma Rainey's Black Bottom*." *Text & Presentation* 14 (1993): 21–26.

Emmanouelidou, Maria. "Voice and Narrative: Zora Neale Hurston's Materialisation of Afro-American Oral Tradition and Dialect as Literary References." In *Women, Creators of Culture.* Ed. Ekaterini Georgoudaki and Domna Pastourmatzi. Thessaloniki, Greece: Hellenic Association of American Studies, 1997. 171–80.

English, Daylanne K. "Somebody Else's Foremother: David Haynes and Zora Neale Hurston." *African American Review* 33.2 (1999): 283–97.

Estes, David C. "The Neo-African Vatican: Zora Neale Hurston's New Orleans." In *Literary New Orleans in the Modern World.* Baton Rouge: Louisiana State UP, 1998. 66–82.

Fannin, Alice. "A Sense of Wonder: The Pattern for Psychic Survival in *Their Eyes Were Watching God* and *The Color Purple.*" *Zora Neale Hurston Forum* 1.1 (1986): 1–11. Reprinted in *Alice Walker and Zora Neale Hurston: The Common Bond.* Ed. Lillie P. Howard. Westport, CT: Greenwood Press, 1993. 45–56.

Farrah, David. "The Liberation of Spirit and Story in Zora Neale Hurston's *Their Eyes Were Watching God.*" *Shoin Literary Review* 26 (1993): 45–54.

Faulkner, Howard J. "*Mules and Men*: Fiction as Folklore." *CLA Journal* 34.3 (1991): 331–39.

Felker, Christopher D. " 'Adaptation of the Source': Ethnocentricity and 'The Florida Negro.' " In *Zora in Florida.* Ed. Steve Glassman and Kathryn Lee Seidel. Orlando: U of Central Florida P, 1991. 146–58.

Ferguson, SallyAnn. "Folkloric Men and Female Growth in *Their Eyes Were Watching God.*" *Black American Literature Forum* 21.1–2 (1987): 185–97.

Fischer-Hornung, Dorothea. "An Island Occupied: The U.S. Marine Occupation of Haiti in Zora Neale Hurston's *Tell My Horse* and Katherine Dunham's *Island Possessed.*" In *Holding Their Own: Perspectives on the Multi-Ethnic Literature of the United States.* Ed. Dorothea Fischer-Hornung and Heiki Raphael-Hernandez. Stauffenburg, Germany: Tubingen, 2000. 153–68.

Flores, Toni. "Claiming and Making: Ethnicity, Gender, and the Common Sense in Leslie Marmon Silko's *Ceremony* and Zora Neale Hurston's *Their Eyes Were Watching God.*" *Frontiers* 10.3 (1989): 52–58.

Fodde, Luisanna, and Paola Boi. "Zora Neale Hurston, The Black Woman Writer in the Thirties and Forties." In *Looking Inward, Looking Outward: From the 1930s through the 1940s.* Ed. Steve Ickringill. Amsterdam: VU UP, 1990. 127–35.

Ford, Nick Aaron. "Postscript." In *The Contemporary Negro Novel: A Study in Race Relations.* Boston: Meador, 1936. 94–100; reprint, College

Park, MD: McGrath, 1968. 94–100. Reprinted as "A Study in Race Relations—A Meeting with Zora Neale Hurston." In *Modern Critical Views: Zora Neale Hurston*. Ed. Harold Bloom. New York: Chelsea House, 1986. 7–10.

Ford, Sarah. "Necessary Chaos in Hurston's *Their Eyes Were Watching God*." *CLA Journal* 43.4 (2000): 407–19.

Foreman, P. Gabrielle. "Looking Back from Zora, or Talking Out Both Sides My Mouth for Those Who Have Two Ears." *Black American Literature Forum* 24.4 (1990): 649–66.

Fox-Genovese, Elizabeth. "Myth and History: Discourse of Origins in Zora Neale Hurston and Maya Angelou." *Black American Literature Forum* 24.2 (1990): 221–35.

Fox-Genovese, Elizabeth. "To Write My Self: The Autobiographies of Afro-American Women." In *Feminist Issues in Literary Scholarship*. Ed. Shari Benstock. Bloomington: Indiana UP, 1987. 161–80.

Freeman, Alma S. "Zora Neale Hurston and Alice Walker: A Spiritual Kinship." *SAGE: A Scholarly Journal on Black Women* 2.1 (1985): 37–40.

Gabbin, Joanne V. "A Laying on of Hands: Black Women Writers Exploring the Roots of Their Folk and Cultural Tradition." In *Wild Women in the Whirlwind: Afra-American Culture and the Contemporary Literary Renaissance*. Ed. Joanne M. Braxton and Andree Nicola McLaughlin. New Brunswick, NJ: Rutgers UP, 1990. 246–63.

Gambrell, Alice. "Serious Fun: Recent Work on Zora Neale Hurston." *Studies in the Novel* 29.2 (1997): 238–44.

Gates, Henry Louis, Jr. "Color Me Zora: Alice Walker's (Re)Writing of the Speakerly Text." In *Intertextuality and Contemporary American Fiction*. Ed. Patrick O'Donnell and Robert Con Davis. Baltimore: Johns Hopkins UP, 1989. 144–67.

Gates, Henry Louis, Jr. "Zora Neale Hurston: 'A Negro Way of Saying.' " Afterword to editions of *Jonah's Gourd Vine*. New York: Harper & Row, 1990. 207–17; *Moses, Man of the Mountain*. New York: Harper & Row, 1990. 289–99; *Mules and Men*. New York: Harper & Row, 1991. 287–97; *Tell My Horse*. New York: Harper & Row, 1990. 289–99; *Their Eyes Were Watching God*. New York: Harper & Row, 1990. 185–95; *Seraph on the Suwanee*. New York: Harper & Row, 1991. 353–63; and *The Complete Stories: Zora Neale Hurston*. New York: HarperCollins, 1995. 285–94.

Gates, Henry Louis, Jr. "Zora Neale Hurston and the Speakerly Text." In *The Signifying Monkey*. New York: Oxford UP, 1988. 170–216. Reprinted in *Southern Literature and Literary Theory*. Ed. Jefferson Humphries. Athens: U of Georgia P, 1990. 142–69; and *Zora Neale*

Hurston: Critical Perspectives Past and Present. Ed. Henry Louis Gates Jr. and K.A. Appiah. New York: Amistad Press, 1993. 154–203.

Gates, Henry Louis, Jr., and Sieglinde Lemke. "Establishing the Canon." Introduction to *The Complete Stories: Zora Neale Hurston.* New York: HarperCollins, 1995, paperback 1996 by HarperPerennial. ix-xxiii.

Gayle, Addison, Jr. "The Outsider." In *The Way of the New World: The Black Novel in America.* Garden City, NY: Anchor Press, 1975. 139–48. Reprinted in *Modern Critical Views: Zora Neale Hurston.* Ed. Harold Bloom. New York: Chelsea House, 1986. 35–46.

Gayle, Addison. "Zora Neale Hurston: The Politics of Freedom." In *A Rainbow Round Her Shoulder: The Zora Neale Hurston Symposium Papers.* Ed. Ruthe T. Sheffey. Baltimore: Morgan State UP, 1982. 21–26.

Gilbert, Sandra M., and Susan Gubar. "Ain't I a New Woman? Feminism and the Harlem Renaissance." In *No Man's Land: The Place of the Woman Writer in the Twentieth Century, Vol. 3: Letters from the Front.* New Haven: Yale UP, 1994. 121–65.

Giles, James R. "The Significance of Time in Zora Neale Hurston's *Their Eyes Were Watching God.*" *Negro American Literature Forum* 6.2 (1972): 52–53+.

Gloster, Hugh M. "Zora Neale Hurston, Novelist and Folklorist." *Phylon* 4.2 (1943): 153–59. Reprinted in *The Harlem Renaissance 1920–1940, Vol. 6: Analysis and Assessment, 1940–1979.* Ed. Cary D. Wintz. New York: Garland, 1996. 477–83.

Goldenberg, Myrna. "The Barnard Connection: Zora Neale Hurston and Annie Nathan Meyer." In *All About Zora.* Ed. Alice Morgan Grant. Winter Park, FL: Four-G, 1991. 69–78.

Goldstein, Philip. "Critical Realism or Black Modernism? The Reception of *Their Eyes Were Watching God.*" *Reader: Essays in Reader-Oriented Theory, Criticism, and Pedagogy* 41 (1999): 54–73.

Gombar, Christina. "Zora Neale Hurston: Genius of the South." *Great Women Writers, 1900–1950.* New York: Facts on File, 1996. 81–104.

Goodwyn, Floyd. "Nature Imagery in *Their Eyes Were Watching God.*" *Publications of the Mississippi Philological Association* (1990): 90–96.

Gordon, Deborah. "The Politics of Ethnographic Authority: Race and Writing in the Ethnography of Margaret Mead and Zora Neale Hurston." In *Modernist Anthropology: From Fieldwork to Text.* Ed. Marc Manganaro. Princeton, NJ: Princeton UP, 1990. 146–62.

Green, Suzanne D. "Fear, Freedom and the Perils of Ethnicity: Otherness in Kate Chopin's 'Beyond the Bayou' and Zora Neale Hurston's 'Sweat.' " *Southern Studies* 5.3–4 (1994): 105–24.

Haas, Robert. "Might Zora Neale Hurston's Janie Woods Be Dying of Rabies? Considerations from Historical Medicine." *Literature and Medicine* 19.2 (2000): 205–28.

Haddox, Thomas F. "The Logic of Expenditure in *Their Eyes Were Watching God.*" *Mosaic: A Journal for the Interdisciplinary Study of Literature* 34.1 (2001): 19–34.

Hale, Anthony R. "Framing the Folk: Zora Neale Hurston, John Millington Synge, and the Politics of Aesthetic Ethnography." *The Comparatist* 20 (1996): 50–61.

Hale, David G. "Hurston's 'Spunk' and *Hamlet.*" *Studies in Short Fiction* 30.3 (1993): 397–98.

Hapke, Laura. "Hurston: Romance as Antiromance." In *Daughters of the Great Depression: Women, Work and Fiction in the American 1930s.* Athens: U of Georgia P, 1995. 134–41.

Harris, Trudier. "Africanizing the Audience: Hurston's Transformation of White Folks in *Mules and Men.*" *Zora Neale Hurston Forum* 8.1 (1993): 43–58.

Harris, Trudier. "Our People, Our People." In *Alice Walker and Zora Neale Hurston: The Common Bond.* Ed. Lillie P. Howard. Westport, CT: Greenwood Press, 1993. 31–42.

Harris, Trudier. "Performing Personae and Southern Hospitality: Zora Neale Hurston in *Mules and Men.*" In *The Power of the Porch: The Storyteller's Craft in Zora Neale Hurston, Gloria Naylor, and Randall Kenan.* Athens: U of Georgia P, 1996. 1–50.

Harrison, Beth. "Zora Neale Hurston and Mary Austin: A Case Study in Ethnography, Literary Modernism, and Contemporary Ethnic Fiction." *MELUS* 21.2 (1996): 89–106.

Harrison, Elizabeth Jane. "Zora Neale Hurston and Mary Hunter Austin's Ethnographic Fiction: New Modernist Narratives." In *Unmanning Modernism: Gendered Re-Readings.* Ed. Elizabeth Jane Harrison and Shirley Peterson. Knoxville: U of Tennessee P, 1997. 44–58.

Hassall, Kathleen. "Text and Personality in Disguise and in the Open: Zora Neale Hurston's *Dust Tracks on a Road.*" In *Zora in Florida.* Ed. Steve Glassman and Kathryn Lee Seidel. Orlando: U of Central Florida P, 1991. 159–73.

Hastings, Alec. "High John, High Jane: Joining Folklore and Literature in *Their Eyes Were Watching God.*" *Zora Neale Hurston Forum* 8.2 (1994): 1–12.

Hattenhauer, Darryl. "Hurston's *Their Eyes Were Watching God.*" *Explicator* 50.2 (1992): 111–12.

Hayes, Elizabeth T. " 'Like Seeing You Buried': Persephone in *The Bluest Eye, Their Eyes Were Watching God,* and *The Color Purple.*" In *Images*

of Persephone: Feminist Readings in Western Literature. Ed. Elizabeth
T. Hayes. Gainesville: U of Florida P, 1994. 170–94.

Headon, David. " 'Beginning to See Things Really': The Politics of Zora
Neale Hurston." In *Zora in Florida.* Ed. Steve Glassman and Kathryn
Lee Seidel. Orlando: U of Central Florida P, 1991. 28–37.

Helmick, Evelyn. "Zora Neale Hurston." *The Carrell* 11.1–2 (1970): 1–19.
Reprinted in *Feminist Criticism: Essays on Theory, Poetry, and Prose.*
Ed. Cheryl L. Brown and Karen Olson. Metuchen, NJ: Scarecrow,
1978. 254–71.

Hemenway, Robert E. "Crayon Enlargements of Life." In *Modern Critical
Views: Zora Neale Hurston.* Ed. Harold Bloom. New York: Chelsea
House, 1986. 71–81.

Hemenway, Robert. "Folklore Field Notes From Zora Neale Hurston."
Black Scholar 7.7 (1976): 39–46.

Hemenway, Robert. Introduction to *Dust Tracks on a Road.* Urbana: U of
Illinois P, 1984. ix–xxxix.

Hemenway, Robert. "Hurston's Buzzards and Elijah's Ravens." In *A Rainbow Round Her Shoulder: The Zora Neale Hurston Symposium Papers.*
Ed. Ruthe T. Sheffey. Baltimore: Morgan State UP, 1982. 28–41.

Hemenway, Robert. "The Personal Dimension in *Their Eyes Were Watching
God.*" In *New Essays on Their Eyes Were Watching God.* Ed. Michael
Awkward. Cambridge: Cambridge UP, 1990. 29–49.

Hemenway, Robert E. "That Which the Soul Lives By." Introduction to
Mules and Men. Bloomington: Indiana UP, 1978. xi–xxviii. Re-
printed in *Modern Critical Views: Zora Neale Hurston.* Ed. Harold
Bloom. New York: Chelsea House, 1986. 83–95.

Hemenway, Robert. "Zora Neale Hurston and the Eatonville Anthology."
In *The Harlem Renaissance Remembered.* Ed. Arna Bontemps. New
York: Dodd, Mead, 1972. 190–214. Reprinted in *The Harlem Ren-
aissance, 1920–40, Vol. 5: Remembering the Harlem Renaissance.* Ed.
Cary D. Wintz. New York: Garland, 1996. 314–38.

Hemmingway, Beulah S. "Through the Prism of Africanity: A Preliminary
Investigation of Zora Neale Hurston's *Mules and Men.*" In *Zora in
Florida.* Ed. Steve Glassman and Kathryn Lee Seidel. Orlando: U of
Central Florida P, 1991. 38–45.

Henderson, Mae Gwendolyn. "Speaking in Tongues: Dialogics, Dialectics,
and the Black Woman Writer's Literary Tradition." In *Changing Our
Own Words: Essays on Criticism, Theory, and Writing by Black
Women.* Ed. Cheryl A. Wall. New Brunswick, NJ: Rutgers UP, 1989.
16–37. Reprinted in *Aesthetics in Feminist Perspective.* Ed. Hilde
Hein and Carolyn Korsmeyer. Bloomington: Indiana UP, 1993.
119–38.

Hernandez, Graciela. "Multiple Subjectivities and Strategic Positionality: Zora Neale Hurston's Experimental Ethnographies." In *Women Writing Culture*. Ed. Ruth Behar and Deborah A. Gordon. Berkeley: U of California P, 1995. 148–65.

Hickok, Kathy. "*Dust Tracks on a Road*: Phantom and Reality." In *All About Zora*. Ed. Alice Morgan Grant. Winter Park, FL: Four-G, 1991. 109–15.

Hicks, John. "Jumping at 'De Sun'—The Trials of a Genius of the South." (Orlando) *Sentinel Star Florida Magazine*, 9 Oct. 1977: 4–6+. Reprinted as *Zora Neale Hurston: A Portrait*. Orlando: Sentinel Star, 1978.

Hillman, Michael Craig. "*Dust Tracks on a Road* as Literary Biography." *Zora Neale Hurston Forum* 10 (1996): 7–20.

Hite, Molly. "Romance, Marginality, Matrilineage: Alice Walker's *The Color Purple* and Zora Neale Hurston's *Their Eyes Were Watching God*." *Novel* 22.3 (1989): 257–73. Reprinted in *Reading Black, Reading Feminist*. Ed. Henry Louis Gates Jr. New York: Meridian, 1990. 431–53.

Holland, Sharon P. " 'Whose God am I, God?': A Reading of Zora Neale Hurston's *Their Eyes Were Watching God*." In *All About Zora*. Ed. Alice Morgan Grant. Winter Park, FL: Four-G, 1991. 3–15.

Holloway, Karla. "The Emergent Voice: The Word within Its Texts." In *Zora Neale Hurston: Critical Perspectives Past and Present*. Ed. Henry Louis Gates Jr. and K.A. Appiah. New York: Amistad Press, 1993. 67–75.

Holloway, Karla F.C. "Holy Heat: Rituals of the Spirit in Zora Neale Hurston's *Their Eyes Were Watching God*." *Religion and Literature* 23.3 (1991): 127–41.

Holloway, Karla F.C. "Hurston, Zora Neale (1891–1960)." In *The Oxford Companion to Women's Writing in the United States*. Ed. Cathy N. Davidson and Linda Wagner-Martin. New York: Oxford UP, 1995. 408–10.

Holmes, Carolyn L. "Reassessing African American Literature through an Afrocentric Paradigm: Zora N. Hurston and James Baldwin." In *Language and Literature in the African American Imagination*. Ed. Carol Aisha Blackshire-Belay. Westport, CT: Greenwood, 1992. 37–51.

Holmes, Gloria. "Zora Neale Hurston's Divided Vision: The Influence of Afro-Christianity and the Blues." *Zora Neale Hurston Forum* 8.2 (1994): 26–40.

Holt, Elvin. "Zora Neale Hurston (1891–1960)." In *Fifty Southern Writers After 1900: A Bio-Bibliographical Sourcebook*. Ed. Joseph M. Flora and Robert Bain. New York: Greenwood Press, 1987. 259–69.

Holt, Elvin. "Zora Neale Hurston's Essays on Jim Crow and Democracy." *Zora Neale Hurston Forum* 2.2 (1988): 16–21.

hooks, bell. "Saving Black Folk Culture: Zora Neale Hurston as Anthropologist and Writer." In *Yearning: Race, Gender and Cultural Politics.* Boston: South End Press, 1990. 135–43.

hooks, bell. "Zora Neale Hurston: A Subversive Reading." *Matatu* 3.6 (1989): 5–23. Reprinted in *Moving Beyond Boundaries, Vol. 2: Black Women's Diasporas.* Ed. Carole Boyce Davies. New York: New York UP, 1995. 244–55.

Howard, Lillie P., ed. "Introduction: Alice and Zora—'The Call and the Response.' " In *Alice Walker and Zora Neale Hurston: The Common Bond.* Westport, CT: Greenwood Press, 1993. 3–12.

Howard, Lillie P. "Marriage: Zora Neale Hurston's System of Values." *CLA Journal* 21.2 (1977): 256–68.

Howard, Lillie P. "Nanny and Janie: Will the Twain Ever Meet?" *Journal of Black Studies* 12.4 (1982): 403–14.

Howard, Lillie. "*Seraph on the Suwanee.*" Reprinted in *Zora Neale Hurston: Critical Perspectives Past and Present.* Ed. Henry Louis Gates Jr. and K.A. Appiah. New York: Amistad Press, 1993. 267–79.

Howard, Lillie P. " 'Them Big Old Lies.' " *Callaloo* 2.2 (May 1979): 95–97.

Howard, Lillie P. "Zora Neale Hurston."*Dictionary of Literary Biography: Afro-American Writers from the Harlem Renaissance to 1940.* Vol. 51. Ed. Trudier Harris. Detroit: Gale Research, 1987. 133–45.

Howard, Lillie P. "Zora Neale Hurston: Just Being Herself." *Essence* (Nov. 1980): 100–101+.

Hubbard, Dolan. " ' . . . Ah said Ah'd save de text for you': Recontextualizing the Sermon to Tell (Her)story in Zora Neale Hurston's *Their Eyes Were Watching God.*" *African American Review* 27.2 (1993): 167–78. Reprinted in *The Sermon and the African American Literary Imagination.* Columbia: U of Missouri P, 1994. 47–63; and *Critical Essays on Zora Neale Hurston.* Ed. Gloria L. Cronin. New York: G. K. Hall, 1998. 100–114.

Hudson, Gossie Harold. "Zora Neale Hurston and Alternative History." *MAWA Review* 1.2–3 (1982): 60–64.

Hudson, Gossie Harold. "Zora Neale Hurston: Historian, Too." In *A Rainbow Round Her Shoulder: The Zora Neale Hurston Symposium Papers.* Ed. Ruthe T. Sheffey. Baltimore: Morgan State UP, 1982. 91–102.

Hughes, Langston. *The Big Sea.* New York: Knopf, 1940. Pp. 238–40 discuss Hurston. Reprinted as "A Perfect Book of Entertainment in Herself." In *Modern Critical Views: Zora Neale Hurston.* Ed. Harold Bloom. New York: Chelsea House, 1986. 13–14.

Hurd, Myles Raymond. "What Goes Around Comes Around: Characterization, Climax, and Closure in Hurston's 'Sweat.' " *Langston Hughes Review* 12.2 (1993): 7–15.

Hurst, Fannie. Introduction to *Jonah's Gourd Vine*. Philadelphia: J.B. Lippincott, 1934. 7–8.

Hurst, Fannie. "Zora Hurston: A Personality Sketch." *Yale University Library Gazette* 35.1 (1960): 17–22. Reprinted in *Modern Critical Views: Zora Neale Hurston*. Ed. Harold Bloom. New York: Chelsea House, 1986. 21–24.

Hutchings, Kevin D. "Transforming 'Sorrow's Kitchen': Gender and Hybridity in Two Novels by Zora Neale Hurston." *English Studies in Canada* 23.2 (1997): 175–99.

Inman, James A. "Love and Awareness in Hurston's Janie: An Archetypal Connection." *Zora Neale Hurston Forum* 10 (1996): 1–6.

Jablon, Madelyn. "The Zora Aesthetic." *Zora Neale Hurston Forum* 6.1 (1991): 1–15.

Jackson, Blyden. Introduction to *Moses, Man of the Mountain*. Urbana: U of Illinois P, 1984. vii–xix. Reprinted as "Moses, Man of the Mountain: A Study of Power." In *Modern Critical Views: Zora Neale Hurston*. Ed. Harold Bloom. New York: Chelsea House, 1986. 151–55.

Jackson, Blyden. "Some Negroes in the Land of Goshen." *Tennessee Folklore Society Bulletin* 19 (1953): 103–7.

Jackson, Chuck. "Waste and Whiteness: Zora Neale Hurston and the Politics of Eugenics." *African American Review* 34.4 (2000): 639–60.

Jackson, Tommie. "Authorial Ambivalence in Zora Neale Hurston's *Dust Tracks on a Road* and *Their Eyes Were Watching God*." *Zora Neale Hurston Forum* 7.1 (1992): 17–39.

Jacobs, Karen. "From 'Spy-Glass' to 'Horizon': Tracking the Anthropological Gaze in Zora Neale Hurston." *Novel* 30.3 (1997): 329–60.

Johnson, Barbara. "Metaphor, Metonymy and Voice in *Their Eyes Were Watching God*." In *Black Literature and Literary Theory*. Ed. Henry Louis Gates Jr. New York: Methuen, 1984. 205–19. Reprinted in *Textual Analysis: Some Readers Reading*. Ed. Mary Ann Caws. New York: Modern Language Association, 1986. 232–44; *Modern Critical Views: Zora Neale Hurston*. Ed. Harold Bloom. New York: Chelsea House, 1986. 157–73; *Modern Critical Interpretations: Zora Neale Hurston's* Their Eyes Were Watching God. Ed. Harold Bloom. New York: Chelsea House, 1987. 41–57; and *A World of Difference*. Baltimore: Johns Hopkins UP, 1987. 155–71.

Johnson, Barbara. "Moses and Intertextuality: Sigmund Freud, Zora Neale Hurston, and the Bible." In *Poetics of the Americas: Race, Founding, and Textuality*. Ed. Bainard Cowan and Jefferson Humphries. Baton Rouge: Louisiana State UP, 1997. 15–29.

Johnson, Barbara. "Thresholds of Difference: Structures of Address in Zora Neale Hurston." *Critical Inquiry* 12.1 (1985): 278–89. Reprinted in *"Race," Writing, and Difference.* Ed. Henry Louis Gates Jr. Chicago: U of Chicago P, 1986. 317–28; *A World of Difference.* Baltimore: Johns Hopkins UP, 1987. 172–83; and *Zora Neale Hurston: Critical Perspectives Past and Present.* Ed. Henry Louis Gates Jr. and K.A. Appiah. New York: Amistad Press, 1993. 130–40.

Johnson, Barbara, and Henry Louis Gates Jr. "A Black and Idiomatic Free Indirect Discourse." *Reading Zora: Discourse and Rhetoric in* Their Eyes Were Watching God. New York, Methuen, 1987. Reprinted in *Modern Critical Interpretations: Zora Neale Hurston's* Their Eyes Were Watching God. Ed. Harold Bloom. New York: Chelsea House, 1987. 73–85.

Johnson, Lonnell. "The Defiant Black Heroine: Ollie Miss and Janie Mae— Two Portraits from the 30's." *Zora Neale Hurston Forum* 4.2 (1990): 41–46.

Johnson, Maria J. " 'The World in a Jug and the Stopper in (Her) Hand': *Their Eyes Were Watching God* as Blues Performance." *African American Review* 32.3 (1998): 401–14.

Jones, Evora. "Ascent and Immersion: Narrative Expression in *Their Eyes Were Watching God.*" *CLA Journal* 39.3 (1996): 369–79.

Jones, Evora W. "The Pastoral and the Picaresque in Zora Neale Hurston's 'The Gilded Six-Bits.' " *CLA Journal* 35.3 (1992): 316–24.

Jones, Gayl. "Breaking out of the Conventions of Dialect: Paul L. Dunbar and Zora Neale Hurston." *Presence Africaine: Cultural Review of the Negro World* 144 (1987): 32–46. Reprinted in *Liberating Voices: Oral Tradition in African American Literature.* Cambridge, MA: Harvard UP, 1991. 57–69; *Zora Neale Hurston: Critical Perspectives Past and Present.* Ed. Henry Louis Gates Jr. and K.A. Appiah. New York: Amistad Press, 1993. 141–53; and *Zora Neale Hurston: "Sweat."* Ed. Cheryl A. Wall. New Brunswick, NJ: Rutgers UP, 1997. 153–68.

Jones, Gayl. "Dialect and Narrative: Zora Neale Hurston's *Their Eyes Were Watching God.*" In *Liberating Voices: Oral Tradition in African American Literature.* Cambridge, MA: Harvard UP, 1991. 125–39.

Jones, Kirkland C. "Folk Humor as Comic Relief in Hurston's *Jonah's Gourd Vine.*" *Zora Neale Hurston Forum* 1.1 (fall 1986): 26–31.

Jordan, Casper LeRoy, comp. "Hurston, Zora Neale (1891–1960)." In *A Bibliographical Guide to African American Women Writers.* Westport, CT: Greenwood Press, 1993. 133–40.

Jordan, Jennifer. "Feminist Fantasies: Zora Neale Hurston's *Their Eyes Were Watching God.*" *Tulsa Studies in Women's Literature* 7.1 (1988): 105–17.

Jordan, June. "On Richard Wright and Zora Neale Hurston: Notes Toward a Balancing of Love and Hatred." *Black World* 23.10 (1974): 4–8. Reprinted in *Civil Wars*. Boston: Beacon Press, 1981: 84–89 and New York: Touchstone, 1995. 84–89.

Jordan, Rosan Augusta. "Not into Cold Space: Zora Neale Hurston and J. Frank Dobie as Holistic Folklorists." *Southern Folklore* 49.2 (1992): 109–31.

Joyce, Joyce Ann. "Change, Chance, and God in Zora Neale Hurston's *Their Eyes Were Watching God*." In *A Rainbow Round Her Shoulder: The Zora Neale Hurston Symposium Papers*. Ed. Ruthe T. Sheffey. Baltimore: Morgan State UP, 1982. 69–79.

Kadlec, David. "Zora Neale Hurston and the Federal Folk." *Modernism/ Modernity* 7.3 (2000): 471–85.

Kafka, Phillipa. " 'Dis ain't no business proposition. Dis is Uh Love Game': Zora Neale Hurston's Disjunctive Conjunctions and European American Success Myths in *Their Eyes Were Watching God*." In *The Great White Way: African American Women and American Success Mythologies*. New York: Garland, 1993. 155–90.

Kaiser, Laurie. "The Black Madonna: Notions of True Womanhood from Jacobs to Hurston." *South Atlantic Review* 60.1 (1995): 97–105.

Kalb, John D. "The Anthropological Narrator in Hurston's *Their Eyes Were Watching God*." *Studies in American Fiction* 16.2 (1988): 169–80.

Kanwar, Asha S. "Zora: An Indian Perspective." *Zora Neale Hurston Forum* 9.2 (1995): 1–12.

Kaplan, Carla. "The Erotics of Talk: 'That Oldest Human Longing' in *Their Eyes Were Watching God*." *American Literature* 67.1 (1995): 115–42. Reprinted as " 'That Oldest Human Longing': The Erotics of Talk in *Their Eyes Were Watching God*" in *The Erotics of Talk: Women's Writing and Feminist Paradigms*. New York: Oxford UP, 1996. 99–122.

Kaplan, Deborah. "Zora Neale Hurston." In *Critical Survey of Long Fiction: English Language Series*. Vol. 4. Ed. Frank N. Magill. Englewood Cliffs, NJ: Salem Press, 1983. 1389–97.

Karanja, Ayana. "Zora Neale Hurston and Alice Walker: A Transcendent Relationship—*Jonah's Gourd Vine* and *The Color Purple*." In *Alice Walker and Zora Neale Hurston: The Common Bond*. Ed. Lillie P. Howard. Westport, CT: Greenwood Press, 1993. 121–37.

Kayano, Yoshiko. "Burden, Escape, and Nature's Role: A Study of Janie's Development in *Their Eyes Were Watching God*." *Publications of the Mississippi Philological Association* (1998): 36–44.

Kellner, Bruce. " 'Refined Racism': White Patronage in the Harlem Renaissance." In *The Harlem Renaissance Reexamined*. Ed. Victor A. Kramer. New York: AMS Press, 1987. 93–106.

Kennedy, Stetson. "Postscript: The Mark of Zora." In *Reading Black, Reading Feminist: A Critical Anthology*. Ed. Henry Louis Gates Jr. New York: Meridian, 1990. 27–29.

Kennedy, Stetson. "A Star Fell on Florida." In *All About Zora*. Ed. Alice Morgan Grant. Winter Park, FL: Four-G, 1991. 1–2.

Kennedy, Stetson. "Working With Zora." In *All About Zora*. Ed. Alice Morgan Grant. Winter Park, FL: Four-G, 1991. 61–68.

Kilson, Marion. "The Transformation of Eatonville's Ethnographer." *Phylon* 33.2 (1972): 112–19.

Kim, Myung Ja. "Zora Neale Hurston's Search for Self: *Their Eyes Were Watching God.*" *Journal of English Language and Literature* 36.3 (1990): 491–513.

King, Sigrid. "Naming and Power in Zora Neale Hurston's *Their Eyes Were Watching God.*" *Black American Literature Forum* 24.4 (1990): 683–96. Reprinted in *Critical Essays on Zora Neale Hurston*. Ed. Gloria L. Cronin. New York: G.K. Hall, 1998. 115–27.

Kitch, Sally L. "Gender and Language: Dialect, Silence, and the Disruption of Discourse." *Women's Studies* 14.1 (1987): 66–78.

Knudsen, Janice L. "The Tapestry of Living: A Journey of Self-Discovery in Hurston's *Their Eyes Were Watching God.*" *CLA Journal* 40.2 (1996): 214–29.

Kodat, Catheine Gunther. "Biting the Hand That Writes You: Southern African-American Folk Narrative and the Place of Women in *Their Eyes Were Watching God.*" In *Haunted Bodies: Gender and Southern Texts*. Ed. Anne Goodwyn Jones and Susan V. Donaldson. Charlottesville: UP of Virginia, 1997. 319–42.

Krasner, James. "The Life of Women: Zora Neale Hurston and Female Autobiography." *Black American Literature Forum* 23.1 (1989): 113–26.

Kraut, Anthea. "Reclaiming the Body: Representations of Black Dance in Three Plays by Zora Neale Hurston." *Theatre Studies* 43 (1998): 23–36.

Kubitschek, Missy Dehn. " 'Save de Text': History, Storytelling, and the Female Quest in *Their Eyes Were Watching God.*" In *Claiming the Heritage: African-American Women Novelists and History*. Jackson: UP of Mississippi, 1991. 52–68.

Kubitschek, Missy Dehn. " 'Tuh de Horizon and Back': The Female Quest in *Their Eyes Were Watching God.*" *Black American Literature Forum* 17.3 (1983): 109–15. Reprinted in *Modern Critical Interpretations: Zora Neale Hurston's* Their Eyes Were Watching God. Ed. Harold Bloom. New York: Chelsea House, 1987. 19–33.

Kunishiro, Tadao. " 'So Much of Life in Its Meshes!': Alice Walker's *The Color Purple* and Zora Neale Hurston's *Their Eyes Were Watching*

God." *Marjorie Kinnan Rawlings Journal of Florida Literature* 7 (1996): 67–83.

Kuyk, Betty M. "From Coon Hide to Mink Skin: Understanding an Afro-American 'Sense of Place' Through *Their Eyes Were Watching God.*" In *A Rainbow Round Her Shoulder: The Zora Neale Hurston Symposium Papers.* Ed. Ruthe T. Sheffey. Baltimore: Morgan State UP, 1982. 81–90.

Kuyk, Dirk, Jr. "A Novel from an Oral Tradition: Zora Neale Hurston's *Their Eyes Were Watching God.*" In *A Rainbow Round Her Shoulder: The Zora Neale Hurston Symposium Papers.* Ed. Ruthe T. Sheffey. Baltimore: Morgan State UP, 1982. 42–57.

Lamothe, Daphne. "Vodou Imagery, African-American Tradition and Cultural Transformation in Zora Neale Hurston's *Their Eyes Were Watching God.*" *Callaloo* 22.1 (1999): 157–75.

Lanser, Susan Sniader. "African-American Personal Voice." In *Fictions of Authority: Women Writers and Narrative Voice.* Ithaca, NY: Cornell UP, 1992. 201–6.

Lawrence, David Todd. "Folkloric Representation and Extended Context in the Experimental Ethnography of Zora Neale Hurston." *Southern Folklore* 57.2 (2000): 119–34.

Lee, Valerie Gray. "The Use of Folktalk in Novels by Black Women Writers." *CLA Journal* 23.3 (1980): 266–72.

Lemke, Sieglinde. "Blurring Generic Boundaries: Zora Neale Hurston: A Writer of Fiction and Anthropologist." *REAL: The Yearbook of Research in English and American Literature* 12 (1996): 163–77.

Lenz, Gunther H. "Southern Exposures: The Urban Experience and the Re-Construction of Black Folk Culture and Community in the Works of Richard Wright and Zora Neale Hurston." *New York Folklore* 7.1–2 (1981): 3–39.

LeSeur, Geta. "Janie as Sisyphus: Existential Heroism in *Their Eyes Were Watching God.*" *Zora Neale Hurston Forum* 4.2 (1990): 33–40.

Lester, Neal A. "Sounds of Silent Performances: Homoeroticism in Zora Neale Hurston's 'Story in Harlem Slang: Jelly's Tale.' " *Southern Quarterly* 36.3 (1998): 10–20.

Levecq, Christine. " 'Mighty Strange Threads in Her Loom': Laughter and Subversive Heteroglossia in Zora Neale Hurston's *Moses, Man of the Mountain.*" *Texas Studies in Literature and Language* 36.4 (1994): 436–61.

Levecq, Christine. " 'You Heard Her, You Ain't Blind': Subversive Shifts in Zora Neale Hurston's *Their Eyes Were Watching God.*" *Tulsa Studies in Women's Literature* 13.1 (1994): 87–111.

Lewis, Vashti Crutcher. "The Declining Significance of the Mulatto Female as Major Character in the Novels of Zora Neale Hurston." *CLA Journal* 28.2 (1984): 127–49.

Lillios, Anna. "Excursions into Zora Neale Hurston's Eatonville." In *Zora in Florida*. Ed. Steve Glassman and Kathryn Lee Seidel. Orlando: U of Central Florida P, 1991. 13–27.

Lillios, Anna. " 'The Monstropolous Beast': The Hurricane in Zora Neale Hurston's *Their Eyes Were Watching God.*" *Southern Quarterly* 36.3 (1998): 89–93.

Lindroth, James R. "Generating the Vocabulary of Hoodoo: Zora Neale Hurston and Ishmael Reed." *Zora Neale Hurston Forum* 2.1 (1987): 27–34.

Lionnet, Francoise. "Autoethnography: The An-Archic Style of *Dust Tracks on a Road.*" In *Autobiographical Voices: Race, Gender, Self-Portraiture*. Ithaca, NY: Cornell UP, 1989. 97–129. Reprinted in *Reading Black, Reading Feminist: A Critical Anthology*. Ed. Henry Louis Gates Jr. New York: Meridian, 1990. 382–414; *African American Autobiography*. Ed. William L. Andrews. Englewood Cliffs, NJ: Prentice Hall, 1993. 113–37; and (under the name Francoise Lionnet-McCumber) in *Zora Neale Hurston: Critical Perspectives Past and Present*. Ed. Henry Louis Gates Jr. and K.A. Appiah. New York: Amistad Press, 1993. 241–66.

Love, Theresa R. "Zora Neale Hurston's America." *Papers on Language and Literature* 12.4 (1976): 422–37. Reprinted in *Modern Critical Views: Zora Neale Hurston*. Ed. Harold Bloom. New York: Chelsea House, 1986. 47–61.

Lowe, John. "From Mule Bones to Funny Bones: The Plays of Zora Neale Hurston." *Southern Quarterly* 33.2–3 (1995): 65–78.

Lowe, John. "Humor and Identity in Ethnic Autobiography: Zora Neale Hurston and Jerre Mangione." In *Cultural Difference and the Literary Text: Pluralism and the Limits of Authenticity in North American Literatures*. Ed. Winfried Siemerling and Katrin Schwenk. Iowa City: U of Iowa P, 1996. 75–99.

Lowe, John. "Hurston, Humor, and the Harlem Renaissance." In *The Harlem Renaissance Reexamined*. Ed. Victor A. Kramer. New York: AMS Press, 1987. 283–313.

Lowe, John. "Seeing Beyond Seeing: Zora Neale Hurston's Religion(s)." *Southern Quarterly* 36.3 (1998): 77–87.

Lowe, John. "Zora Neale Hurston." In *American Playwrights, 1880–1945: A Research and Production Sourcebook*. Ed. William W. Demastes. Westport, CT: Greenwood Press, 1995. 206–13.

Lupton, Mary Jane. "Black Women and Survival in *Comedy, American Style* and *Their Eyes Were Watching God.*" *Zora Neale Hurston Forum* 1.1 (1986): 38–44.

Lupton, Mary Jane. "Zora Neale Hurston and the Survival of the Female." *Southern Literary Journal* 15.1 (1982): 45–54.

Lurie, Susan. "Antiracist Rhetorics and the Female Subject: The Trials of

Zora Neale Hurston." In *Unsettled Subjects: Restoring Feminist Politics to Poststructuralist Critique*. Durham, NC: Duke UP, 1997. 44–77.

MacKethan, Lucinda H. "Mother Wit: Humor in Afro-American Women's Autobiography." *Studies in American Humor* 4.1–2 (1985): 51–61.

MacKethan, Lucinda H. "Prodigal Daughters: The Journeys of Ellen Glasgow, Zora Neale Hurston, and Eudora Welty." In *Daughters of Time: Creating Woman's Voice in Southern Story*. Athens: U of Georgia P, 1990. 37–63.

Maekawa, Yuji. "Zora Neale Hurston's Biography Revisited." *Zora Neale Hurston Forum* 9.2 (1995): 14–26.

Manuel, Carme. "*Mule Bone*: Langston Hughes and Zora Neale Hurston's Dream Deferred, an African-American Theatre of the Black Word." *African American Review* 35.1 (2001): 77–92.

Marks, Donald R. "Sex, Violence, and Organic Consciousness in Zora Neale Hurston's *Their Eyes Were Watching God*." *Black American Literature Forum* 19.4 (1985): 152–57.

Marsh-Lockett, Carol P. "What Ever Happened to Jochebed? Motherhood as Marginality in Zora Neale Hurston's *Seraph on the Suwanee*." In *Southern Mothers: Fact and Fictions in Southern Women's Writing*. Ed. Nagueyalti Warren and Sally Wolff. Baton Rouge: Louisiana State UP, 1999. 100–110.

Matza, Diane. "Zora Neale Hurston's *Their Eyes Were Watching God* and Toni Morrison's *Sula*: A Comparison." *MELUS* 12.3 (1985): 43–54.

Maxwell, William J. " 'Is It True What They Say About Dixie?': Richard Wright, Zora Neale Hurston, and Rural/Urban Exchange in Modern African-American Literature." In *Knowing Your Place: Rural Identity and Cultural Hierarchy*. Ed. Barbara Ching and Gerald W. Creed. New York: Routledge, 1997. 71–104.

McCarthy, Kevin M. "Three Legal Entanglements of Zora Neale Hurston." In *Zora in Florida*. Ed. Steve Glassman and Kathryn Lee Seidel. Orlando: U of Central Florida P, 1991. 174–82.

McCaskill, Barbara. "The Folklore of the Coasts in Black Women's Fiction of the Harlem Renaissance." *CLA Journal* 39.3 (1996): 273–301.

McCredie, Wendy J. "Authority and Authorization in *Their Eyes Were Watching God*." *Black American Literature Forum* 16.1 (1982): 25–28.

McDowell, Deborah E. Foreword to *Moses, Man of the Mountain*. New York: HarperPerennial, 1991. vii–xxii. Reprinted as "Lines of Descent/Dissenting Lines." In *Zora Neale Hurston: Critical Perspectives Past and Present*. Ed. Henry Louis Gates, Jr. and K.A. Appiah. New York: Amistad Press, 1993. 218–29.

McGowan, Todd. "Liberation and Domination: *Their Eyes Were Watching God* and the Evolution of Capitalism." *MELUS* 24.1 (1999): 109–28.

McKay, Nellie Y. "The Autobiographies of Zora Neale Hurston and Gwendolyn Brooks: Alternate Versions of the Black Female Self." In *Wild Women in the Whirlwind: Afra-American Culture and the Contemporary Literary Renaissance.* Ed. Joanne M. Braxton and Andree Nicola McLaughlin. New Brunswick, NJ: Rutgers UP, 1990. 264–81.

McKay, Nellie. " 'Crayon Enlargements of Life': Zora Neale Hurston's *Their Eyes Were Watching God* as Autobiography." In *New Essays on* Their Eyes Were Watching God. Ed. Michael Awkward. Cambridge: Cambridge UP, 1990. 51–70.

McKay, Nellie. "Race, Gender, and Cultural Context in Zora Neale Hurston's *Dust Tracks on a Road.*" In *Life/Lines: Theorizing Women's Autobiography.* Ed. Bella Brodzki and Celeste Schenck. Ithaca: Cornell UP, 1988. 175–88.

McVicker, Jeanette. "Dislocating the Discourse of Modernism: The Examples of Woolf and Hurston." In *Virginia Woolf: Emerging Perspectives: Selected Papers from the Third Annual Conference on Virginia Woolf.* Ed. Mark Hussey and Vara Neverow. New York: Pace UP, 1994. 313–18.

Meese, Elizabeth A. "Orality and Textuality in *Their Eyes Were Watching God.*" In *Crossing the Double-Cross: The Practice of Feminist Criticism.* Chapel Hill: U of North Carolina P, 1986. 39–53. Reprinted in *Modern Critical Interpretations: Zora Neale Hurston's* Their Eyes Were Watching God. Ed. Harold Bloom. New York: Chelsea House, 1987. 59–71.

Meisenhelder, Susan. "Conflict and Resistance in Zora Neale Hurston's *Mules and Men.*" *Journal of American Folklore* 109.433 (1996): 267–88.

Meisenhelder, Susan. " 'Eating Cane' in Gloria Naylor's *The Women of Brewster Place* and Zora Neale Hurston's 'Sweat.' " *Notes on Contemporary Literature* 23.2 (1993): 5–7.

Meisenhelder, Susan. "Hurston's Critique of White Culture in *Seraph on the Suwanee.*" In *All About Zora.* Ed. Alice Morgan Grant. Winter Park, FL: Four-G, 1991. 79–92.

Menke, Pamela Glenn. " 'The Lips of Books': Hurston's *Tell My Horse* and *Their Eyes Were Watching God* as Metalingual Texts." *The Literary Griot* 4.1–2 (1992): 75–99.

Messent, Peter B. "A Medley of Voices: Zora Neale Hurston's *Their Eyes Were Watching God.*" In *New Readings of the American Novel: Narrative Theory and Its Application.* New York: St. Martin's, 1990. 243–87.

Mikell, Gwendolyn. "The Anthropological Imaginations of Zora Neale Hurston." *Western Journal of Black Studies* 7.1 (1983): 27–35.

Mikell, Gwendolyn. "When Horses Talk: Reflections on Zora Neale Hurston's Haitian Anthropology." *Phylon* 43.3 (1982): 218–30. Reprinted in *Zora Neale Hurston Forum* 5.2 (1991): 1–9; and under the name Gwendolyn Mikell-Remy in *A Rainbow Round Her Shoulder: The Zora Neale Hurston Symposium Papers*. Ed. Ruthe T. Sheffey. Baltimore: Morgan State UP, 1982. 119–32.

Miller, James A. "Janie's Blues: The Blues Motif in *Their Eyes Were Watching God*." In *A Rainbow Round Her Shoulder: The Zora Neale Hurston Symposium Papers*. Ed. Ruthe T. Sheffey. Baltimore: Morgan State UP, 1982. 59–67.

Monroe, Barbara. "Courtship, Comedy, and African-American Expressive Culture in Zora Neale Hurston's Fiction." In *Look Who's Laughing: Gender and Comedy*. Ed. Gail Finney. Langhorne, PA: Gordon and Breach, 1994. 173–88.

Morgan, Kathleen. " 'An Ox upon the Tongue': An Allusion to Aeschylus' *Agamemnon* in Zora Neale Hurston's *Their Eyes Were Watching God*." *Classical and Modern Literature* 15.1 (1994): 57–65.

Morris, Ann R., and Margaret M. Dunn. "Carnival in Eatonville." In *All About Zora*. Ed. Alice Morgan Grant. Winter Park, FL: Four-G, 1991. 17–22.

Morris, Ann R., and Margaret M. Dunn. "Flora and Fauna in Hurston's Florida Novels. In *Zora in Florida*. Ed. Steve Glassman and Kathryn Lee Seidel. Orlando: U of Central Florida P, 1991. 1–12.

Morris, Robert J. "Zora Neale Hurston's Ambitious Enigma: *Moses, Man of the Mountain*." *CLA Journal* 40.3 (1997): 305–35.

Morrison, Toni. "Rootedness: The Ancestor as Foundation." In *Black Women Writers (1950–1980)*. Ed. Mari Evans. Garden City, NY: Doubleday, 1984. 339–45.

Navarro, Mary L., and Mary H. Sims. "Settling the Dust: Tracking Zora Through Alice Walker's 'The Revenge of Hannah Kemhuff.' " In *Alice Walker and Zora Neale Hurston: The Common Bond*. Ed. Lillie P. Howard. Westport, CT: Greenwood Press, 1993. 21–29.

Naylor, Carolyn A. "Cross-Gender Significance of the Journey Motif in Selected Afro-American Fiction." *Colby Library Quarterly* 18.1 (1982): 26–38.

Neal, Larry. Introduction to *Jonah's Gourd Vine*. Philadelphia: J.B. Lippincott, 1971. 5–7. Reprinted as "The Spirituality of *Jonah's Gourd Vine*." In *Modern Critical Views: Zora Neale Hurston*. Ed. Harold Bloom. New York: Chelsea House, 1986. 25–27.

Neal, Larry. "A Profile: Zora Neale Hurston." *Southern Exposure* 1.3-4 (1974): 160–68. Reprinted as "Eatonville's Zora Neale Hurston: A

Profile." In *Visions of a Liberated Future: Black Arts Movement Writings*. New York: Thunder's Mouth Press, 1989. 81–96.

Newson, Adele S. " 'The Fiery Chariot': A One-Act Play by Zora Neale Hurston." *Zora Neale Hurston Forum* 1.1 (1986): 32–37.

Neyland, Leedell W. "Zora Neale Hurston, Author and Folklorist." In *Twelve Black Floridians*. Tallahassee: Florida A & M Foundation, 1970. 43–51.

Nicholls, David G. "Migrant Labor, Folklore, and Resistance in Hurston's Polk County: Reframing *Mules and Men*." *African American Review* 33.3 (1999): 457–79.

Norman, Wilbert Reuben, Jr. "The Use of African American Culture as a Foundation for Community Cohesion and Self-Esteem in *Their Eyes Were Watching God*." *Zora Neale Hurston Forum* 5.1 (1990): 30–37.

North, Michael. " 'Characteristics of Negro Expression': Zora Neale Hurston and the *Negro* Anthology." In *The Dialect of Modernism: Race, Language, and Twentieth-Century Literature*. New York: Oxford UP, 1994. 175–95.

Olaniyan, Tejumola. "God's Weeping Eyes: Hurston and the Anti-Patriarchal Form." *Obsidian II* 5.2 (1990): 30–45.

Olson, Kirby. "Surrealism, Haiti, and Zora Neale Hurston's *Their Eyes Were Watching God*." *Real: The Journal of Liberal Arts* 25.2 (2000): 80–93.

Orlow-Klein, Ingrid M. " 'Witnessing the Ceremony': The Writing of Folklore and Hoodoo in Zora Neale Hurston's *Mules and Men*." *Bulletin of Faculty of Commerce* 38.2 (1994): 33–51.

Orr, Elaine Neil. "Our Confounded Identities: Negotiating Audience in Zora Neale Hurston's *Their Eyes Were Watching God*." *Subject to Negotiation: Reading Feminist Criticism and American Women's Fictions*. Charlottesville: UP of Virginia, 1997. 46–66.

Orser, Frank. "Tracy L'Engle Angas and Zora Neale Hurston: Correspondence and Friendship." *Southern Quarterly* 36.3 (1998): 61–67.

Osinubi, Viktor. "African American Writers and the Use of Dialect in Literature: The Foregrounding of Ethnicity." *Journal of Commonwealth and Postcolonial Studies* 4.1 (1996): 65–77.

O'Sullivan, Maurice J., Jr., and Jack C. Lane. "Zora Neale Hurston at Rollins College." In *Zora in Florida*. Ed. Steve Glassman and Kathryn Lee Seidel. Orlando: U of Central Florida P, 1991. 130–45.

Oxindine, Annette. "Pear Trees Beyond Eden: Women's Knowing Reconfigured in Woolf's *To the Lighthouse* and Hurston's *Their Eyes Were Watching God*." In *Approaches to Teaching Woolf's* To the Lighthouse. Ed. Beth Rigel Daugherty and Mary Beth Pringle. New York: Modern Language Association, 2001. 163–68.

Paquet, Sandra Pouchet. "The Ancestor as Foundation in *Their Eyes Were Watching God* and *Tar Baby*." *Callaloo* 13.3 (1990): 499–515. Reprinted in *Toni Morrison's Fiction: Contemporary Criticism*. Ed. David L. Middleton. New York: Garland, 1997. 183–206.

Patterson, Gordon. "Zora Neale Hurston as English Teacher: A Lost Chapter Found." *Marjorie Kinnan Rawlings Journal of Florida Literature* 5 (1993): 51–60. Reprinted in *Zora Neale Hurston Forum* 7.2 (1993): 39–51.

Pavloska, Susanna. "Zora Neale Hurston's Ethnological Fiction." In *Modern Primitives: Race and Language in Gertrude Stein, Ernest Hemingway and Zora Neale Hurston*. New York: Garland, 2000. 75–98.

Perry, Margaret. "The Short Story." In *Silence to the Drums: A Survey of the Literature of the Harlem Renaissance*. Westport, CT: Greenwood Press, 1976. Pp. 121–24 discuss Hurston.

Peters, Pearlie M. " 'Ah Got the Law in My Mouth': Black Women and Assertive Voice in Hurston's Fiction and Folklore." *Zora Neale Hurston Forum* 6.2 (1992): 11+. Reprinted in *CLA Journal* 37.3 (1994): 293–302.

Plant, Deborah G. "Cultural Collision, Africanity, and the Black Baptist Preacher in *Jonah's Gourd Vine* and *In My Father's House*." *Griot* 14.1 (1995): 10–17.

Plant, Deborah G. "The Folk Preacher and Folk Sermon Form in Zora Neale Hurston's *Dust Tracks on a Road*." *Folklore Forum* 21.1 (1988): 3–19.

Pondrom, Cyrena N. "The Role of Myth in Hurston's *Their Eyes Were Watching God*." *American Literature* 58.2 (1986): 181–202.

Popkin, Michael, ed. "Hurston, Zora Neale (1903–1960)." In *Modern Black Writers: A Library of Literary Criticism*. New York: Frederick Ungar, 1978. 242–47.

Potter, Rich. "Zora Neale Hurston and African American Folk Identity in *Their Eyes Were Watching God*." *Griot* 15.1 (1996): 15–26.

Pratt, Theodore. "A Memoir: Zora Neale Hurston, Florida's First Distinguished Author." *Negro Digest* (Feb. 1962): 52–56.

Pratt, Theodore. "Zora Neale Hurston." *Florida Historical Quarterly* 40.1 (1961–62): 35–40.

Preu, Dana McKinnon. "A Literary Reading of *Mules and Men*, Part I." In *Zora in Florida*. Ed. Steve Glassman and Kathryn Lee Seidel. Orlando: U of Central Florida P, 1991. 46–61.

Pryse, Marjorie. "Zora Neale Hurston, Alice Walker, and the 'Ancient Power' of Black Women." *Conjuring: Black Women, Fiction, and Literary Tradition*. Ed. Marjorie Pryse and Hortense J. Spillers. Bloomington: Indiana UP, 1985. 1–24.

Racine, Maria J. "Voice and Interiority in Zora Neale Hurston's *Their Eyes*

Were Watching God." *African American Review* 28.2 (1994): 283–92.

Rambeau, James. "The Fiction of Zora Neale Hurston." *Markham Review* 5 (summer 1976): 61–64.

Rampersad, Arnold. Foreword to *Mules and Men.* New York: Quality Paperbacks, 1990. xv–xviii.

Rampersad, Arnold. *The Life of Langston Hughes. Vol. 1: 1902–1941: I, Too, Sing America.* New York: Oxford UP, 1986. 150–200. Discusses Hughes's relationship with Hurston.

Ramsey, William M. "The Compelling Ambivalence of Zora Neale Hurston's *Their Eyes Were Watching God.*" *Southern Literary Journal* 27.1 (1994): 36–50.

Raynaud, Claudine. "Autobiography as a 'Lying' Session: Zora Neale Hurston's *Dust Tracks on a Road.*" In *Studies in Black American Literature, Vol. 3: Black Feminist Criticism and Critical Theory.* Ed. Joe Weixlmann and Houston A. Baker, Jr. Greenwood, FL: Penkevill Publishing, 1988. 111–38.

Raynaud, Claudine. " 'Rubbing a Paragraph with a Soft Cloth'? Muted Voices and Editorial Constraints in *Dust Tracks on a Road.*" In *De/Colonizing the Subject: The Politics of Gender in Women's Autobiography.* Ed. Sidonie Smith and Julia Watson. Minneapolis: U of Minnesota P, 1992. 34–64.

Rayson, Ann L. "*Dust Tracks on a Road*: Zora Neale Hurston and the Form of Black Autobiography." *Negro American Literature Forum* 7 (1973): 39–45.

Rayson, Ann L. "The Novels of Zora Neale Hurston." *Studies in Black Literature* 5.3 (1974): 1–10.

Reed, Ishmael. Foreword to *Tell My Horse.* New York: HarperPerennial, 1990. xi–xv.

Reed, Ishmael. "Zora Neale Hurston, Writer." In *Airing Dirty Laundry.* Reading, MA: Addison-Wesley, 1993: 146–51.

Refoe, Annye L. "Their Eyes Were Watching God: The Journey to Self." In *All About Zora.* Ed. Alice Morgan Grant. Winter Park, FL: Four-G, 1991. 23–30.

Reich, Alice. "Pheoby's Hungry Listening." *Women's Studies* 13.1–2 (1986): 163–69.

Reith, Nicole E. "*Dust Tracks on a Road*: Zora Neale Hurston's Autobiography and the Rhetoric of 'Feather-Bed Resistance.' " In *Writing Lives: American Biography and Autobiography.* Ed. Hans Bak and Hans Krabbendam. Amsterdam, Netherlands: VU UP, 1998. 75–81.

Roark, Chris. "Hurston's Shakespeare: 'Something Like a King, Only Bigger and Better.' " *CLA Journal* 40.2 (1996): 197–213.

Roberts, Margaret O. "Nella and Zora: Sisters and Comrades, Writing to Liberate." *Zora Neale Hurston Forum* 2.2 (1988): 1–5.

Robey, Judith. "Generic Strategies in Zora Neale Hurston's *Dust Tracks on a Road.*" *Black American Literature Forum* 24.4 (1990): 667–82.

Rodriguez, Barbara. "On the Gatepost: Literal and Metaphorical Journeys in Zora Neale Hurston's *Dust Tracks on a Road.*" In *Women, America, and Movement: Narratives of Relocation.* Ed. Susan L. Roberson. Columbia: U of Missouri P, 1998. 235–57.

Roemer, Julie. "Celebrating the Black Female Self: Zora Neale Hurston's American Classic (*Their Eyes Were Watching God*)." *English Journal* (Nov. 1989): 70–72.

Rosenberg, Rachel A. "Looking for Zora's *Mule Bone*: The Battle for Artistic Authority in the Hurston-Hughes Collaboration." *Modernism/Modernity* 6.2 (1999): 79–105.

Rosenblatt, Jean. "Charred Manuscripts Tell Zora Neale Hurston's Poignant and Powerful Story." *Chronicle of Higher Education*, 5 June 1991: B4–5.

Rosenblatt, Roger. "*Their Eyes Were Watching God.*" In *Black Fiction.* Cambridge, MA: Harvard UP, 1974. 84–90. Reprinted in *Modern Critical Views: Zora Neale Hurston.* Ed. Harold Bloom. New York: Chelsea House, 1986. 29–33.

Rudolphi, Maria Frias. " 'Marriage Doesn't Make Love': Zora Neale Hurston's *Their Eyes Were Watching God.*" *REDEN* 6.9 (1995): 37–43.

Russell, Sandi. "A Jump at de Sun." In *Render Me My Song: African-American Women Writers from Slavery to the Present.* New York: St. Martin's, 1990. 35–46.

Ryan, Bonnie Crarey. "Zora Neale Hurston—A Checklist of Secondary Sources." *Bulletin of Bibliography* 45.1 (1988): 33–39.

Sadoff, Diane F. "Black Matrilineage: The Case of Alice Walker and Zora Neale Hurston." *Signs* 11.1 (1985): 4–26. Reprinted in *Black Women in America: Social Science Perspectives.* Ed. Micheline R. Malson, Elisabeth Mudimbe-Boyi, Jean F. O'Barr, and Mary Wyer. Chicago: U of Chicago P, 1990. 197–219.

Samuels, Wilfred D. "The Light of Daybreak: Heterosexual Relationships in Hurston's Short Stories." In *Critical Essays on Zora Neale Hurston.* Ed. Gloria L. Cronin. New York: G. K. Hall, 1998. 239–53.

Sanchez-Eppler, Benigno. "Telling Anthropology: Zora Neale Hurston and Gilberto Freyre Disciplined in Their Field-Home-Work." *American Literary History* 4.3 (1992): 464–88.

Saunders, James Robert. "Womanism as the Key to Understanding Zora Neale Hurston's *Their Eyes Were Watching God* and Alice Walker's *The Color Purple.*" *Hollins Critic* 25.4 (1988): 1–11.

Schamburger, Nancy E. "Beyond *Jane Eyre*: The Maturity of Tea Cake and

Janie in *Their Eyes Were Watching God.*" *Zora Neale Hurston Forum* 6.2 (1992): 1–9.

Schmidt, Rita T. "The Fiction of Zora Neale Hurston: An Assertion of Black Womanhood." *Ilha do Desterro: A Journal of Language and Literature* 14.2 (1985): 53–70.

Schwalbenberg, Peter. "Time as Point of View in Zora Neale Hurston's *Their Eyes Were Watching God.*" *Negro American Literature Forum* 10.3 (1976): 104–5+.

Seidel, Kathryn Lee. "The Artist in the Kitchen: The Economics of Creativity in Hurston's 'Sweat.' " In *Zora in Florida.* Ed. Steve Glassman and Kathryn Lee Seidel. Orlando: U of Central Florida P, 1991. 110–20. Reprinted in *Zora Neale Hurston: "Sweat."* Ed. Cheryl A. Wall. New Brunswick, NJ: Rutgers UP, 1997. 169–81.

Setterberg, Fred. "Zora Neale Hurston in the Land of 1,000 Dances." *Georgia Review* 46.4 (1992): 627–43. Reprinted in *The Roads Taken: Travels through America's Literary Landscapes.* Athens: U of Georgia P, 1993. 104–31.

Sheffey, Ruthe T. "Behold the Dreamers: Katherine Dunham and Zora Neale Hurston Among the Maroons." In *Trajectory: Fueling the Future and Preserving the African-American Past: Essays in Criticism (1962–1986).* Baltimore: Morgan State UP, 1989. 183–201. Reprinted in *Zora Neale Hurston Forum* 5.2 (1991): 20–29.

Sheffey, Ruthe T. "Zora Hurston and Langston Hughes's 'Mule Bone': An Authentic Folk Comedy and the Compromised Tradition." Reprinted in *Trajectory: Fueling the Future and Preserving the African-American Past: Essays in Criticism (1962–1986).* Baltimore: Morgan State UP, 1989. 211–31.

Sheffey, Ruthe T. "Zora Neale Hurston: The Morgan Connection." *MAP: Multi-Ethnicity in American Publishing,* Middle Atlantic Region (winter 1976). Reprinted in *A Rainbow Round Her Shoulder: The Zora Neale Hurston Symposium Papers.* Ed. Ruthe T. Sheffey. Baltimore: Morgan State UP, 1982. 15–20; and *Trajectory: Fueling the Future and Preserving the African-American Past: Essays in Criticism (1962–1986).* Baltimore: Morgan State UP, 1989. 203–9.

Sheffey, Ruthe T. "Zora Neale Hurston's *Moses, Man of the Mountain*: A Fictionalized Manifesto on the Imperatives of Black Leadership." *CLA Journal* 29.2 (1985): 206–20. Reprinted in *Trajectory: Fueling the Future and Preserving the African-American Past: Essays in Criticism (1962–1986).* Baltimore: Morgan State UP, 1989. 165–81; and *Critical Essays on Zora Neale Hurston.* Ed. Gloria L. Cronin. New York: G.K. Hall, 1998. 154–64.

Sheppard, David M. "Living by Comparison: Janie and Her Discontents." *English Language Notes* 30.2 (1992): 63–75.

Siferd, Nancy B. "Zora Neale Hurston: Foremost Foremother of African-American Women's Fiction." In *All About Zora.* Ed. Alice Morgan Grant. Winter Park, FL: Four-G, 1991. 43–50.

Simpson, Valerie. "Zora Neale Hurston: Social Advocate." *Publications of the Mississippi Philological Association* (1999): 34–38.

Smart, Nick. "Other Jonahs: Rhetoric and Redemption in *Jonah's Gourd Vine.*" In *Proceedings of the Northeast Regional Meeting of the Conference on Christianity and Literature.* Weston, MA: Regis College, 1996. 108–13.

Smith, Barbara. "Sexual Politics and the Fiction of Zora Neale Hurston." *Radical Teacher* 8 (May 1978): 26–30.

Smith, Sidonie. "Diasporan Subjectivity and Identity Politics in Zora Neale Hurston's *Dust Tracks on a Road.*" In *Subjectivity, Identity, and the Body: Women's Autobiographical Practices in the Twentieth Century.* Bloomington: Indiana UP, 1993. 103–25.

Smith-Wright, Geraldine. "In Spite of the Klan: Ghosts in the Fiction of Black Women Writers." In *Haunting the House of Fiction: Feminist Perspectives on Ghost Stories by American Women.* Ed. Lynette Carpenter and Wendy K. Kolmar. Knoxville: U of Tennessee P, 1991. 142–65.

Smith-Wright, Geraldine. "Revision as Collaboration: Zora Neale Hurston's *Their Eyes Were Watching God* as Source for Alice Walker's *The Color Purple.*" *SAGE* 4.2 (1987): 20–25.

Snyder, Phillip A. "Zora Neale Hurston's *Dust Tracks*: Autobiography and Artist Novel." In *Critical Essays on Zora Neale Hurston.* Ed. Gloria L. Cronin. New York: G.K. Hall, 1998. 173–89.

Sollors, Werner. "Anthropological and Sociological Tendencies in American Literature of the 1930's and 1940's: Richard Wright, Zora Neale Hurston and American Culture." In *Looking Inward, Looking Outward: From the 1930s through the 1940s.* Ed. Steve Ickringill. Amsterdam: VU UP, 1990. 22–75.

Southerland, Ellease. "The Influence of Voodoo on the Fiction of Zora Neale Hurston." In *Sturdy Black Bridges: Visions of Black Women in Literature.* Ed. Roseann P. Bell, Bettye J. Parker, and Beverly Guy-Sheftall. Garden City, NY: Anchor Press, 1979. 172–83.

Southerland, Ellease. "The Novelist-Anthropologist's Life/Works: Zora Neale Hurston." *Black World* 23.10 (1974): 20–30.

Speisman, Barbara. "From 'Spears' to *The Great Day*: Zora Neale Hurston's Vision of a Real Negro Theater." *Southern Quarterly* 36.3 (1998): 34–46.

Speisman, Barbara. "A Tea with Zora and Marjorie: A Series of Vignettes Based on the Unique Friendship of Zora Neale Hurston and Marjorie Kinnan Rawlings." *Rawlings Journal* 1 (1988): 67–100.

Speisman, Barbara. "Voodoo as Symbol in *Jonah's Gourd Vine*." In *Zora in Florida*. Ed. Steve Glassman and Kathryn Lee Seidel. Orlando: U of Central Florida P, 1991. 86–93.

St. Clair, Janet. "The Courageous Undertow of Zora Neale Hurston's *Seraph on the Suwanee*." *Modern Language Quarterly* 50.1 (1989): 38–57. Reprinted in *Critical Essays on Zora Neale Hurston*. Ed. Gloria L. Cronin. New York: G.K. Hall, 1998. 197–212.

Stanford, Ann Folwell. "Dynamics of Change: Men and Co-Feeling in the Fiction of Zora Neale Hurston and Alice Walker." In *Alice Walker and Zora Neale Hurston: The Common Bond*. Ed. Lillie P. Howard. Westport, CT: Greenwood Press, 1993. 109–19.

Staub, Michael E. "Zora Neale Hurston: Talking Black, Talking Back." In *Voices of Persuasion: Politics of Representation in 1930s America*. Cambridge: Cambridge UP, 1994. 79–109.

Stein, Rachel. "Rerooting the Sacred Tree: Nature, Black Women, and Voodoo in Zora Neale Hurston's *Tell My Horse* and *Their Eyes Were Watching God*." In *Shifting the Ground: American Women Writers' Revisions of Nature, Gender, and Race*. Charlottesville: UP of Virginia, 1997. 53–83.

Stepto, Robert. "Distrust of the Reader in Afro-American Narratives." In *Reconstructing American Literary History*. Ed. Sacvan Bercovitch. Cambridge, MA: Harvard UP, 1986. 300–322.

Stepto, Robert. *From Behind the Veil: A Study of Afro-American Narrative*. Urbana: U of Illinois P, 1979. 164–67. Reprinted as "Ascent, Immersion, Narration." In *Modern Critical Interpretations: Zora Neale Hurston's* Their Eyes Were Watching God. Ed. Harold Bloom. New York: Chelsea House, 1987. 5–8.

Stetson, Erlene. "*Their Eyes Were Watching God*: A Woman's Story." *Regionalism and the Female Imagination* 4.1 (1978): 30–36.

Story, Ralph D. "Gender and Ambition: Zora Neale Hurston in the Harlem Renaissance." *Black Scholar* 20.2 (1989): 25–31. Reprinted in *Critical Essays on Zora Neale Hurston*. Ed. Gloria L. Cronin. New York: G.K. Hall, 1998. 128–38.

Story, Ralph D. "Patronage and the Harlem Renaissance: You Get What You Pay For." *CLA Journal* 32.3 (1989): 284–95.

Sundahl, Daniel J. "Zora Neale Hurston: A Voice of Her Own/An Entertainment in Herself." *Southern Studies* N.S. 1.3 (1990): 243–56.

Sundquist, Eric J. " 'The Drum with the Man Skin': *Jonah's Gourd Vine*." In *The Hammers of Creation: Folk Culture in Modern African-American Fiction*. Athens: U of Georgia P, 1992. 49–91. Reprinted in *Zora Neale Hurston: Critical Perspectives Past and Present*. Ed. Henry Louis Gates Jr. and K.A. Appiah. New York: Amistad Press, 1993. 13–15.

Szeto, Dominic. "Haiti as Historical Sign and Allegorical Symbol of Resistance Culture in the Writings of Zora Neale Hurston and Aime Cesaire." *Zora Neale Hurston Forum* 11 (1997): 20–33.

Tate, Claudia. "Hitting 'A Straight Lick with a Crooked Stick': *Seraph on the Suwanee*, Zora Neale Hurston's Whiteface Novel." In *The Psychoanalysis of Race*. Ed. Christopher Lane. New York: Columbia UP, 1998. 380–94.

Tate, Claudia. "Mourning, Humor, and Reparation: Detecting the Joke in *Seraph on the Suwanee*, by Zora Neale Hurston." In *Psychoanalysis and Black Novels*. New York: Oxford UP, 1998. 148–77.

Tate, Claudia. "To Vote and to Marry: Locating a Gendered and Historicized Model of Interpretation." In *Domestic Allegories of Political Desire: The Black Heroine's Text at the Turn of the Century*. New York: Oxford UP, 1992. 70–96.

Thomas, Marion A. "Reflections on the Sanctified Church as Portrayed by Zora Neale Hurston." *Black American Literature Forum* 25.1 (1991): 35–41. Reprinted in *Critical Essays on Zora Neale Hurston*. Ed. Gloria L. Cronin. New York: G.K. Hall, 1998. 215–21.

Thompson, Gordon E. "Projecting Gender: Personification in the Works of Zora Neale Hurston." *American Literature* 66.4 (1994): 737–63.

Thornton, Jerome E. " 'Goin' on de Muck': The Paradoxical Journey of the Black American Hero." *CLA Journal* 31.3 (1988): 261–80.

Townsend, Rosemary. "The Writing of Their Lives: A Comparative Exploration of Two Women Writers." In *Juxtapositions: The Harlem Renaissance and the Lost Generation*. Ed. Lesley Marx, Loes Nas, and Chandre Carstens. Cape Town, South Africa: University of Cape Town, 2000. 136–47.

Traub, Valerie. "Rainbows of Darkness: Deconstructing Shakespeare in the Work of Gloria Naylor and Zora Neale Hurston." In *Cross-Cultural Performances: Differences in Women's Re-Visions of Shakespeare*. Ed. Marianne Novy. Urbana: U of Illinois P, 1993. 150–64.

Trefzer, Annette. "Floating Homes and Signifiers in Hurston's and Rawlings's Autobiographies." *Southern Quarterly* 36.3 (1998): 68–76.

Trefzer, Annette. " 'Let Us All Be Kissing-Friends?': Zora Neale Hurston and Race Politics in Dixie." *Journal of American Studies* 31.1 (1997): 69–78.

Trefzer, Annette. "Possessing the Self: Caribbean Identities in Zora Neale Hurston's *Tell My Horse*." *African American Review* 34.2 (2000): 299–312.

Trombold, John. "The Minstrel Show Goes to the Great War: Zora Neale Hurston's Mass Cultural Other." *MELUS* 24.1 (1999): 85–107.

Turner, Darwin T. Foreword to *Dust Tracks on a Road*. New York: Arno Press, 1969. i–v.

Turner, Darwin T. "The Negro Novelist and the South." *Southern Humanities Review* 1 (1967): 21–29.

Turner, Darwin T. "Zora Neale Hurston: One More Time." *Langston Hughes Review* 11.2 (1992): 34–37.

Turner, Darwin T. "Zora Neale Hurston: The Wandering Minstrel." In *In a Minor Chord: Three Afro-American Writers and Their Search for Identity.* Carbondale: Southern Illinois UP, 1971. 89–120.

Unter, Jennifer. "Virginia Woolf's Clarissa and Zora Neale Hurston's Janie: Images of Women in Literature." *Mount Olive Review* 6 (1992): 56–60.

Urgo, Joseph R. " 'The Tune is the Unity of the Thing': Power and Vulnerability in Zora Neale Hurston's *Their Eyes Were Watching God.*" *Southern Literary Journal* 23.2 (1991): 40–54.

Vickers, Anita M. "The Reaffirmation of African-American Dignity Through the Oral Tradition in Zora Neale Hurston's *Their Eyes Were Watching God.*" *CLA Journal* 37.3 (1994): 303–15.

Wainwright, Mary Katherine. "The Aesthetics of Community: The Insular Black Community as Theme and Focus in Hurston's *Their Eyes Were Watching God.*" In *The Harlem Renaissance: Revaluations.* Ed. Amritjit Singh, William S. Shiver, and Stanley Brodwin. New York: Garland, 1989. 233–43.

Wainwright, Mary Katherine. " 'The Map of Dixie on my Tongue' and Other Challenges to Autobiographical Conventions in Hurston's *Dust Tracks on a Road.*" In *All About Zora.* Ed. Alice Morgan Grant. Winter Park, FL: Four-G, 1991. 117–26.

Wainwright, Mary Katherine. "Subversive Female Folk Tellers in *Mules and Men.*" In *Zora in Florida.* Ed. Steve Glassman and Kathryn Lee Seidel. Gainesville: U of Florida P, 1991. 62–75.

Wald, Priscilla. " 'Becoming Colored': The Self-Authorized Language of Difference in Zora Neale Hurston." *American Literary History* 2.1 (1990): 79–100.

Walker, Alice. "Looking for Zora." *Ms.* (Mar. 1975): 74–79+. Reprinted in *I Love Myself When I Am Laughing . . . and Then Again When I Am Looking Mean and Impressive: A Zora Neale Hurston Reader.* Ed. Alice Walker. Old Westbury, NY: Feminist Press, 1979. 297–313; *Chant of Saints: A Gathering of Afro-American Literature, Art, and Scholarship.* Ed. Michael S. Harper and Robert B. Stepto. Urbana: U of Illinois P, 1979. 377–92; *In Search of Our Mothers' Gardens.* San Diego: Harcourt, Brace, Jovanovich, 1983. 93–116; *Between Women: Biographers, Novelists, Critics, Teachers, and Artists Write about Their Work on Women.* Ed. Carol Ascher, Louise DeSalvo, and Sara Ruddick. Boston: Beacon Press, 1984. 431–47; *Modern Critical Views: Zora Neale Hurston.* Ed. Harold Bloom. New

York: Chelsea House, 1986. 107–22; and *Zora Neale Hurston: "Sweat."* Ed. Cheryl A. Wall. New Brunswick, NJ: Rutgers UP, 1997. 211–30.

Walker, Alice. "On Refusing to Be Humbled by Second Place in a Contest You Did Not Design." In *I Love Myself When I Am Laughing . . . and Then Again When I Am Looking Mean and Impressive: A Zora Neale Hurston Reader.* Ed. Alice Walker. Old Westbury, NY: Feminist Press, 1979. 1–5. Reprinted in *Modern Critical Views: Zora Neale Hurston.* Ed. Harold Bloom. New York: Chelsea House, 1986. 103–6.

Walker, Alice. "Zora Neale Hurston: A Cautionary Tale and a Partisan View." Foreword to Robert E. Hemenway's *Zora Neale Hurston: A Literary Biography.* Urbana: U of Illinois P, 1980. xi-xviii. Reprinted in *In Search of Our Mothers' Gardens.* San Diego: Harcourt, Brace, Jovanovich, 1983. 83–92; *Modern Critical Views: Zora Neale Hurston.* Ed. Harold Bloom. New York: Chelsea House, 1986. 63–69; and *Alice Walker and Zora Neale Hurston: The Common Bond.* Ed. Lillie P. Howard. Westport, CT: Greenwood Press, 1993. 13–19.

Walker, Pierre A. "Zora Neale Hurston and the Post-Modern Self in *Dust Tracks on a Road.*" *African American Review* 32.3 (1998): 387–99.

Walker, S. Jay. "Zora Neale Hurston's *Their Eyes Were Watching God*: Black Novel of Sexism." *Modern Fiction Studies* 20.4 (1974–75): 519–27.

Wall, Cheryl A. Introduction to *Zora Neale Hurston: "Sweat."* New Brunswick, NJ: Rutgers UP, 1997. 3–19.

Wall, Cheryl. "*Mules and Men* and Women: Zora Neale Hurston's Strategies of Narration and Visions of Female Empowerment." *Black American Literature Forum* 23.4 (1989): 661–80. Reprinted in *Critical Essays on Zora Neale Hurston.* Ed. Gloria L. Cronin. New York: G.K. Hall, 1998. 53–70.

Wall, Cheryl A. "Zora Neale Hurston." In *African-American Writers.* Ed. Valerie Smith, Lea Baechler, and A. Walton Litz. New York: Charles Scribner's Sons, 1991. 205–18.

Wall, Cheryl. "Zora Neale Hurston: Changing Her Own Words" In *American Novelists Revisited: Essays in Feminist Criticism.* Ed. Fritz Fleischmann. Boston: G.K. Hall, 1982. 371–93. Reprinted in *Zora Neale Hurston: Critical Perspectives Past and Present.* Ed. Henry Louis Gates Jr. and K.A. Appiah. New York: Amistad Press, 1993. 76–97.

Wall, Cheryl A. "Zora Neale Hurston's Traveling Blues." In *Women of the Harlem Renaissance.* Bloomington: U of Indiana P, 1995. 139–99.

Wallace, Michele. "Who Dat Say Who Dat When I Say Who Dat?: Zora Neale Hurston Then and Now." *Village Voice Literary Supplement* (Apr. 1988): 18–21.

Wallerstein, Nicholas. "Feminist/Womanist Liberation Hermeneutics and the Kyriologic of Zora Neale Hurston." *Literary Griot* 11.2 (1999): 97–115.

Walters, Keith. " 'He Can Read My Writing but He Sho' Can't Read My Mind': Zora Neale Hurston's Revenge in *Mules and Men*." *Journal of American Folklore* 112.445 (1999): 343–71.

Ward, Cynthia. "From the Suwanee to Egypt, There's No Place like Home." *PLMA* 115.1 (2000): 75–88.

Washington, Mary Helen. Foreword to *Their Eyes Were Watching God*. New York: Harper & Row, 1990. vii-xiv.

Washington, Mary Helen. " 'I Love the Way Janie Crawford Left Her Husbands': Zora Neale Hurston's Emergent Female Hero." In *Invented Lives: Narratives of Black Women 1860–1960*. Ed. Mary Helen Washington. New York: Doubleday, 1987. 237–54. Reprinted in *Zora Neale Hurston: Critical Perspectives Past and Present*. Ed. Henry Louis Gates Jr. and K.A. Appiah. New York: Amistad Press, 1993. 98–109; and *Zora Neale Hurston: "Sweat."* Ed. Cheryl A. Wall. New Brunswick, NJ: Rutgers UP, 1997. 193–209.

Washington, Mary Helen. "A Woman Half in Shadow." In *I Love Myself When I Am Laughing . . . and Then Again When I Am Looking Mean and Impressive: A Zora Neale Hurston Reader*. Ed. Alice Walker. Old Westbury, NY: Feminist Press, 1979. 7–25. Reprinted in *Modern Critical Views: Zora Neale Hurston*. Ed. Harold Bloom. New York: Chelsea House, 1986. 123–38.

Washington, Mary Helen. "Zora Neale Hurston: The Black Woman's Search for Identity." *Black World* 21.10 (1972): 68–75.

Watson, Carol McAlpine. "Looking Within: Race Consciousness and Self-Criticism, 1921–1945." In *Prologue: The Novels of Black American Women, 1891–1965*. Westport, CT: Greenwood Press, 1985. 33–69.

Watson, Reginald. "Mulatto as Object in Zora Neale Hurston's *Their Eyes Were Watching God* and John O. Killens's *The Cotillion*." *CLA Journal* 43.4 (2000): 383–406.

Welsh-Asante, Kariamu. "Dance as Metaphor in Zora Neale Hurston's *Their Eyes Were Watching God*." *Zora Neale Hurston Forum* 4.2 (1990): 18–31.

Werner, Craig. "Zora Neale Hurston." In *Modern American Women Writers*. Ed. Elaine Showalter, Lea Baechler, and A. Walton Litz. New York: Charles Scribner's Sons, 1991. 221–33.

Whitlow, Roger. *Black American Literature: A Critical History*. Chicago: Nelson Hall, 1973, Rev. ed. 1976. 103–6.

Wilentz, Gay. "Defeating the False God: Janie's Self-Determination in Zora Neale Hurston's *Their Eyes Were Watching God*." In *Faith of a (Woman) Writer*. Ed. Alice Kessler-Harris and William McBrien. New York: Greenwood, 1988. 285–91.

Wilentz, Gay. "White Patron and Black Artist: The Correspondence of Fannie Hurst and Zora Neale Hurston." *Library Chronicle of the University of Texas* 35 (1986): 20–43.

Williams, Delores S. "Black Women's Literature and the Task of Feminist Theology." In *Immaculate & Powerful: The Female in Sacred Image and Social Reality*. Ed. Clarissa W. Atkinson, Constance H. Buchanan, and Margaret R. Miles. Boston: Beacon Press, 1985. 88–110.

Williams, Donna M. "Our Love/Hate Relationship with Zora Neale Hurston." *Black Collegian* 24.3 (1994): 86+.

Williams, Sherley Anne. Foreword to *Their Eyes Were Watching God*. Urbana: U of Illinois P, 1978. Reprinted as "Janie's Burden." In *Modern Critical Views: Zora Neale Hurston*. Ed. Harold Bloom. New York: Chelsea House, 1986. 97–102.

Williams, Sherley Anne. Introduction to *Their Eyes Were Watching God*. Urbana: U of Illinois P, 1991. xiii–xxxii.

Willis, Miriam Decosta. "Folklore and the Creative Artist: Lydia Cabrera and Zora Neale Hurston." *CLA Journal* 27.1 (1983): 81–90.

Willis, Susan. "Wandering: Zora Neale Hurston's Search for Self and Method." *Specifying: Black Women Writing the American Experience*. Madison: U of Wisconsin P, 1987. 26–52. Reprinted in *Zora Neale Hurston: Critical Perspectives Past and Present*. Ed. Henry Louis Gates Jr. and K.A. Appiah. New York: Amistad Press, 1993. 110–29.

Wilson, Mary Ann. " 'That Which the Soul Lives By': Spirituality in the Works of Zora Neale Hurston." In *Alice Walker and Zora Neale Hurston: The Common Bond*. Ed. Lillie P. Howard. Westport, CT: Greenwood Press, 1993. 57–67.

Wolff, Maria Tai. "Listening and Living: Reading and Experience in *Their Eyes Were Watching God*." *Black American Literature Forum* 16.1 (1982): 29–33. Reprinted in *Zora Neale Hurston: Critical Perspectives Past and Present*. Ed. Henry Louis Gates, Jr. and K.A. Appiah. New York: Amistad Press, 1993. 218–29.

Woodson, Jon. "Zora Neale Hurston's *Their Eyes Were Watching God* and the Influence of Jens Peter Jacobsen's *Marie Grubbe*." *African American Review* 26.4 (1992): 619–35.

Young, James O. *Black Writers of the Thirties*. Baton Rouge: Louisiana State UP, 1973. 219–23.

Reviews of Hurston's Books and Plays

The Great Day

Ruhl, Arthur. Review of *The Great Day*. *New York Herald Tribune*, 17 Jan. 1932: 1+.

Jonah's Gourd Vine

Booklist 30.11 (July 1934): 351.

[Rev. of *Jonah's Gourd Vine*.] *Boston Chronicle*, 5 May 1934.

Brickell, Herschel. [Rev. of *Jonah's Gourd Vine*.] *North American Review*, 23 July 1934: 95–96.

Burris, Andrew. [Rev. of *Jonah's Gourd Vine*.] *Crisis*, 3 June 1934: 166–67. Reprinted in *Zora Neale Hurston: Critical Perspectives Past and Present*. Ed. Henry Louis Gates, Jr. and K.A. Appiah. New York: Amistad Press, 1993. 6–8; and in *Critical Essays on Zora Neale Hurston*. Ed. Gloria L. Cronin. New York: G.K. Hall, 1998. 35–36.

Felton, Estelle. [Rev. of *Jonah's Gourd Vine*.] *Opportunity* (Aug. 1934). Reprinted in *Zora Neale Hurston: Critical Perspectives Past and Present*. Ed. Henry Louis Gates Jr. and K.A. Appiah. New York: Amistad Press, 1993. 4–5.

Gannett, Lewis. "Books and Things." *New York Herald Tribune*, 3 May 1934: 15.

Gruening, Martha. "Darktown Strutter." *New Republic*, 11 July 1934. 244–45. Reprinted in *Zora Neale Hurston: Critical Perspectives Past and Present*. Ed. Henry Louis Gates Jr. and K.A. Appiah. New York: Amistad Press, 1993. 3–4.

[Rev. of *Jonah's Gourd Vine*.] *Nation*, 13 June 1934: 683–84.

Pinckney, Josephine. "A Pungent, Poetic Novel About Negroes." *New York Herald Tribune Books*, 6 May 1934: 7. Reprinted in *Critical Essays on Zora Neale Hurston*. Ed. Gloria L. Cronin. New York: G.K. Hall, 1998. 33–34.

Plomer, William. [Rev. of *Jonah's Gourd Vine*.] *Spectator*, 4 Jan. 1935: 25.

Skeel, E.F. [Rev. of *Jonah's Gourd Vine*.] *The Crisis* (July 1934).

[Rev. of *Jonah's Gourd Vine*.] *Times Literary Supplement*, 18 Oct. 1934: 716–17.

Wallace, Margaret. "Real Negro People." *New York Times Book Review*, 6 May 1934: 6–7. Reprinted in *Zora Neale Hurston: Critical Perspectives Past and Present*. Ed. Henry Louis Gates Jr. and K.A. Appiah. New York: Amistad Press, 1993. 6–8.

Mules and Men

Brickell, Herschel. "A Negro Writer and Her People." *New York Post*, 26 Oct. 1935: 7.

Brock, H.I. "The Full, True Flavor of Life in a Negro Community." *New York Times Book Review*, 10 Nov. 1935: 4. Reprinted in *Zora Neale Hurston: Critical Perspectives Past and Present*. Ed. Henry Louis Gates Jr. and K.A. Appiah. New York: Amistad Press, 1993. 13–15; excerpted in *Black American Prose Writers of the Harlem Renais-*

sance. Ed. Harold Bloom. New York: Chelsea House, 1994. 79; and in *Critical Essays on Zora Neale Hurston.* Ed. Gloria L. Cronin. New York: G.K. Hall, 1998. 39–40.

Brogan, D.W. "Both Sides of the Medal." *Spectator,* 6 Mar. 1936: 403.

Chubb, Thomas Caldecot. [Rev. of *Mules and Men.*] *Times Literary Supplement,* 7 Mar. 1936: 200; and *North American Review* 241 (Mar. 1936): 181–83.

Daniels, Jonathan. "Black Magic and Dark Laughter." *Saturday Review of Literature,* 19 Oct. 1935: 12.

Fallaize, E.N. "Negro Folklore." *Manchester Guardian,* 7 Apr. 1936: 7.

Gannett, Lewis. "Books and Things." *New York Herald Tribune Weekly Book Review,* 11 Oct. 1935: 27. Reprinted in *Zora Neale Hurston: Critical Perspectives Past and Present.* Ed. Henry Louis Gates Jr. and K.A. Appiah. New York: Amistad Press, 1993. 11–13.

McNeill, B.C. [Rev. of *Mules and Men.*] *Journal of Negro History* 21.2 (April 1936): 223–25. Reprinted in *Critical Essays on Zora Neale Hurston.* Ed. Gloria L. Cronin. New York: G.K. Hall, 1998. 41–42.

Moon, Henry Lee. "Big Old Lies." *New Republic,* 11 Dec. 1935: 142. Reprinted in *Zora Neale Hurston: Critical Perspectives Past and Present.* Ed. Henry Louis Gates Jr. and K.A. Appiah. New York: Amistad Press, 1993. 10.

Roberts, John. [Rev. of *Mules and Men.*] *Journal of American Folklore* 93: 370 (Oct.-Dec. 1980): 463–67.

Stoney, Samuel Gaillard. "Wit, Wisdom and Folklore." *New York Herald Tribune Books,* 13 Oct. 1935: 7.

Their Eyes Were Watching God

Brickell, Herschel. [Rev. of *Their Eyes Were Watching God.*] *New York Post,* 14 Sept. 1937.

Brown, Sterling A. "Luck is a Fortune." *Nation,* 16 Oct. 1937: 409–10. Reprinted in *Zora Neale Hurston: Critical Perspectives Past and Present.* Ed. Henry Louis Gates Jr. and K.A. Appiah. New York: Amistad Press, 1993. 20–21; and excerpted in *Black American Prose Writers of the Harlem Renaissance.* Ed. Harold Bloom. New York: Chelsea House, 1994. 80.

Ferguson, Otis. "You Can't Hear Their Voices." *New Republic,* 13 Oct. 1937: 276. Reprinted in *Zora Neale Hurston: Critical Perspectives Past and Present.* Ed. Henry Louis Gates Jr. and K.A. Appiah. New York: Amistad Press, 1993. 22–23; and in *Critical Essays on Zora Neale Hurston.* Ed. Gloria L. Cronin. New York: G.K. Hall, 1998. 77–78.

Hibben, Sheila. "Vibrant Book Full of Nature and Salt." *New York Herald Tribune Weekly Book Review,* 26 Sept. 1937: 2. Reprinted in *Zora*

Neale Hurston: Critical Perspectives Past and Present. Ed. Henry Louis Gates Jr. and K.A. Appiah. New York: Amistad Press, 1993. 21–22; and in *Critical Essays on Zora Neale Hurston.* Ed. Gloria L. Cronin. New York: G.K. Hall, 1998. 73–74.

Locke, Alain. "Jingo, Counter-Jingo, and Us." *Opportunity* (Jan. 1938): 7–11+. Reprinted in *Zora Neale Hurston: Critical Perspectives Past and Present.* Ed. Henry Louis Gates Jr. and K.A. Appiah. New York: Amistad Press, 1993. 18.

Stevens, George. "Negroes by Themselves." *Saturday Review of Literature,* 18 Sept. 1937: 3.

Thompson, Ralph. "Books of the Times." *New York Times,* 6 Oct. 1937: 23.

Tompkins, Lucy. "In the Florida Everglades." *New York Times Book Review,* 26 Sept. 1937: 29. Reprinted in *Zora Neale Hurston: Critical Perspectives Past and Present.* Ed. Henry Louis Gates Jr. and K.A. Appiah. New York: Amistad Press, 1993. 18–19.

Wright, Richard. "Between Laughter and Tears." *New Masses,* 5 Oct. 1937: 22+. Reprinted in *Zora Neale Hurston: Critical Perspectives Past and Present.* Ed. Henry Louis Gates Jr. and K.A. Appiah. New York: Amistad Press, 1993. 16–17; excerpted in *Black American Prose Writers of the Harlem Renaissance.* Ed. Harold Bloom. New York: Chelsea House, 1994. 80–81; and in *Critical Essays on Zora Neale Hurston.* Ed. Gloria L. Cronin. New York: G.K. Hall, 1998. 75–76.

Tell My Horse

Carmer, Carl. *New York Herald Tribune Books,* 23 Oct. 1938: 2. Reprinted in *Critical Essays on Zora Neale Hurston.* Ed. Gloria L. Cronin. New York: G.K. Hall, 1998. 143–44.

Courlander, Harold. *Saturday Review of Literature* 18 (15 October 1938): 6. Reprinted in *Critical Essays on Zora Neale Hurston.* Ed. Gloria L. Cronin. New York: G.K. Hall, 1998. 141–42.

Davis, Elmer. "Witchcraft in the Caribbean Islands." *Saturday Review of Literature,* 15 Oct. 1938: 6–7. Reprinted in *Zora Neale Hurston: Critical Perspectives Past and Present.* Ed. Henry Louis Gates Jr. and K.A. Appiah. New York: Amistad Press, 1993. 24–25.

Locke, Alain. "The Negro: 'New' or Newer." *Opportunity* (Feb. 1939): 36–42. [*Tell My Horse* is discussed on p. 38.]

[Rev. of *Tell My Horse.*] *New Yorker,* 15 Oct. 1938: 71.

Woodson, C.G. Review of *Tell My Horse. Journal of Negro History* 24.1 (Jan. 1939): 116–18. Reprinted in *Critical Essays on Zora Neale Hurston.* Ed. Gloria L. Cronin. New York: G.K. Hall, 1998. 145–46.

Moses, Man of the Mountain

Carmer, Carl. "Biblical Story in Negro Rhythm." *New York Herald Tribune Books*, 26 Nov. 1939: 5.

Gates, Henry Louis, Jr. "A Negro Way of Saying." *New York Times Book Review*, 21 Apr. 1985: 1+.

Hutchison, Percy. "Led His People Free." *New York Times Book Review*, 19 Nov. 1939: 21. Reprinted in *Zora Neale Hurston: Critical Perspectives Past and Present*. Ed. Henry Louis Gates Jr. and K.A. Appiah. New York: Amistad Press, 1993. 27–29; and in *Critical Essays on Zora Neale Hurston*. Ed. Gloria L. Cronin. New York: G.K. Hall, 1998. 149–51.

Slomovitz, Philip. "The Negro's Moses." *Christian Century*, 6 Dec. 1939: 1504. Reprinted in *Critical Essays on Zora Neale Hurston*. Ed. Gloria L. Cronin. New York: G.K. Hall, 1998. 152–53.

Untermeyer, Louis. "Old Testament Voodoo." *Saturday Review of Literature*, 11 Nov. 1939: 11. Reprinted in *Zora Neale Hurston: Critical Perspectives Past and Present*. Ed. Henry Louis Gates Jr. and K.A. Appiah. New York: Amistad Press, 1993. 26–27.

Dust Tracks on a Road

[Rev. of *Dust Tracks on a Road*.] *Booklist*, 1 Dec. 1942: 120.

Chamberlain, John. [Rev. of *Dust Tracks on a Road*.] *New York Times*, 7 Nov. 1942: 13.

Farrison, W. Edward. [Rev. of *Dust Tracks on a Road*.] *Journal of Negro History* 28.3 (July 1943): 352–55. Reprinted in *Critical Essays on Zora Neale Hurston*. Ed. Gloria L. Cronin. New York: G.K. Hall, 1998. 170–72.

Gates, Henry Louis, Jr. "A Negro Way of Saying." *New York Times Book Review*, 21 Apr. 1985: 1+.

[Rev. of *Dust Tracks on a Road*.] *Library Journal*, 1 Nov. 1942: 950.

[Rev. of *Dust Tracks on a Road*.] *New Yorker*, 14 Nov. 1942: 71.

Preece, Harold. "Dust Tracks on a Road." *Tomorrow* 1 (Feb. 1943): 58–59.

Sherman, Beatrice. "Zora Hurston's Story." *New York Times Book Review*, 29 Nov. 1942: 44. Reprinted in *Zora Neale Hurston: Critical Perspectives Past and Present*. Ed. Henry Louis Gates Jr. and K.A. Appiah. New York: Amistad Press, 1993. 32–33.

Strong, Phil. "Zora Hurston Sums Up." *Saturday Review of Literature*, 28 Nov. 1942: 6–7. Reprinted in *Zora Neale Hurston: Critical Perspectives Past and Present*. Ed. Henry Louis Gates Jr. and K.A. Appiah. New York: Amistad Press, 1993. 30–32; and in *Critical Essays on*

Zora Neale Hurston. Ed. Gloria L. Cronin. New York: G.K. Hall, 1998. 167–69.

Seraph on the Suwanee

Brickell, Herschel. "A Woman Saved." *Saturday Review of Literature,* 6 Nov. 1948: 19. Reprinted in *Critical Essays on Zora Neale Hurston.* Ed. Gloria L. Cronin. New York: G.K. Hall, 1998. 195–96.

Hedden, Worth Tuttle. "Turpentine and Moonshine: Love Conquers Caste Between Florida Crackers and Aristocrats." *New York Herald Tribune Weekly Book Review,* 10 Oct. 1948: 2. Reprinted in *Zora Neale Hurston: Critical Perspectives Past and Present.* Ed. Henry Louis Gates Jr. and K.A. Appiah. New York: Amistad Press, 1993. 35–36; and excerpted in *Black American Prose Writers of the Harlem Renaissance.* Ed. Harold Bloom. New York: Chelsea House, 1994. 83.

Rugg, Winnifred King. Review of *Seraph on the Suwanee. Christian Science Monitor,* 23 Dec. 1948: 11.

Slaughter, Frank G. "Freud in Turpentine." *New York Times Book Review,* 31 Oct. 1948: 24. Reprinted in *Zora Neale Hurston: Critical Perspectives Past and Present.* Ed. Henry Louis Gates Jr. and K.A. Appiah. New York: Amistad Press, 1993. 34–35; and in *Critical Essays on Zora Neale Hurston.* Ed. Gloria L. Cronin. New York: G.K. Hall, 1998. 193–94.

Mule Bone

Gates, Henry Louis, Jr. "Why the *Mule Bone* Debate Goes On." *New York Times Book Review,* 10 Feb. 1991: Sec. II, 5+. Reprinted in *Critical Essays on Zora Neale Hurston.* Ed. Gloria L. Cronin. New York: G.K. Hall, 1998. 225–28.

Pacheco, Patrick. "A Discovery Worth the Wait." *Los Angeles Times,* 24 Feb. 1991: 4. Reprinted in *Critical Essays on Zora Neale Hurston.* Ed. Gloria L. Cronin. New York: G.K. Hall, 1998. 232–36.

Rich, Frank. "A Difficult Birth for *Mule Bone." New York Times,* 15 Feb. 1991: 1. Reprinted in *Critical Essays on Zora Neale Hurston.* Ed. Gloria L. Cronin. New York: G.K. Hall, 1998. 229–31.

Index

About the Author

ROBERT W. CROFT is Associate Professor of English at Gainesville College in Gainesville, GA. He has written two previous books, both published by Greenwood Press: *Anne Tyler: A Bio-Bibliography* (1995) and *An Anne Tyler Companion* (1998).